Sunday Missal for Young Catholics

2026-2027

I want to know Jesus better.

This missal will help you take part in the Mass on Sundays and important feast days. Pages 2 through 43 contain the words and explain the gestures that are the same for every Mass. The rest of the book gives you the Scripture readings for each Sunday of the year.

Look over the readings with your family before you go to church. This is an excellent way to use this book and a wonderful way to prepare for Mass.

The most important thing about this little book is that it will help you to know Jesus better. Jesus came to bring God's love into the world. And his Spirit continues to fill us with love for one another.

We hope the short notes in this book will help you to participate more fully in the Mass. May the Mass become an important part of your life as you grow up, and may the readings and prayers you find in this missal inspire you to love and serve others just as Jesus did.

I0805530

WHAT WE NEED TO CELEBRATE THE MASS

The **altar** is the table where the priest consecrates bread and wine. The **priest** makes Jesus present and acts in his name.

A group of Christians. You are a Christian by your baptism.

Two **books** are used at Mass: the missal contains the prayers of the Mass, and the lectionary contains the readings.

One **cruet** contains water, while the other cruet contains wine.

The **ambo** is the place where the word of God is proclaimed.

Holy vessels

chalice

ciborium

paten

Bread and wine
The Mass is the commemoration of what Jesus did during the Last Supper with his disciples, before he died. The bread is shaped like a small disc and is called a "host."

or they offer it for themselves
and all who are dear to them:
for the redemption of their souls,
in hope of health and well-being,
and paying their homage to you,
the eternal God, living and true.

On the Nativity of the Lord and throughout the Octave add:
Celebrating the most sacred night (day)
on which blessed Mary the immaculate Virgin
brought forth the Savior for this world,
and

On the Epiphany of the Lord add:
Celebrating the most sacred day
on which your Only Begotten Son,
eternal with you in your glory,
appeared in a human body, truly sharing
our flesh,
and

From the Mass of the Easter Vigil until the Second Sunday of Easter add:
Celebrating the most sacred night (day)
of the Resurrection of our Lord Jesus Christ
in the flesh,
and

On the Ascension of the Lord add:
Celebrating the most sacred day
on which your Only Begotten Son, our Lord,
placed at the right hand of your glory
our weak human nature,
which he had united to himself,
and

On Pentecost Sunday add:
Celebrating the most sacred day of Pentecost,
on which the Holy Spirit
appeared to the Apostles in tongues of fire,
and

In communion with those whose memory
we venerate,
especially the glorious ever-Virgin Mary,

Mother of our God and Lord, Jesus Christ,
and blessed Joseph, her Spouse,
your blessed Apostles and Martyrs,
Peter and Paul, Andrew,
(James, John,
Thomas, James, Philip,
Bartholomew, Matthew,
Simon and Jude;
Linus, Cletus, Clement, Sixtus,
Cornelius, Cyprian,
Lawrence, Chrysogonus,
John and Paul,
Cosmas and Damian)
and all your Saints;
we ask that through their merits and prayers,
in all things we may be defended
by your protecting help.
(Through Christ our Lord. Amen.)

Therefore, Lord, we pray:
graciously accept this oblation of our service,
that of your whole family;

From the Mass of the Easter Vigil until the Second Sunday of Easter add:
which we make to you
also for those to whom you have
been pleased to give
the new birth of water and the Holy Spirit,
granting them forgiveness of all their sins;

order our days in your peace,
and command that we be delivered
from eternal damnation
and counted among the flock of those
you have chosen.
(Through Christ our Lord. Amen.)

Be pleased, O God, we pray,
to bless, acknowledge,
and approve this offering in every respect;
make it spiritual and acceptable,
so that it may become for us
the Body and Blood of your most beloved Son,
our Lord Jesus Christ.

On the day before he was to suffer,
he took bread in his holy and venerable hands,
and with eyes raised to heaven
to you, O God, his almighty Father,
giving you thanks, he said the blessing,
broke the bread
and gave it to his disciples, saying:

TAKE THIS, ALL OF YOU, AND EAT OF IT,
FOR THIS IS MY BODY,
WHICH WILL BE GIVEN UP FOR YOU.

In a similar way, when supper was ended,
he took this precious chalice
in his holy and venerable hands,
and once more giving you thanks,
he said the blessing
and gave the chalice to his disciples, saying:

TAKE THIS, ALL OF YOU, AND DRINK FROM IT,
FOR THIS IS THE CHALICE OF MY BLOOD,
THE BLOOD OF THE NEW AND ETERNAL **COVENANT**,
WHICH WILL BE POURED OUT FOR YOU AND FOR MANY
FOR THE **FORGIVENESS OF SINS**.

DO THIS IN MEMORY OF ME.

The mystery of faith.

Everyone: We proclaim your Death, O Lord,
and profess your Resurrection
until you come again.

(For other acclamations, see page 21)

Priest: Therefore, O Lord,
as we celebrate the **memorial** of the blessed Passion,
the Resurrection from the dead,
and the glorious Ascension into heaven
of Christ, your Son, our Lord,
we, your servants and your holy people,
offer to your glorious majesty
from the gifts that you have given us,
this pure victim,
this holy victim,
this spotless victim,

the holy Bread of **eternal life**
and the Chalice of everlasting salvation.

Be pleased to look upon these offerings
with a serene and kindly countenance,
and to accept them,
as once you were pleased to accept
the gifts of your servant Abel the just,
the sacrifice of Abraham, our father in faith,
and the offering of your high priest Melchizedek,
a holy sacrifice, a spotless victim.

In humble prayer we ask you, almighty God:
command that these gifts be borne
by the hands of your holy Angel
to your altar on high
in the sight of your divine majesty,
so that all of us, who through this participation
at the altar
receive the most holy Body and Blood of your Son,
may be filled with every grace
and heavenly blessing.
(Through Christ our Lord. Amen.)

Remember also, Lord, your servants N. and N.,
who have gone before us with the sign of faith
and rest in the sleep of peace.
(Pause)
Grant them, O Lord, we pray,
and all who sleep in Christ,
a place of refreshment, light and peace.
(Through Christ our Lord. Amen.)

To us, also, your servants, who, though sinners,
hope in your abundant mercies,
graciously grant some share
and fellowship with your holy Apostles and Martyrs:
with John the Baptist, Stephen,
Matthias, Barnabas,
(Ignatius, Alexander,
Marcellinus, Peter,
Felicity, Perpetua,
Agatha, Lucy,
Agnes, Cecilia, Anastasia)
and all your Saints;

admit us, we beseech you,
into their company,
not weighing our merits,
but granting us your pardon,
through Christ our Lord.

Through whom
you continue to make all these good things, O Lord;
you sanctify them, fill them with life,
bless them, and bestow them upon us.

Through him, and with him, and in him,
O God, almighty Father,
in the unity of the Holy Spirit,
all glory and honor is yours,
for ever and ever. Amen.

(Turn to the Lord's Prayer, page 37)

Eucharistic Prayer II

The priest may use the preface below, or another may be chosen.

Priest: *(Preface)*
It is truly right and just, our duty and our salvation,
always and everywhere to give you thanks,
Father most holy,
through your beloved Son, Jesus Christ,
your Word through whom you made all things,
whom you sent as our Savior and Redeemer,
incarnate by the Holy Spirit and born of the Virgin.

Fulfilling your will and gaining for you a holy people,
he stretched out his hands as he endured
his Passion,
so as to break the bonds of death and manifest
the resurrection.

And so, with the Angels and all the Saints
we declare your glory,
as with one voice we acclaim:

Everyone: Holy, Holy, Holy Lord God of hosts... *(page 22)*

Priest: You are indeed Holy, O Lord,
the fount of all holiness.

Make holy, therefore, these gifts, we pray,
by sending down your Spirit upon them
like the dewfall,
so that they may become for us
the Body and Blood of our Lord Jesus Christ.

At the time he was betrayed
and entered willingly into his Passion,
he took bread and, giving thanks, broke it,
and gave it to his disciples, saying:

TAKE THIS, ALL OF YOU, AND EAT OF IT,
FOR THIS IS MY BODY
WHICH WILL BE GIVEN UP FOR YOU.

In a similar way, when supper was ended,
he took the chalice
and, once more giving thanks,
he gave it to his disciples, saying:

TAKE THIS, ALL OF YOU, AND DRINK FROM IT,
FOR THIS IS THE CHALICE OF MY BLOOD,
THE BLOOD OF THE NEW AND ETERNAL **COVENANT**,
WHICH WILL BE POURED OUT FOR YOU AND FOR MANY
FOR THE **FORGIVENESS OF SINS**.

DO THIS IN MEMORY OF ME.

The mystery of faith.

Everyone: When we eat this Bread and drink this Cup,
we proclaim your Death, O Lord,
until you come again.

(For other acclamations, see page 21)

Priest: Therefore, as we celebrate
the **memorial** of his Death and Resurrection,
we offer you, Lord,
the Bread of life and the Chalice of salvation,
giving thanks that you have held us worthy
to be in your presence and minister to you.

Humbly we pray
that, partaking of the Body and Blood of Christ,
we may be **gathered into one by the Holy Spirit.**
Remember, Lord, your Church,
spread throughout the world,
and bring her to the fullness of charity,
together with N. our Pope and N. our Bishop
and all the clergy.

Remember also our brothers and sisters
who have fallen asleep in the hope of the resurrection,
and all who have died in your mercy:
welcome them into the light of your face.
Have mercy on us all, we pray,
that with the Blessed Virgin Mary, Mother of God,
with blessed Joseph, her Spouse,
with the blessed Apostles,
and all the Saints who have pleased you
throughout the ages,
we may merit to be co-heirs to **eternal life**,
and may praise and glorify you
through your Son, Jesus Christ.

Through him, and with him, and in him,
O God, almighty Father,
in the unity of the Holy Spirit,
all glory and honor is yours,
for ever and ever.

Everyone: Amen.

(Turn to the Lord's Prayer, page 37)

Eucharistic Prayer III

The priest chooses a preface according to the liturgical calendar.

Everyone: Holy, Holy, Holy Lord God of hosts… *(page 22)*

Priest: You are indeed Holy, O Lord,
and all you have created
rightly gives you praise,
for through your Son our Lord Jesus Christ,

by the power and working of the Holy Spirit,
you give life to all things and make them holy,
and you never cease to gather a people to yourself,
so that from the rising of the sun to its setting
a pure sacrifice may be offered to your name.

Therefore, O Lord, we humbly implore you:
by the same Spirit graciously make holy
these gifts we have brought to you for consecration,
that they may become the Body and Blood
of your Son our Lord Jesus Christ,
at whose command we celebrate these mysteries.

For on the night he was betrayed
he himself took bread,
and, giving you thanks, he said the blessing,
broke the bread and gave it to his disciples, saying:

> TAKE THIS, ALL OF YOU, AND EAT OF IT,
> FOR THIS IS MY BODY,
> WHICH WILL BE GIVEN UP FOR YOU.

In a similar way, when supper was ended,
he took the chalice,
and, giving you thanks, he said the blessing,
and gave the chalice to his disciples, saying:

> TAKE THIS, ALL OF YOU, AND DRINK FROM IT,
> FOR THIS IS THE CHALICE OF MY BLOOD,
> THE BLOOD OF THE NEW AND ETERNAL **COVENANT**,
> WHICH WILL BE POURED OUT FOR YOU AND FOR MANY
> FOR THE **FORGIVENESS OF SINS**.
>
> **DO THIS IN MEMORY OF ME.**

The mystery of faith.

Everyone: Save us, Savior of the world,
for by your Cross and Resurrection
you have set us free.

(For other acclamations, see page 21)

Priest: Therefore, O Lord, as we celebrate the **memorial**
of the saving Passion of your Son,
his wondrous Resurrection
and Ascension into heaven,

and as we look forward to his second coming,
we offer you in thanksgiving
this holy and living sacrifice.

Look, we pray, upon the oblation of your Church
and, recognizing the sacrificial Victim
by whose death
you willed to reconcile us to yourself,
grant that we, who are nourished
by the Body and Blood of your Son
and filled with his Holy Spirit,
may become one body, one spirit in Christ.

May he make of us
an eternal offering to you,
so that we may obtain an inheritance with your elect,
especially with the most Blessed Virgin Mary,
Mother of God,
with blessed Joseph, her Spouse,
with your blessed Apostles and glorious Martyrs
(with Saint N.)
and with all the Saints,
on whose constant intercession in your presence
we rely for unfailing help.

May this Sacrifice of our reconciliation,
we pray, O Lord,
advance the peace and salvation of all the world.
Be pleased to confirm in faith and charity
your pilgrim Church on earth,
with your servant N. our Pope and N. our Bishop,
the Order of Bishops, all the clergy,
and the entire people you have gained for your own.

Listen graciously to the prayers of this family,
whom you have summoned before you:
in your compassion, O merciful Father,
gather to yourself all your children
scattered throughout the world.

To our departed brothers and sisters
and to all who were pleasing to you
at their passing from this life,
give kind admittance to your kingdom.
There we hope to enjoy for ever the fullness
of your glory

through Christ our Lord,
through whom you bestow on the world all that is good.

Through him, and with him, and in him,
O God, almighty Father,
in the unity of the Holy Spirit,
all glory and honor is yours,
for ever and ever. Amen.

(Turn to the Lord's Prayer, page 37)

Eucharistic Prayer IV

This Eucharistic Prayer has its own fixed preface.

Priest: *(Preface)*
It is truly right to give you thanks,
truly just to give you glory, Father most holy,
for you are the one God living and true,
existing before all ages and abiding for all eternity,
dwelling in unapproachable light;
yet you, who alone are good, the source of life,
have made all that is,
so that you might fill your creatures with blessings
and bring joy to many of them by the glory
of your light.

And so, in your presence are countless hosts
of Angels,
who serve you day and night
and, gazing upon the glory of your face,
glorify you without ceasing.
With them we, too, confess your name in exultation,
giving voice to every creature under heaven,
as we acclaim:

Everyone: Holy, Holy, Holy Lord God of hosts... *(page 22)*

Priest: We give you praise, Father most holy,
for you are great
and you have fashioned all your works
in wisdom and in love.
You formed man in your own image

and entrusted the whole world to his care,
so that in serving you alone, the Creator,
he might have dominion over all creatures.

And when through disobedience he had lost
your friendship,
you did not abandon him to the domain of death.
For you came in mercy to the aid of all,
so that those who seek might find you.
Time and again you offered them covenants
and through the prophets
taught them to look forward to salvation.

And you so loved the world, Father most holy,
that in the fullness of time
you sent your Only Begotten Son to be our Savior.
Made incarnate by the Holy Spirit
and born of the Virgin Mary,
he shared our human nature
in all things but sin.
To the poor he proclaimed the good news of salvation,
to prisoners, freedom,
and to the sorrowful of heart, joy.
To accomplish your plan,
he gave himself up to death,
and, rising from the dead,
he destroyed death and restored life.

And that we might live no longer for ourselves
but for him who died and rose again for us,
he sent the Holy Spirit from you, Father,
as the first fruits for those who believe,
so that, bringing to perfection his work
in the world,
he might sanctify creation to the full.

Therefore, O Lord, we pray:
may this same Holy Spirit
graciously sanctify these offerings,
that they may become
the Body and Blood of our Lord Jesus Christ
for the celebration of this great mystery,
which he himself left us
as an eternal covenant.

For when the hour had come
for him to be glorified by you, Father most holy,
having loved his own who were in the world,
he loved them to the end:
and while they were at supper,
he took bread, blessed and broke it,
and gave it to his disciples, saying:

TAKE THIS, ALL OF YOU, AND EAT OF IT,
FOR THIS IS MY BODY,
WHICH WILL BE GIVEN UP FOR YOU.

In a similar way,
taking the chalice filled with the fruit of the vine,
he gave thanks,
and gave the chalice to his disciples, saying:

TAKE THIS, ALL OF YOU, AND DRINK FROM IT,
FOR THIS IS THE CHALICE OF MY BLOOD,
THE BLOOD OF THE NEW AND ETERNAL **COVENANT**,
WHICH WILL BE POURED OUT FOR YOU AND FOR MANY
FOR THE **FORGIVENESS OF SINS**.

DO THIS IN MEMORY OF ME.

The mystery of faith.

Everyone: We proclaim your Death, O Lord,
and profess your Resurrection
until you come again.

(For other acclamations, see page 21)

Priest: Therefore, O Lord,
as we now celebrate the **memorial** of our redemption,
we remember Christ's Death
and his descent to the realm of the dead,
we proclaim his Resurrection
and his Ascension to your right hand,
and, as we await his coming in glory,
we offer you his Body and Blood,
the sacrifice acceptable to you
which brings salvation to the whole world.

Look, O Lord, upon the Sacrifice
which you yourself have provided for your Church,
and grant in your loving kindness
to all who partake of this one Bread and one Chalice
that, **gathered into one body by the Holy Spirit,**
they may truly become a living sacrifice in Christ
to the praise of your glory.

Therefore, Lord, remember now
all for whom we offer this sacrifice:
especially your servant N. our Pope,
N. our Bishop, and the whole Order of Bishops,
all the clergy,
those who take part in this offering,
those gathered here before you,
your entire people,
and all who seek you with a sincere heart.

Remember also
those who have died in the peace of your Christ
and all the dead,
whose faith you alone have known.

To all of us, your children,
grant, O merciful Father,
that we may enter into a heavenly inheritance
with the Blessed Virgin Mary, Mother of God,
with blessed Joseph, her Spouse,
and with your Apostles and Saints in your kingdom.
There, with the whole of creation,
freed from the corruption of sin and death,
may we glorify you through Christ our Lord,
through whom you bestow on the world
all that is good.

Through him, and with him, and in him,
O God, almighty Father,
in the unity of the Holy Spirit,
all glory and honor is yours,
for ever and ever. Amen.

(Turn to the Lord's Prayer, page 37)

What Does It Mean?

Covenant
When two people enter into a covenant, they promise to be faithful to one another. God entered into a covenant with us. He is our God and we are his people.

Forgiveness of sins
This is the forgiveness that comes from God, whose love is greater than our sins.

Do this in memory of me
Jesus asked the disciples to remember him by reliving what he said and did during the Last Supper.

The mystery of faith
Together we proclaim our belief in Christ, who was born and died for us, rose to life, and will return one day.

Memorial
Memorial means to remember. When we remember at Mass, we're not just thinking about something that happened a long time ago. To remember Jesus' death and resurrection at Mass means that those events are real and happening now, in our celebration, in our hearts. It doesn't mean that Jesus is repeating his passion, death, and resurrection for us at each Mass, but that, at each Mass, the Holy Spirit makes the powerful saving mystery of Jesus' death and resurrection present to us. No one can explain this or fully understand it. It is part of the mystery of faith.

Gathered into one by the Holy Spirit
In the Mass, the Holy Spirit draws us into unity—communion—not only with Jesus, but with all the members of his Body—with the pope and our bishop and all the bishops and clergy, with every member of the Church throughout the world, with all members of the Body of Christ who share in eternal life, including the Blessed Virgin Mary, the apostles, and all the saints. When we gather at Mass, even though we can't see them, we know in faith that the whole Body of Christ is with us praising and worshiping God.

Eternal life
This is life with God, which will be given to us fully after death.

We Say the Lord's Prayer

Jesus has taught us that God is the Father of all human beings and that we can call upon God at any time. Together we recite or sing this prayer. To help us to be truly ready to receive Jesus in Communion, we need to ask for forgiveness and to forgive those who have hurt us.

Priest: At the **Savior's** command
and formed by divine teaching,
we dare to say:

Everyone: Our Father, who art in **heaven**,
hallowed be thy name;
thy kingdom come,
thy will be done
on earth as it is in heaven.
Give us this day our daily bread,
and forgive us our **trespasses**,
as we forgive those who trespass against us;
and lead us not into **temptation**,
but deliver us from evil.

Priest: Deliver us, Lord, we pray, from every evil,
graciously grant peace in our days,
that, by the help of your mercy,
we may be always free from sin
and safe from all distress,
as we await the blessed hope
and the coming of our Savior, Jesus Christ.

Everyone: For the **kingdom**,
the power and the glory are yours
now and for ever.

What Does It Mean?

Savior
This is one of the names we give to Jesus because he saves us from evil and death.

Heaven
Heaven is a special way of being with God after our life on earth is over.

Trespasses
These refer to our lack of love and to the sins we commit.

Temptation
This is a desire we sometimes feel to do things we know are wrong.

Kingdom
Jesus speaks of God as king when he says: "The kingdom of God is at hand." With his life, Jesus shows us that God is present in our midst as a king who loves us. When we live as Jesus did, we welcome the kingdom of God.

Act of Contrition

O my God,
I am sorry and repent with all my heart.
for all the wrong I have done
and for the good I have failed to do,
because by sinning I have offended you,
who are all good and worthy to be loved above all things.
I firmly resolve, with the help of your grace,
to do penance,
to sin no more,
and to avoid the occasions of sin.
Through the merits of the Passion of our Savior Jesus Christ,
Lord, have mercy.

The Lord's Prayer

Our Father, who art in heaven,
hallowed be thy name;
thy kingdom come,
thy will be done
on earth as it is in heaven.
Give us this day our daily bread,
and forgive us our trespasses,
as we forgive those who trespass against us;
and lead us not into temptation,
but deliver us from evil. Amen.

Come, Holy Spirit

Come, Holy Spirit,
fill the hearts of your faithful
and kindle in them the fire of your love.
Send forth your Spirit and they shall be created,
and you shall renew the face of the earth. Amen.

Glory Be to the Father

Glory be to the Father,
and to the Son,
and to the Holy Spirit;
as it was in the beginning,
is now, and ever shall be,
world without end. Amen.

LIVING OUR FAITH EVERY DAY

As Mass ends, the priest dismisses us with one of several prayers: "Go forth, the Mass is ended," for example, or "Go and announce the Gospel of the Lord." As people of faith, we are called to carry all that we have celebrated at Mass out into our daily lives.

There are several ways to do this:

- Prepare for Mass by reading the coming Sunday's first and second readings, the psalm, and the gospel in advance, so that you are familiar with what you will hear at Mass. Try imagining yourself in the gospel story, witnessing first-hand the story you will hear. Who might you be? What would your reaction be if you were to hear Jesus tell a parable? How would you feel if you were to witness Jesus perform a miracle? What must it have been like to travel with Jesus and listen to him teach and preach?
- After you have heard the gospel proclaimed at Mass, ask yourself what message or idea really made an impression on you. Think about that throughout the week. If there is a phrase or passage that particularly appealed to you, try reciting it to yourself throughout the week. Think of ways it relates to you and to the world today.
- Listen closely to the priest's homily and ask yourself what you have learned from it. Reflect on that point throughout the week.
- Listen to the Prayer of the Faithful and remember who and what were being prayed for at Mass. Keep these petitions in mind as you say your prayers during the week. As you leave Mass, say to yourself, "This week I will pray for ________________."

THE FOUR MAIN PARTS OF THE MASS

On the following pages you will find the words that the priest says and the responses we say together during each part of the Mass. You will also find explanations and responses to many questions that people ask about the Mass.

The Introductory Rites

The Lord brings us together.
We ask God for forgiveness.
We give glory to God.

The Liturgy of the Word

We listen to the word of God.
We profess our faith.
We pray for the whole world.

The Liturgy of the Eucharist

We offer bread and wine to God.
We give thanks to God.
We say the Lord's Prayer.
We share the peace of Christ.
We receive Jesus in communion.

The Concluding Rites

The Lord sends us forth to live the gospel.

The Lord Brings Us Together (Greeting)

We come together in church with family, friends, neighbors, and strangers. We are here because Jesus has invited us to be here.

When the priest comes in, we stand and sing. Then we make the sign of the cross along with the priest.

Priest: In the name of the Father, and of the Son,
and of the Holy Spirit.

Everyone: Amen.

The priest will choose one of these greetings:

1 **Priest:** The grace of our Lord Jesus Christ,
and the love of God,
and the communion of the Holy Spirit
be with you all.

Everyone: And with your spirit.

2 **Priest:** Grace to you and peace from God our Father
and the Lord Jesus Christ.

Everyone: And with your spirit.

3 **Priest:** The Lord be with you.

Everyone: And with your spirit.

Questions

Why do we celebrate Mass on Sunday?
Jesus rose from the dead on Sunday, the day after the Sabbath. This is why Christians gather on that day. Over time, people started to call it "the Lord's day."

Why do we celebrate Mass in a church?
Churches are built specially for Christians to gather in. If needed, Mass can be celebrated in other places: a home, a school, a plaza, a jail, a hospital, a park...

Why do we need a priest to celebrate Mass?
We believe that Jesus is present in the person of the priest when Christians gather for the Mass. He presides over the celebration of the Lord's supper in the name of Jesus Christ.

Gestures

Standing
We stand to welcome Jesus, who is present among us when we gather in his name.

The sign of the cross
With our right hand we make the sign of the cross (from our forehead to our chest, from our left shoulder to our right) and say "In the name of the Father, and of the Son, and of the Holy Spirit." This is how all Catholic prayer begins.

Singing
This is a joyful way to pray together.

We Ask God for Forgiveness (Penitential Act)

We recognize that we have done wrong. We ask for forgiveness for our misdeeds. God, who knows and loves us, forgives us.

Priest: Brethren (brothers and sisters), let us acknowledge our sins,
and so prepare ourselves to celebrate the sacred mysteries.

After a brief pause for silence, one of the following forms is used:

1 **Everyone:** I **confess** to almighty God
and to you, my brothers and sisters,
that I have greatly sinned,
in my thoughts and in my words,
in what I have done and in what I have failed to do,
(tap the heart) through my fault,
through my fault,
through my most grievous fault;
therefore I ask blessed Mary ever-Virgin,
all the Angels and Saints,
and you, my brothers and sisters,
to pray for me to the Lord our God.

Priest: May almighty God have mercy on us,
forgive us our sins,
and bring us to everlasting life.

Everyone: Amen.

2 **Priest:** Have mercy on us, O Lord.

Everyone: For we have sinned against you.

Priest: Show us, O Lord, your mercy.

Everyone: And grant us your salvation.

Priest: May almighty God have mercy on us,
forgive us our sins,
and bring us to everlasting life.

Everyone: Amen.

3 *The celebrant says the following or other prayers:*

Priest: You were sent to heal the contrite of heart:
Lord, have mercy. **Or** Kyrie, eleison.

Everyone: Lord, have mercy. **Or** Kyrie, eleison.

Priest: You came to call sinners:
Christ, have mercy. **Or** Christe, eleison.

Everyone: Christ, have mercy. **Or** Christe, eleison.

Priest: You are seated at the right hand of the Father
to intercede for us:
Lord, have mercy. **Or** Kyrie, eleison.

Everyone: Lord, have mercy. **Or** Kyrie, eleison.

Priest: May almighty God have mercy on us,
forgive us our sins,
and bring us to everlasting life.

Everyone: Amen.

The following prayers are said, in either English or the ancient Greek, unless they were just said in a formula of the Penitential Act:

Priest: Lord, have mercy. **Or** Kyrie, eleison.

Everyone: Lord, have mercy. **Or** Kyrie, eleison.

Priest: Christ, have mercy. **Or** Christe, eleison.

Everyone: Christ, have mercy. **Or** Christe, eleison.

Priest: Lord, have mercy. **Or** Kyrie, eleison.

Everyone: Lord, have mercy. **Or** Kyrie, eleison.

What Does It Mean?

Confess
We recognize before others that we have turned away from God, who is love.

Mercy
We know God is full of mercy—that he loves us even when we have sinned. God's mercy is always there for us.

Amen
This is a Hebrew word meaning "Yes, I agree. I commit myself."

Lord
This is a name that we give to God. Christians call Jesus "Lord" because we believe he is the Son of God.

Christ or Messiah
In the Bible, these words designate someone who has been blessed with perfumed oil. This blessing is a sign that God has given a mission to the person. Christians give this name to Jesus.

Gestures

Tapping our heart
This is a way of showing we are very sorry for our sins.

We Give Glory to God

We recognize God's greatness when we say "Glory to God." This prayer begins with the hymn the angels sang when they announced Jesus' birth to the shepherds.

Everyone: **Glory** to God in the highest,
and on earth peace to people of good will.

We **praise** you,
we bless you,
we adore you,
we glorify you,
we give you thanks for your great glory,
Lord God, heavenly King,
O God, **almighty** Father.

Lord Jesus Christ, Only Begotten Son,
Lord God, Lamb of God, Son of the Father,
you take away the **sins of the world**,
have mercy on us;
you take away the sins of the world,
receive our prayer;
you are seated at the right hand of the Father,
have mercy on us.

For you alone are the Holy One,
you alone are the Lord,
you alone are the Most High,
Jesus Christ,
with the **Holy Spirit**,
in the glory of God the Father.
Amen.

Priest: Let us pray.

The priest invites us to pray. He then says a prayer in the name of all of us and finishes like this:

Through our Lord Jesus Christ, your Son, who lives and reigns with you in the unity of the Holy Spirit, God, for ever and ever.

Everyone: Amen.

What Does It Mean?

Glory
With this word, we indicate the greatness of a person. It shows that a person is important. When we say "Glory to God" we are recognizing that God is important in our lives.

Praise
To praise is to speak well and enthusiastically of someone.

Almighty
When we say that God is almighty, we mean that nothing is impossible for God.

Sins of the world
This expression refers to all the evil that is done in the world.

Holy Spirit
This is the Spirit of God, our heavenly guide, who fills us with love for Jesus.

We Listen to the Word of God

This is the moment when we listen to several readings from the **Bible.** We welcome God who speaks to us today.

You can follow the readings in this book. Look for the Sunday that corresponds to the day's date.

The First Two Readings

We sit down for these readings. The first reading is usually taken from the Old Testament. The second is from a letter written by an apostle to the first Christians. Between these two readings, we pray with the responsorial **Psalm**, *which we do best when it is sung.*

The Gospel

We stand and sing **Alleluia!** *(except during Lent) as we prepare to listen carefully to a reading from one of the gospels.*

Priest: The Lord be with you.

Everyone: And with your spirit.

Priest: A reading from the holy **Gospel** according to N.

Everyone: Glory to you, O Lord.

We trace three small crosses with our thumb: one on our forehead, one on our lips, and another on our heart. When the reading is finished, the priest kisses the book and says:

Priest: The Gospel of the Lord.

Everyone: Praise to you, Lord Jesus Christ.

The Homily

We sit down to listen to the comments of the priest, which help us to understand and apply the word of God in our lives.

What Does It Mean?

Bible
This is the holy book of all Christians. The Old Testament tells the story of the covenant God made with the Jewish people before Jesus' time. The New Testament tells the story of the covenant God made with all people through his son, Jesus Christ.

Psalm
The Psalms are prayers that are found in the Bible. They are meant to be sung.

Alleluia!
This Hebrew word means "May God be praised and thanked."

Gospel
The word "gospel" means "good news." Jesus himself is the Good News who lives with us. The first four books of the New Testament are called "gospels." They transmit the good news to us.

Gestures

The sign of the cross that we make on our forehead, lips, and heart
This sign means that we want to make the gospel so much a part of our life that we can proclaim it to all around us with all our being.

Kissing the book of the gospels
When the priest does this, he says in a low voice: "Through the words of the Gospel may our sins be wiped away."

We Profess Our Faith (Nicene Creed)

We have just listened to the word of God. To respond to it, we proclaim the **Creed**.

We stand up and profess our faith:

Everyone: I believe in one God,
the Father almighty,
maker of heaven and earth,
of all things visible and invisible.

I believe in one Lord Jesus Christ,
the Only Begotten Son of God,
born of the Father before all ages.
God from God, Light from Light,
true God from true God,
begotten, not made, consubstantial with the Father;
through him all things were made.
For us men and for our salvation
he came down from heaven,
(At the words that follow, up to and including "and became man," all bow.)
and by the Holy Spirit was incarnate of the Virgin Mary,
and became man.

For our sake he was **crucified** under **Pontius Pilate**,
he suffered death and was buried,
and rose again on the third day
in accordance with the Scriptures.
He ascended into heaven
and is seated at the right hand of the Father.
He will come again in glory
to judge the living and the dead
and his kingdom will have no end.

I believe in the Holy Spirit, the Lord, the giver of life,
who proceeds from the Father and the Son,
who with the Father and the Son is adored and glorified,
who has spoken through the prophets.

I believe in one, holy, **catholic** and apostolic **Church**.
I confess one Baptism for the forgiveness of sins
and I look forward to the **resurrection** of the dead
and the life of the world to come. Amen.

What Does It Mean?

Creed
From the Latin verb *credo*, meaning "I believe." The Creed is the prayer that expresses our faith as Christians.

Crucified
Jesus died by crucifixion, meaning he was nailed to a cross.

Pontius Pilate
This is the name of the Roman governor who ordered that Jesus be crucified.

Catholic
In Greek, this word means "universal." The Church is open to all people in the world.

Church
The "Church" with a big C refers to the whole Christian community throughout the world. The "church" with a little c is a building where we gather to worship God.

Resurrection
This means coming back to life after having died. God raised Jesus from the dead and gave him new life for ever. Jesus shares that life with us.

We Pray for the Whole World

This is the moment of the Universal Prayer of the Faithful, when we present our **petitions** to God. We pray for the Church, for all of humanity, for those who are sick or lonely, for children who are abandoned, for those who suffer through natural disasters...

After each petition we respond with a phrase, such as:

Everyone: Lord, hear our prayer.

Reader: For the needs of the Church...

For peace in every country...

For the hungry and the homeless...

For ourselves and for all God's children...

What Does It Mean?

Petitions
Petitions are prayers asking for something specific. Each week at Mass, the petitions change because the needs of the world and our community change. We stand for the petitions and answer "Amen" at the end. Sometimes we call these prayers intentions.

Why do we call the Prayer of the Faithful "universal"?
It is a universal prayer because it includes everyone: we pray for all the people of the world.

Why do we take up a collection?
Christians help out with the maintenance of the church building and also help people who are in need. These gifts are brought to the altar with the bread and the wine.

We Offer Bread and Wine to God (Preparation of Gifts)

We sing the Offertory Chant while members of the community bring the bread and wine and the gifts collected (to relieve the needs of the Church and the poor) to the altar to be offered to God. At the altar, the priest receives the gifts and then with him we bless God for the bread and wine that will become the Body and Blood of Jesus.

We sit down. The priest lifts up the bread and wine, saying:

Priest: **Blessed** are you, Lord God of all creation,
for through your goodness we have received
the bread we offer you:
fruit of the earth and work of human hands,
it will become for us the bread of life.

Everyone: Blessed be God for ever.

Priest: Blessed are you, Lord God of all creation,
for through your goodness we have received
the wine we offer you:
fruit of the vine and work of human hands,
it will become our spiritual drink.

Everyone: Blessed be God for ever.

The priest washes his hands. Then we all stand and the priest says:

Priest: Pray brethren (brothers and sisters),
that my sacrifice and yours
may be acceptable to God,
the almighty Father.

Everyone: May the Lord accept the **sacrifice** at your hands
for the praise and glory of his name,
for our good,
and the good of all his holy Church.

The priest, with hands extended, says a prayer over the bread and wine. He usually ends the prayer by saying:

Priest: Through Christ our Lord.

Everyone: Amen.

What Does It Mean?

Eucharist
A Greek word that means "gratefulness, thanksgiving." The Mass is also called the Eucharist.

Blessed
To bless means to speak well of someone. To bless God is to give thanks for everything God gives us.

Sacrifice
God does not ask for animal sacrifice, as in the old days written about in the Bible. Nor does God ask us to die on a cross, like Jesus did. Instead, God asks us to offer our daily life, with Jesus, as a beautiful gift.

Gestures

Procession with the bread and the wine
With this gesture we present to God the fruit of our work and we give thanks for the gift of life that comes from God.

Drops of water in the wine
With this sign, the priest prays that our life be united with God's life.

Washing of hands
Before saying the most important prayer of the Mass, the priest washes his hands and asks God to wash away his sins.

We Give Thanks to God (Eucharistic Prayer)

At this moment we give thanks to God for his Son, Jesus Christ, for life, and for all that he gives us. This is how the great Eucharistic Prayer begins.

Priest: The Lord be with you.

Everyone: And with your spirit.

Priest: Lift up your hearts.

Everyone: We lift them up to the Lord.

Priest: Let us give thanks to the Lord our God.

Everyone: It is right and just.

The Eucharistic Prayer for Masses with Children is one way of celebrating the Eucharist with young Catholics. Eucharistic Prayers 1-4 are used to celebrate the Eucharist with grown-ups.

The priest chooses a preface, a special prayer said at the beginning of the Liturgy of the Eucharist to help everyone give thanks to God. Then everyone sings the Sanctus ("Holy, Holy, Holy").

Eucharistic Prayer for Masses with Children I
(Father, you are always thinking about your people…) page 19

Eucharistic Prayer 1
(To you, therefore…) page 22

Eucharistic Prayer 2
(You are indeed Holy, O Lord, the fount of all holiness…) page 27

Eucharistic Prayer 3
(You are indeed Holy, O Lord, and all you have created…) page 29

Eucharistic Prayer 4
(We give you praise…) page 32

Eucharistic Prayer for Masses with Children I

Priest: *(Preface)*
God our Father,
you have brought us here together
so that we can give you thanks and praise
for all the wonderful things you have done.

We thank you for all that is beautiful in the world
and for the happiness you have given us.
We praise you for daylight
and for your word which lights up our minds.
We praise you for the earth,
and all the people who live on it,
and for our life which comes from you.

We know that you are good.
You love us and do great things for us.

So we all sing together:

Everyone: Holy, Holy, Holy Lord God of hosts.
Heaven and earth are full of your glory.
Hosanna in the highest.

Priest: Father,
you are always thinking about your people;
you never forget us.
You sent us your Son Jesus,
who gave his life for us
and who came to save us.
He cured sick people;
he cared for those who were poor
and wept with those who were sad.
He forgave sinners
and taught us to forgive each other.
He loved everyone
and showed us how to be kind.
He took children in his arms and blessed them.

So we are glad to sing:

Everyone: Blessed is he who comes in the name of the Lord.
Hosanna in the highest.

Priest: God our Father,
all over the world your people praise you.
So now we pray with the whole Church:
with **N.**, our Pope and **N.**, our Bishop.
In heaven the Blessed Virgin Mary,
the Apostles and all the Saints
always sing your praise.
Now we join with them and with the Angels
to adore you as we sing:

Everyone: Holy, Holy, Holy Lord God of hosts.
Heaven and earth are full of your glory.
Hosanna in the highest.
Blessed is he who comes in the name of the Lord.
Hosanna in the highest.

Priest: God our Father,
you are most holy
and we want to show you that we are grateful.
We bring you bread and wine
and ask you to send your Holy Spirit
to make these gifts
the Body and Blood of Jesus your Son.
Then we can offer to you
what you have given to us.

On the night before he died,
Jesus was having supper with his Apostles.
He took bread from the table.
He gave you thanks and praise.
Then he broke the bread,
gave it to his friends, and said:

TAKE THIS, ALL OF YOU, AND EAT OF IT,
FOR THIS IS MY BODY
WHICH WILL BE GIVEN UP FOR YOU.

When supper was ended,
Jesus took the chalice that was filled with wine.
He thanked you, gave it to his friends, and said:

TAKE THIS, ALL OF YOU, AND DRINK FROM IT,
FOR THIS IS THE CHALICE OF MY BLOOD,
THE BLOOD OF THE NEW AND ETERNAL **COVENANT**,
WHICH WILL BE POURED OUT FOR YOU AND FOR MANY
FOR THE **FORGIVENESS OF SINS**.

Then he said to them:

DO THIS IN MEMORY OF ME.

We do now what Jesus told us to do.
We remember his Death
and his Resurrection
and we offer you, Father,
the bread that gives us life,
and the cup that saves us.
Jesus brings us to you;
welcome us as you welcome him.

Let us proclaim our faith:

Everyone: We proclaim your Death, O Lord,
and profess your Resurrection,
until you come again.

Or
When we eat this Bread and drink this Cup,
we proclaim your Death, O Lord,
until you come again.

Or
Save us, Savior of the world,
for by your Cross and Resurrection
you have set us free.

Priest: Father,
because you love us,
you invite us to come to your table.
Fill us with the joy of the Holy Spirit
as we receive the Body and Blood of your Son.

Lord,
you never forget any of your children.
We ask you to take care of those we love,
especially of **N.** and **N.**,
and we pray for those who have died.
Remember everyone who is suffering
from pain or sorrow.

Remember Christians everywhere
and all other people in the world.

We are filled with wonder and praise
when we see what you do for us

through Jesus your Son,
and so we sing:

Through him, and with him, and in him,
O God, almighty Father,
in the unity of the Holy Spirit,
all glory and honor is yours,
for ever and ever.

Everyone: Amen.

(Turn to the Lord's Prayer, page 37)

Eucharistic Prayer I

The priest chooses a preface according to the liturgical calendar.

Everyone: Holy, Holy, Holy Lord God of hosts.
Heaven and earth are full of your glory.
Hosanna in the highest.
Blessed is he who comes in the name of the Lord.
Hosanna in the highest.

Priest: To you, therefore, most merciful Father,
we make humble prayer and petition
through Jesus Christ, your Son, our Lord:
that you accept
and bless these gifts, these offerings,
these holy and unblemished sacrifices,
which we offer you firstly
for your holy catholic Church.
Be pleased to grant her peace,
to guard, unite and govern her
throughout the whole world,
together with your servant **N.** our Pope
and **N.** our Bishop,
and all those who, holding to the truth,
hand on the catholic and apostolic faith.

Remember, Lord, your servants **N.** and **N.**
and all gathered here,
whose faith and devotion are known to you.
For them, we offer you this sacrifice of praise

We Share the Peace of Christ

God is our Father and we are brothers and sisters in Christ. In order to show that we are one family, the priest invites us to offer each other a sign of peace.

Priest: Lord Jesus Christ,
who said to your Apostles:
Peace I leave you, my peace I give you,
look not on our sins,
but on the faith of your Church,
and graciously grant her peace and **unity**
in accordance with your will.
Who live and reign for ever and ever.

Everyone: Amen.

Priest: The peace of the Lord be with you always.

Everyone: And with your spirit.

Priest: Let us offer each other the sign of peace.

At this time, by a handshake, a hug, or a bow, we give to those near us a sign of Christ's peace. Immediately after, we sing or say:

Everyone: **Lamb of God**, you take away the sins of the world,
have mercy on us.

Lamb of God, you take away the sins of the world,
have mercy on us.

Lamb of God, you take away the sins of the world,
grant us peace.

What Does It Mean?

Unity
When we get together each Sunday to celebrate the Lord's Supper, we recognize our unity, or oneness, since we are all children of the same loving Father.

Lamb of God
In the Old Testament, believers offered a lamb to God. We call Jesus the Lamb of God because he offers his life to God.

Gestures

The Sign of Peace
We shake hands, hug, or bow to one another to share the peace that comes from Christ. It is a sign of our commitment to live in peace with others.

We Receive Jesus in Communion

When we receive communion, the Bread of Life, Jesus feeds us with his very self.

The priest breaks the host and says:

Priest: Behold the Lamb of God,
behold him who takes away the sins of the world.
Blessed are those called to the supper of the Lamb.

Everyone: Lord, I am not worthy
that you should enter under my roof,
but only say the word
and my soul shall be healed.

It is time to come up to receive communion. The priest or the communion minister says:

Priest: The Body of Christ.

Everyone: Amen.

Questions

Why do we go to communion?
When we eat the bread, we receive Jesus. He gives himself to us this way so we can live for God. Sharing the Body and Blood of Christ in communion creates among us a special "one-ness" with God and with each other.

Why is the bread we share during Mass called a "host"?
The word "host" means "victim who is offered." The consecrated host is Jesus Christ, who offers himself in order to give life to others.

Gestures

The priest breaks the bread
The priest breaks the bread in the same way that Jesus did during the Last Supper, in order to share it. The early Christians used to call the Mass "the breaking of the bread."

Receiving the host
The priest or communion minister places the host in your open left hand. You pick the host up with your right hand, put the host in your mouth, eat the bread carefully, and return to your place. You take a few moments of quiet prayer to thank God for this Bread of Life.

The Lord Sends Us Forth (Dismissal)

After announcements, the priest blesses us in the name of God. We are then sent to live out our faith among all the people we meet during the week.

Priest: The Lord be with you.

Everyone: And with your spirit.

Priest: May almighty God bless you,
the Father, and the Son, and the Holy Spirit.

Everyone: Amen.

Then the priest sends us out, using one of these options:

1. **Priest:** Go forth, the Mass is ended.

   Everyone: Thanks be to God.

2. **Priest:** Go and announce the Gospel of the Lord.

   Everyone: Thanks be to God.

3. **Priest:** Go in peace, glorifying the Lord by your life.

   Everyone: Thanks be to God.

4. **Priest:** Go in peace.

   Everyone: Thanks be to God.

What Does It Mean?

The word "Mass"
The word "Mass" comes from the second word in the Latin phrase that was once used by the priest to announce the end of the Sunday celebration: *Ite missa est*—Go forth, the Mass is ended.

Communion for the sick
Sometimes people who are sick cannot be present at Sunday Mass. Certain members of the parish, known as communion ministers, can take consecrated hosts to the homes of sick people so that they can receive communion and be assured that the rest of the community is praying for them.

Gestures

Blessing
The priest makes the sign of the cross over the people in church. With this blessing we are sent out with the loving strength of God to live a life of love and service to others.

Dismissal
We cannot stay together in the church all week. When the Mass is ended, we must go our separate ways, in peace and love, to witness to the risen Jesus in the world today.

November 29

1st Sunday of Advent

First Reading (Isaiah 63:16b-17, 19b; 64:2-7)

You, LORD, are our father,
our **redeemer** you are named forever.
Why do you let us wander, O LORD, from your ways,
and harden our hearts so that we fear you not?
Return for the sake of your servants,
the tribes of your heritage.
Oh, that you would rend the heavens and come down,
with the mountains quaking before you,
while you wrought awesome deeds we could not hope for,
such as they had not heard of from of old.
No ear has ever heard, no eye ever seen, any God but you
doing such deeds for those who wait for him.
Would that you might meet us doing right,
that we were mindful of you in our ways!
Behold, you are angry, and we are sinful;
all of us have become like unclean people,
all our good deeds are like polluted rags;
we have all withered like leaves,
and our guilt carries us away like the wind.
There is none who calls upon your name,
who rouses himself to cling to you;
for you have **hidden your face** from us
and have delivered us up to our guilt.
Yet, O LORD, you are our father;
we are the clay and you the potter:
we are all the work of your hands.

The word of the Lord. **Thanks be to God.**

Responsorial Psalm (Psalm 80:2-3, 15-16, 18-19)

℟. **Lord, make us turn to you; let us see your face and we shall be saved.**

O shepherd of Israel, hearken,
from your throne upon the **cherubim**, shine forth.
Rouse your power,
and come to save us. ℟.

Once again, O LORD of hosts,
look down from heaven, and see;
take care of this vine,
and protect what your right hand has planted,
the son of man whom you yourself made strong. ℟.

May your help be with the man of your right hand,
with the son of man whom you yourself made strong.
Then we will no more withdraw from you;
give us new life, and we will call upon your name. ℟.

Second Reading (1 Corinthians 1:3-9)

Brothers and sisters: Grace to you and peace from God our Father and the Lord Jesus Christ.

I give thanks to my God always on your account for the grace of God bestowed on you in Christ Jesus, that in him you were enriched in every way, with all discourse and all knowledge, as the testimony to Christ was confirmed among you, so that you are not lacking in any spiritual gift as you wait for the revelation of our Lord Jesus Christ. He will keep you firm to the end, irreproachable on **the day of our Lord Jesus Christ**. God is faithful, and by him you were called to fellowship with his Son, Jesus Christ our Lord.

The word of the Lord. **Thanks be to God.**

Gospel (Mark 13:33-37)

A reading from the holy Gospel according to Mark.
Glory to you, O Lord.

Jesus said to his disciples: "Be watchful! Be alert! You do not know when the time will come. It is like a man traveling abroad. He leaves home and places his servants in charge, each with his own work, and orders the gatekeeper to be on the watch. Watch, therefore; you do not know when the lord of the house is coming, whether in the evening, or at midnight, or at cockcrow, or in the morning. May he not come suddenly and find you sleeping. What I say to you, I say to all: 'Watch!'"

The Gospel of the Lord. **Praise to you, Lord Jesus Christ.**

Key Words

With the season of **Advent**, which means "coming," we begin a new liturgical year. Advent lasts four weeks and during this time the liturgical color is violet or purple. Purple is the color of waiting; it reminds us to prepare our hearts to celebrate the birth of Jesus at Christmas and his return at the end of time.

To redeem is to buy something back or to pay to free someone. God is called our **redeemer** because God freed Israel from slavery in Egypt. Christ is our Redeemer, for by his resurrection he freed us from the power of death.

When the Bible says that God has **hidden his face**, it means that we think God has turned away or is angry. But we know that God is always near and we are the ones who have turned our backs to God.

Cherubim (the plural of cherub) are a type of angel. In the Bible they are the ones who watch over the entrance to the Garden of Eden. To show that God is above everything, the psalmist says that God's throne is above the cherubim.

When Saint Paul refers to **the day of our Lord Jesus Christ**, he is speaking about the end of the world—the day human history will end and we will see God face to face.

The **Gospel of Mark** is the earliest and the shortest of the four gospels. The other gospels were written by Matthew, Luke, and John. This year, most of the gospel readings will come from Mark.

December 6

2nd Sunday of Advent

First Reading (Isaiah 40:1-5, 9-11)

Comfort, give comfort to my people,
says your God.
Speak tenderly to Jerusalem, and proclaim to her
that her service is at an end,
her guilt is expiated;
indeed, she has received from **the hand of the LORD**
double for all her sins.

A voice cries out:
In the desert prepare the way of the LORD!
Make straight in the wasteland a highway for our God!
Every valley shall be filled in,
every mountain and hill shall be made low;
the rugged land shall be made a plain,
the rough country, a broad valley.
Then the glory of the LORD shall be revealed,
and all people shall see it together;
for **the mouth of the LORD** has spoken.

Go up on to a high mountain,
Zion, herald of glad tidings;
cry out at the top of your voice,
Jerusalem, herald of good news!
Fear not to cry out
and say to the cities of Judah:
Here is your God!
Here comes with power
the Lord GOD,
who **rules by his strong arm**;
here is his reward with him,
his recompense before him.
Like a shepherd he feeds his flock;
in his arms he gathers the lambs,
carrying them in his bosom,
and leading the ewes with care.

The word of the Lord. **Thanks be to God.**

Responsorial Psalm (Psalm 85:9-10, 11-12, 13-14)

℟. **Lord, let us see your kindness,
and grant us your salvation.**

I will hear what God proclaims;
the LORD—for he proclaims peace to his people.
Near indeed is his salvation to those who fear him,
glory dwelling in our land. ℟.

Kindness and truth shall meet;
justice and peace shall kiss.
Truth shall spring out of the earth,
and justice shall look down from heaven. ℟.

The LORD himself will give his benefits;
our land shall yield its increase.
Justice shall walk before him,
and prepare the way of his steps. ℟.

Second Reading (2 Peter 3:8-14)

Do not ignore this one fact, beloved, that with the Lord one day is like a thousand years and a thousand years like one day. The Lord does not delay his promise, as some regard "delay," but he is patient with you, not wishing that any should perish but that all should come to repentance. But the day of the Lord will come like a thief, and then the heavens will pass away with a mighty roar and the elements will be dissolved by fire, and the earth and everything done on it will be found out.

Since everything is to be dissolved in this way, what sort of persons ought you to be, conducting yourselves in **holiness** and devotion, waiting for and hastening the coming of the day of God, because of which the heavens will be dissolved in flames and the elements melted by fire. But according to his promise we await new heavens and a new earth in which righteousness dwells. Therefore, beloved, since you await these things, be eager to be found without spot or blemish before him, at peace.

The word of the Lord. **Thanks be to God.**

Gospel (Mark 1:1-8)

A reading from the holy Gospel according to Mark.
Glory to you, O Lord.

The beginning of the gospel of Jesus Christ the Son of God.

As it is written in Isaiah the prophet:
Behold, I am sending my messenger ahead of you;
he will prepare your way.
A voice of one crying out in the desert:
"Prepare the way of the Lord,
make straight his paths."

John the Baptist appeared in the desert proclaiming a baptism of repentance for the forgiveness of sins. People of the whole Judean countryside and all the inhabitants of Jerusalem were going out to him and were being baptized by him in the Jordan River as they acknowledged their sins. John was clothed in camel's hair, with a leather belt around his waist. He fed on locusts and wild honey. And this is what he proclaimed: "One mightier than I is coming after me. I am not worthy to stoop and loosen the thongs of his sandals. I have baptized you with water; he will baptize you **with the Holy Spirit**."

The Gospel of the Lord. **Praise to you, Lord Jesus Christ.**

Key Words

God does not have a body, but to help us understand, the Bible uses parts of the human body to describe God: God acts (**the hand of the Lord**), God communicates with us (**the mouth of the Lord**), God is powerful (he **rules by his strong arm**) and God cares for us (**in his arms he gathers the lambs**).

In the **Second Letter of Saint Peter**, the people are worrying about when Jesus will return. Saint Peter helps them understand that the important thing is not to worry but to live well and to let God decide when the Second Coming (or advent) will take place.

Holiness means living near God and letting the Holy Spirit guide us. To be holy is to live in a God-like manner: with love, mercy, and compassion.

"**Prepare the way of the Lord**" were John the Baptist's words to the people, telling them to change their lives so that they would be ready for the Messiah. John the Baptist used the same words as the Prophet Isaiah had done, to show that Jesus was indeed the Promised One, the Messiah.

John the Baptist was the son of Zechariah and Elizabeth (the cousin of the Virgin Mary), and therefore Jesus' cousin. He told people that Jesus was coming soon. He was called John the Baptist because he baptized many people.

When we are baptized, we are baptized with water and **with the Holy Spirit**. We let God into our lives, and the Holy Spirit is alive in us. John the Baptist knew that baptism in the name of Jesus marked the beginning of a new life!

December 8

Immaculate Conception of the Blessed Virgin Mary

First Reading (Genesis 3:9-15, 20)

After the man, **Adam**, had eaten of the tree, the LORD God called to the man and asked him, "Where are you?" He answered, "I heard you in the garden; but I was afraid, because I was naked, so I hid myself." Then he asked, "Who told you that you were naked? You have eaten, then, from the tree of which I had forbidden you to eat!" The man replied, "The woman whom you put here with me—she gave me fruit from the tree, and so I ate it." The LORD God then asked the woman, "Why did you do such a thing?" The woman answered, "The serpent tricked me into it, so I ate it."

Then the LORD God said to the serpent:
"Because you have done this, you shall be banned
from all the animals
and from all the wild creatures;
on your belly shall you crawl,
and dirt shall you eat
all the days of your life.
I will put enmity between you and the woman,
and between your offspring and hers;
he will strike at your head,
while you strike at his heel."

The man called his wife **Eve**, because she became the mother of all the living.

The word of the Lord. **Thanks be to God.**

Responsorial Psalm (Psalm 98:1, 2-3ab, 3cd-4)

℟. **Sing to the Lord a new song,**
for he has done marvelous deeds.

Sing to the LORD a new song,
for he has done wondrous deeds;
His right hand has won victory for him,
his holy arm. ℟.

The LORD has made his salvation known:
in the sight of the nations he has revealed his justice.
He has remembered his kindness and his faithfulness
toward the house of Israel. ℟.

All the ends of the earth have seen
the salvation by our God.
Sing joyfully to the LORD, all you lands;
break into song; sing praise. ℟.

Second Reading (Ephesians 1:3-6, 11-12)

Brothers and sisters: Blessed be the God and Father of our Lord Jesus Christ, who has blessed us in Christ with every spiritual blessing in the heavens, as he chose us in him, before the foundation of the world, to be holy and without blemish before him. In love he destined us for **adoption** to himself through Jesus Christ, in accord with the favor of his will, for the praise of the glory of his grace that he granted us in the beloved.

In him we were also chosen, destined in accord with the purpose of the One who accomplishes all things according to the intention of his will, so that we might exist for the praise of his glory, we who first hoped in Christ.

The word of the Lord. **Thanks be to God.**

Gospel (Luke 1:26-38)

A reading from the holy Gospel according to Luke.
Glory to you, O Lord.

The angel Gabriel was sent from God to a town of Galilee called Nazareth, to a virgin betrothed to a man named Joseph, of the house of David, and the virgin's name was Mary. And coming to her, he said, "Hail, full of grace! The Lord is with you." But she was greatly troubled at what was said and pondered what sort of greeting this might be. Then the angel said to her, "Do not be afraid, Mary, for you have found favor with God. Behold, you will conceive in your womb and bear a son, and you shall name him Jesus. He will be great and will be called Son of the Most High, and the Lord God will give him the throne of David his father, and he will rule over the house of Jacob forever, and of his Kingdom there will be no end." But Mary said to the angel, "How can this be, since I have no relations with a man?" And the angel said to her in reply, "The Holy Spirit will come upon you, and the power of the Most High will overshadow you. Therefore the child to be born will be called holy, the Son of God. And behold, Elizabeth, your relative, has also conceived a son in her old age, and this is the sixth month for her who was called barren; for nothing will be impossible for God." Mary said, "Behold, I am the handmaid of the Lord. May it be done to me according to your word." Then the angel departed from her.

The Gospel of the Lord.
Praise to you, Lord Jesus Christ.

Key Words

The **Immaculate Conception** is the day we remember that God kept the Virgin Mary free from sin from the very beginning of her life. God did this for Mary because she was the mother of our Savior, Jesus, and it is through Jesus that all of us, including Mary, are redeemed and saved from sin.

Some stories are true on the inside, even if they are not completely true on the outside. The Church does not teach that the story of **Adam** and **Eve** happened just as it is told in this reading. But it does teach that this story tells us a very important truth about how human beings first turned away from God—and often still do.

When God says "**he will strike at your head**," the Church believes that God is speaking about Jesus, who will come and save human beings from sin.

Children without parents can be adopted into new families. A similar process of **adoption** happened in our baptism. Through baptism, we have been adopted by God, our heavenly parent. We have become brothers and sisters of Jesus, brothers and sisters to one another, all of us children of God, called to share God's love and life.

December 13

3rd Sunday of Advent

First Reading (Isaiah 61:1-2a, 10-11)

The spirit of the Lord GOD is upon me,
because the LORD has **anointed** me;
he has sent me to bring glad tidings to the poor,
to heal the brokenhearted,
to proclaim liberty to the captives
and release to the prisoners,
to announce a **year of favor from the LORD**
and a day of vindication by our God.

I rejoice heartily in the LORD,
in my God is the joy of my soul;
for he has clothed me with a robe of salvation
and wrapped me in a mantle of justice,
like a bridegroom adorned with a diadem,
like a bride bedecked with her jewels.
As the earth brings forth its plants,
and a garden makes its growth spring up,
so will the Lord GOD make justice and praise
spring up before all the nations.

The word of the Lord. **Thanks be to God.**

Responsorial Psalm (Luke 1:46-48, 49-50, 53-54)

℟. **My soul rejoices in my God.**

My soul proclaims the greatness of the Lord;
my spirit rejoices in God my Savior,
for he has looked upon his lowly servant.
From this day all generations will call me blessed. ℟.

The Almighty has done great things for me,
and holy is his Name.
He has mercy on those who fear him
in every generation. ℟.

He has filled the hungry with good things,
and the rich he has sent away empty.
He has come to the help of his servant Israel
for he has remembered his promise of mercy. ℟.

Second Reading (1 Thessalonians 5:16-24)

Brothers and sisters: Rejoice always. Pray without ceasing. In all circumstances **give thanks**, for this is the will of God for you in Christ Jesus. Do not quench the Spirit. Do not despise prophetic utterances. Test everything; retain what is good. Refrain from every kind of evil.

May the God of peace make you perfectly holy and may you entirely, spirit, soul, and body, be preserved blameless for the coming of our Lord Jesus Christ. The one who calls you is faithful, and he will also accomplish it.

The word of the Lord. **Thanks be to God.**

Gospel (John 1:6-8, 19-28)

A reading from the holy Gospel according to John.
Glory to you, O Lord.

A man named **John** was sent from God. He came for testimony, to testify to the light, so that all might believe through him. He was not the light, but came to testify to the light.

And this is the testimony of John. When the Jews from Jerusalem sent priests and Levites to him to ask him, "Who are you?" he admitted and did not deny it, but admitted, "I am not the **Christ**." So they asked him, "What are you then? Are you Elijah?" And he said, "I am not." "Are you the Prophet?" He answered, "No." So they said to him, "Who are you, so we can give an answer to those who sent us? What do you have to say for yourself?" He said:

> "I am *the voice of one crying out in the desert,*
> *'make straight the way of the Lord,'*

as Isaiah the prophet said." Some Pharisees were also sent. They asked him, "Why then do you baptize if you are not the Christ or Elijah or the Prophet?" John answered them, "I baptize with water; but there is one among you whom you do not recognize, the one who is coming after me, whose sandal strap I am not worthy to untie." This happened in Bethany across the Jordan, where John was baptizing.

The Gospel of the Lord. **Praise to you, Lord Jesus Christ.**

Key Words

To anoint means to bless with oil. In the Bible it can also mean to give someone a mission, an important job. Christians are **anointed** at baptism and confirmation: our mission is to live as Jesus taught us, bringing good news to the oppressed.

Every 50 years, Israel celebrated a jubilee year, a special time when debts were forgiven and wrongs were pardoned. When Isaiah mentions a **year of favor from the Lord**, he means that, just as in the jubilee year, God is offering forgiveness to all those who are sorry for their wrongs and are seeking pardon.

One way to pray is to **give thanks** to God. We do this, for example, when we say "grace'" before meals—we thank God each day for all the good things God has given us. In many languages, the words for "grace" and "thanks" are the same.

Today's gospel is taken from the **Gospel of John**, the last of the gospels to be written. The author of this gospel was one of the Twelve Apostles. Today we hear of another **John**—John the Baptist, the cousin of Jesus, who preached that everyone had to change their lives and prepare to receive the Messiah. John the Baptist did not write the gospel, but he was the greatest of all the prophets.

Jesus, his disciples, and the people of the time spoke Aramaic. Messiah is an Aramaic word meaning "anointed." The chosen person was anointed or blessed with holy oil and given a special mission. The Greek word for "anointed" is **Christ**.

December 20

4th Sunday of Advent

First Reading (2 Samuel 7:1-5, 8b-12, 14a, 16)

When King David was settled in his palace, and the LORD had given him rest from his enemies on every side, he said to Nathan the prophet, "Here I am living in a house of cedar, while the **ark of God** dwells in a tent!" Nathan answered the king, "Go, do whatever you have in mind, for the LORD is with you." But that night the LORD spoke to Nathan and said: "Go, tell my servant David, 'Thus says the LORD: Should you build me a house to dwell in?

" '**It was I who took you from the pasture** and from the care of the flock to be commander of my people Israel. I have been with you wherever you went, and I have destroyed all your enemies before you. And I will make you famous like the great ones of the earth. I will fix a place for my people Israel; I will plant them so that they may dwell in their place without further disturbance. Neither shall the wicked continue to afflict them as they did of old, since the time I first appointed judges over my people Israel. I will give you rest from all your enemies. The LORD also reveals to you that he will establish a house for you. And when your time comes and you rest with your ancestors, I will raise up your heir after you, sprung from your loins, and I will make his kingdom firm. I will be a father to him, and he shall be a son to me. Your house and your kingdom shall endure forever before me; your throne shall stand firm forever.' "

The word of the Lord. **Thanks be to God.**

Responsorial Psalm (Psalm 89:2-3, 4-5, 27, 29)

℟. **For ever I will sing the goodness of the Lord.**

The promises of the LORD I will sing forever;
through all generations my mouth shall proclaim
your faithfulness.
For you have said, "My kindness is established forever";
in heaven you have confirmed your faithfulness. ℟.

"I have made a covenant with my chosen one,
I have sworn to David my servant:
forever will I confirm your posterity
and establish your throne for all generations." ℟.

"He shall say of me, 'You are my father,
my God, the Rock, my savior.'
Forever I will maintain my kindness toward him,
and my covenant with him stands firm." ℟.

Second Reading (Romans 16:25-27)

Brothers and sisters: To him who can strengthen you, according to my gospel and the proclamation of Jesus Christ, according to the revelation of the mystery kept secret for long ages but now manifested through the prophetic writings and, according to the command of the eternal God, made known to all nations to bring about the obedience of faith, to the only wise God, through Jesus Christ be glory forever and ever. Amen.

The word of the Lord. **Thanks be to God.**

Gospel (Luke 1:26-38)

A reading from the holy Gospel according to Luke.
Glory to you, O Lord.

The angel Gabriel was sent from God to a town of Galilee called Nazareth, to a virgin betrothed to a man named Joseph, of the **house of David**, and the virgin's name was Mary. And coming to her, he said, "Hail, full of grace! The Lord is with you." But she was greatly troubled at what was said and pondered what sort of greeting this might be. Then the angel said to her, "Do not be afraid, Mary, for you have found favor with God.

"Behold, you will conceive in your womb and bear a son, and you shall name him Jesus. He will be great and will be called Son of the Most High, and the Lord God will give him the throne of David his father, and he will rule over the house of Jacob forever, and of his kingdom there will be no end." But Mary said to the angel, "How can this be, since I have no relations with a man?" And the angel said to her in reply, "The Holy Spirit will come upon you, and the power of the Most High will overshadow you. Therefore the child to be born will be called holy, the Son of God. And behold, Elizabeth, your relative, has also conceived a son in her old age, and this is the sixth month for her who was called barren; for nothing will be impossible for God." Mary said, "Behold, I am the handmaid of the Lord. May it be done to me according to your word." Then the angel departed from her.

The Gospel of the Lord. **Praise to you, Lord Jesus Christ.**

Key Words

Samuel, a prophet and judge in Israel, was born over 1,000 years before Jesus. The Lord chose Samuel to anoint Saul, the first king of Israel. Samuel also anointed David, who was king after Saul. The Bible contains two books in his name: 1 Samuel and 2 Samuel.

The **ark of God**, also called the ark of the covenant, was a wooden box in which the Israelites stored important objects reminding them that God was their savior. It was built to contain the two stone tablets on which the Ten Commandments were written, a golden urn of manna (the miraculous bread that fell from heaven when they were living in the desert), and Aaron's staff.

Before he was anointed king of Israel, David was a lowly shepherd. It was by God's grace that David was chosen and not because of anything special David had done to earn the title. When God tells David, "**It was I who took you from the pasture**," God is reminding him that it is God who chooses, not David.

The **Gospel of Luke** was written for people who, like Luke, weren't Jewish before becoming Christian. This gospel tells us the most of what we know of Mary, the mother of Jesus—such as today's wonderful story of the annunciation.

The gospel assures us that Joseph was descended from the **house of David**. This fulfills the promise made by the prophets that the Messiah would be born from among David's descendants. In fact, the Gospel of Matthew opens with a genealogy showing how Jesus is descended from David through Joseph.

December 25

The Nativity of the Lord (Christmas)

Vigil Mass: page 69
Mass During the Night: page 72
Mass at Dawn: page 75
Mass During the Day: page 76

Vigil Mass

First Reading (Isaiah 62:1-5)

For Zion's sake I will not be silent,
  or Jerusalem's sake I will not be quiet,
until her vindication shines forth like the dawn
  and her victory like a burning torch.

Nations shall behold your vindication,
  and all the kings your glory;
you shall be called by a new name
  pronounced by the mouth of the Lord.
You shall be a glorious crown in the hand of the Lord,
  a royal diadem held by your God.
No more shall people call you "Forsaken,"
  or your land "Desolate,"
but you shall be called "My Delight,"
  and your land "Espoused."
For the Lord delights in you
  and makes your land his spouse.
As a young man marries a virgin,
  your Builder shall marry you;
and as a bridegroom rejoices in his bride
  so shall your God rejoice in you.

The word of the Lord. **Thanks be to God.**

Responsorial Psalm (Psalm 89:4-5, 16-17, 27, 29)

℟. **For ever I will sing the goodness of the Lord.**

I have made a covenant with my chosen one,
I have sworn to David my servant:
Forever will I confirm your posterity
and establish your throne for all generations. ℟.

Blessed the people who know the joyful shout;
in the light of your countenance, O LORD, they walk.
At your name they rejoice all the day,
and through your justice they are exalted. ℟.

He shall say of me, "You are my father,
my God, the rock, my savior."
Forever I will maintain my kindness toward him,
and my covenant with him stands firm. ℟.

Second Reading (Acts 13:16-17, 22-25)

When Paul reached Antioch in Pisidia and entered the synagogue, he stood up, motioned with his hand, and said, "Fellow Israelites and you others who are God-fearing, listen. The God of this people Israel chose our ancestors and exalted the people during their sojourn in the land of Egypt. With uplifted arm he led them out of it. Then he removed Saul and raised up David as king; of him he testified, 'I have found David, son of Jesse, a man after my own heart; he will carry out my every wish.' From this man's descendants God, according to his promise, has brought to Israel a savior, Jesus. John heralded his coming by proclaiming a baptism of repentance to all the people of Israel; and as John was completing his course, he would say, 'What do you suppose that I am? I am not he. Behold, one is coming after me; I am not worthy to unfasten the sandals of his feet.'"

The word of the Lord. **Thanks be to God.**

Gospel (Matthew 1:1-25 or 1:18-25)

For the shorter reading, omit the part in brackets.

A reading from the holy Gospel according to Luke.
Glory to you, O Lord.

[The book of the genealogy of Jesus Christ, the son of David, the son of Abraham.

Abraham became the father of Isaac, Isaac the father of Jacob, Jacob the father of Judah and his brothers. Judah became the father of Perez and Zerah, whose mother was Tamar. Perez became the father of Hezron, Hezron the father of Ram, Ram the father of Amminadab. Amminadab became the father of Nahshon, Nahshon the father of Salmon, Salmon the father of Boaz, whose mother was Rahab. Boaz became the father of Obed, whose mother was Ruth. Obed became the father of Jesse, Jesse the father of David the king.

David became the father of Solomon, whose mother had been the wife of Uriah. Solomon became the father of Rehoboam, Rehoboam the father of Abijah, Abijah the father of Asaph. Asaph became the father of Jehoshaphat, Jehoshaphat the father of Joram, Joram the father of Uzziah. Uzziah became the father of Jotham, Jotham the father of Ahaz, Ahaz the father of Hezekiah. Hezekiah became the father of Manasseh, Manasseh the father of Amos, Amos the father of Josiah. Josiah became the father of Jechoniah and his brothers at the time of the Babylonian exile.

After the Babylonian exile, Jechoniah became the father of Shealtiel, Shealtiel the father of Zerubbabel, Zerubbabel the father of Abiud, Abiud became the father of Eliakim, Eliakim the father of Azor, Azor the father of Zadok. Zadok became the father of Achim, Achim the father of Eliud, Eliud the father of Eleazar. Eleazar became the father of Matthan, Matthan the father of Jacob, Jacob the father of Joseph, the husband of Mary. Of her was born Jesus who is called the Christ.

Thus the total number of generations from Abraham to David is fourteen generations; from David to the Babylonian exile, fourteen generations; from the Babylonian exile to the Messiah, fourteen generations.

Now] this is how the birth of Jesus Christ came about. When his mother Mary was betrothed to Joseph, but before they lived together, she was found with child through the Holy Spirit. Joseph her husband, since he was a righteous man, yet unwilling to expose her to shame, decided to divorce her quietly. Such was his intention when, behold, the angel of the Lord appeared to him in a dream and said, "Joseph, son of David, do not be afraid to take Mary your wife into your home. For it is through the Holy Spirit that this child has been conceived in her. She will bear a son and you are to name him Jesus, because he will save his people from their sins." All this took place to fulfill what the Lord had said through the prophet:

Behold, the virgin shall conceive and bear a son,
and they shall name him Emmanuel,

which means "God is with us." When Joseph awoke, he did as the angel of the Lord had commanded him and took his wife into his home. He had no relations with her until she bore a son, and he named him Jesus.

The Gospel of the Lord. **Praise to you, Lord Jesus Christ.**

Mass During the Night

First Reading (Isaiah 9:1-6)

The people who walked in darkness
have seen a great light;
upon those who dwelt in the land of gloom
a light has shone.
You have brought them abundant joy
and great rejoicing,
as they rejoice before you as at the harvest,
as people make merry when dividing spoils.
For the yoke that burdened them,
the pole on their shoulder,
and the rod of their taskmaster
you have smashed, as on the day of Midian.
For every boot that tramped in battle,
every cloak rolled in blood,
will be burned as fuel for flames.

For a child is born to us, a son is given us;
  upon his shoulder dominion rests.
They name him Wonder-Counselor, God-Hero,
  Father-Forever, Prince of Peace.
His dominion is vast
  and forever peaceful,
from David's throne, and over his kingdom,
  which he confirms and sustains
by judgment and justice,
  both now and forever.
The zeal of the LORD of hosts will do this!

The word of the Lord. **Thanks be to God.**

Responsorial Psalm (Psalm 96:1-2, 2-3, 11-12, 13)

℟. **Today is born our Savior, Christ the Lord.**

Sing to the LORD a new song;
  sing to the LORD, all you lands.
Sing to the Lord; bless his name. ℟.

Announce his salvation, day after day.
  Tell his glory among the nations;
  among all peoples, his wondrous deeds. ℟.

Let the heavens be glad and the earth rejoice;
  let the sea and what fills it resound;
  let the plains be joyful and all that is in them!
Then shall all the trees of the forest exult. ℟.

They shall **exult** before the LORD, for he comes;
  for he comes to rule the earth.
He shall rule the world with justice
  and the peoples with his constancy. ℟.

Second Reading (Titus 2:11-14)

Beloved: The grace of God has appeared, saving all and training us to reject godless ways and worldly desires and to live temperately, justly, and devoutly in this age, as we await the blessed hope, the appearance of the glory of our great God and savior Jesus Christ, who gave himself for us to deliver us from all lawlessness and to cleanse for himself a people as his own, eager to do what is good.

The word of the Lord. **Thanks be to God.**

Gospel (Luke 2:1-14)

A reading from the holy Gospel according to Luke.
Glory to you, O Lord.

In those days a decree went out from Caesar Augustus that the whole world should be enrolled. This was the first enrollment, when Quirinius was governor of Syria. So all went to be enrolled, each to his own town. And Joseph too went up from Galilee from the town of Nazareth to Judea, to the city of David that is called Bethlehem, because he was of the house and family of David, to be enrolled with Mary, his betrothed, who was with child. While they were there, the time came for her to have her child, and she gave birth to her firstborn son. She wrapped him in swaddling clothes and laid him in a **manger**, because there was no room for them in the inn.

Now there were shepherds in that region living in the fields and keeping the night watch over their flock. The **angel of the Lord** appeared to them and the glory of the Lord shone around them, and they were struck with great fear. The angel said to them, "Do not be afraid; for behold, I proclaim to you good news of great joy that will be for all the people. For today in the city of David a savior has been born for you who is Christ and Lord. And this will be a sign for you: you will find an infant wrapped in swaddling clothes and lying in a manger." And suddenly there was a multitude of the heavenly host with the angel, praising God and saying:

"Glory to God in the highest
and on earth peace to those on whom his favor rests."

The Gospel of the Lord. **Praise to you, Lord Jesus Christ.**

Mass at Dawn

First Reading (Isaiah 62:11-12)

See, the LORD proclaims
to the ends of the earth:
say to daughter Zion,
your savior comes!
Here is his reward with him,
his recompense before him.
They shall be called the holy people,
the redeemed of the LORD,
and you shall be called "Frequented,"
a city that is not forsaken.

The word of the Lord. **Thanks be to God.**

Responsorial Psalm (Psalm 97:1, 6, 11-12)

℟. **A light will shine on us this day:**
the Lord is born for us.

The LORD is king; let the earth rejoice;
let the many isles be glad.
The heavens proclaim his justice,
and all peoples see his glory. ℟.

Light dawns for the just;
and gladness, for the upright of heart.
Be glad in the LORD, you just,
and give thanks to his holy name. ℟.

Second Reading (Titus 3:4-7)

Beloved:
When the kindness and generous love
of God our savior appeared,
not because of any righteous deeds we had done
but because of his mercy,
he saved us through the bath of rebirth
and renewal by the Holy Spirit,

whom he richly poured out on us
  through Jesus Christ our savior,
so that we might be justified by his grace
  and become heirs in hope of eternal life.

The word of the Lord. **Thanks be to God.**

Gospel (Luke 2:15-20)

A reading from the holy Gospel according to Luke.
Glory to you, O Lord.

When the angels went away from them to heaven, the shepherds said to one another, "Let us go, then, to Bethlehem to see this thing that has taken place, which the Lord has made known to us." So they went in haste and found Mary and Joseph, and the infant lying in the manger. When they saw this, they made known the message that had been told them about this child. All who heard it were amazed by what had been told them by the shepherds. And Mary kept all these things, reflecting on them in her heart. Then the shepherds returned, glorifying and praising God for all they had heard and seen, just as it had been told to them.

The Gospel of the Lord. **Praise to you, Lord Jesus Christ.**

Mass During the Day

First Reading (Isaiah 52:7-10)

How beautiful upon the mountains
  are the feet of him who brings glad tidings,
announcing peace, bearing good news,
  announcing salvation, and saying to Zion,
  "Your God is King!"

Hark! Your sentinels raise a cry,
  together they shout for joy,
for they see directly, before their eyes,
  the LORD restoring Zion.
Break out together in song,
  O ruins of Jerusalem!

For the LORD comforts his people,
    he redeems Jerusalem.
The LORD has bared his holy arm
    in the sight of all the nations;
all the ends of the earth will behold
    the salvation of our God.

The word of the Lord. **Thanks be to God.**

Responsorial Psalm (Psalm 98:1, 2-3, 3-4, 5-6)

℟. **All the ends of the earth have seen the saving power of God.**

Sing to the LORD a new song,
    for he has done wondrous deeds;
his right hand has won victory for him,
    his holy arm. ℟.

The LORD has made his salvation known:
    in the sight of the nations he has revealed
        his justice.
He has remembered his kindness
        and his faithfulness
    toward the house of Israel. ℟.

All the ends of the earth have seen
    the salvation by our God.
Sing joyfully to the LORD, all you lands;
    break into song; sing praise. ℟.

Sing praise to the LORD with the harp,
    with the harp and melodious song.
With trumpets and the sound of the horn
    sing joyfully before the King, the LORD. ℟.

Second Reading (Hebrews 1:1-6)

Brothers and sisters: In times past, God spoke in partial and various ways to our ancestors through the prophets; in these last days, he has spoken to us through the Son, whom he made heir of all things and through whom he created the universe,

who is the refulgence of his glory, the very imprint
of his being,
and who sustains all things by his mighty word.
When he had accomplished purification from sins,
he took his seat at the right hand of the Majesty on high,
as far superior to the angels
as the name he has inherited is more excellent than theirs.

For to which of the angels did God ever say:
You are my son; this day I have begotten you?
Or again:
I will be a father to him, and he shall be a son to me?
And again, when he leads the firstborn into the world, he says:
Let all the angels of God worship him.

The word of the Lord. **Thanks be to God.**

Gospel (John 1:1-18 or 1:1-5, 9-14)

For the shorter reading, omit the indented parts in brackets.

A reading from the holy Gospel according to John.
Glory to you, O Lord.

In the beginning was the Word?,
and the Word was with God,
and the Word was God.
He was in the beginning with God.
All things came to be through him,
and without him nothing came to be.
What came to be through him was life,
and this life was the light of the human race;
the light shines in the darkness,
and the darkness has not overcome it.
[A man named John was sent from God. He came for testimony, to testify to the light, so that all might believe through him. He was not the light, but came to testify to the light.]
The true light, which enlightens everyone, was coming into the world.
He was in the world,
and the world came to be through him,
but the world did not know him.
He came to what was his own,

but his own people did not accept him.
But to those who did accept him he gave power to become children of God, to those who believe in his name, who were born not by natural generation nor by human choice nor by a man's decision but of God.

And the Word became flesh
and made his dwelling among us,
and we saw his glory,
the glory as of the Father's only Son,
full of grace and truth.

[John testified to him and cried out, saying, "This was he of whom I said, 'The one who is coming after me ranks ahead of me because he existed before me.'" From his fullness we have all received, grace in place of grace, because while the law was given through Moses, grace and truth came through Jesus Christ. No one has ever seen God. The only Son, God, who is at the Father's side, has revealed him.]

The Gospel of the Lord. **Praise to you, Lord Jesus Christ.**

Key Words

Christmas Day is celebrated on December 25, but the **Christmas** season lasts for three weeks, ending with the Baptism of Jesus in January. The liturgical color for this season is white, the color of joy and celebration.

Prophets like **Isaiah** were good men and women who spoke for God. Sometimes their messages were demanding: they asked people to change their lives and attitudes to grow closer to God. At other times, they brought words of comfort.

We **exult**, or rejoice, because our hearts are full of happiness: God has come to be with us. In today's psalm, we see that all creation—even the trees!—rejoice and glory in the Lord.

A **manger** is a wooden crate filled with hay to feed the animals in a stable. The baby Jesus was placed in a manger soon after he was born. It was amazing that God would choose to be born in such a simple place.

An **angel of the Lord** is a messenger of God. Angels appear many times in the Bible, as we see angels revealing God's plan in the lives of Jesus, Mary, and Joseph.

December 27

Holy Family of Jesus, Mary & Joseph

These are the readings for Year B. The first reading, psalm, and second reading for Year A (Sirach 3:2-6, 12-14; Psalm 128:1-2, 3, 4-5; Colossians 3:12-21 or 3:12-17) may also be used.

First Reading (Genesis 15:1-6; 21:1-3)

The word of the LORD came to **Abram** in a vision, saying:
"Fear not, Abram!
I am your shield;
I will make your reward very great."

But Abram said, "O Lord GOD, what good will your gifts be, if I keep on being childless and have as my heir the steward of my house, Eliezer?" Abram continued, "See, you have given me no offspring, and so one of my servants will be my heir." Then the word of the LORD came to him: "No, that one shall not be your heir; your own issue shall be your heir." The Lord took Abram outside and said, "Look up at the sky and count the stars, if you can. Just so," he added, "shall your descendants be." Abram put his faith in the LORD, who credited it to him as an act of righteousness.

The LORD took note of Sarah as he had said he would; he did for her as he had promised. Sarah became pregnant and bore Abraham a son in his old age, at the set time that God had stated. Abraham gave the name Isaac to this son of his whom Sarah bore him.

The word of the Lord. **Thanks be to God.**

Responsorial Psalm (Psalm 105:1-2, 3-4, 6-7, 8-9)

℟. **The Lord remembers his covenant for ever.**

Give thanks to the LORD, invoke his name;
make known among the nations his deeds.
Sing to him, sing his praise,
proclaim all his wondrous deeds. ℟.

Glory in his holy name;
rejoice, O hearts that seek the LORD!
Look to the LORD in his strength;
constantly seek his face. ℟.

You descendants of Abraham, his servants,
 sons of Jacob, his chosen ones!
He, the LORD, is our God;
 throughout the earth his judgments prevail. ℟.

He remembers forever his covenant
 which he made binding for a thousand generations
which he entered into with Abraham
 and by his oath to Isaac. ℟.

Second Reading (Hebrews 11:8, 11-12, 17-19)

Brothers and sisters: By **faith** Abraham obeyed when he was called to go out to a place that he was to receive as an inheritance; he went out, not knowing where he was to go. By faith he received power to generate, even though he was past the normal age—and Sarah herself was **sterile**—for he thought that the one who had made the promise was trustworthy. So it was that there came forth from one man, himself as good as dead, descendants as numerous as the stars in the sky and as countless as the sands on the seashore.

By faith Abraham, when put to the test, offered up Isaac, and he who had received the promises was ready to offer his only son, of whom it was said, "Through Isaac descendants shall bear your name." He reasoned that God was able to raise even from the dead, and he received Isaac back as a symbol.

The word of the Lord. **Thanks be to God.**

Gospel (Luke 2:22-40 or 2:22, 39-40)

For the shorter version, omit the indented part in brackets.

A reading from the holy Gospel according to Luke.
Glory to you, O Lord.

When the days were completed for their **purification** according to the law of Moses, they took him up to Jerusalem to present him to the Lord,

> [just as it is written in the law of the Lord, *Every male that opens the womb shall be consecrated to the Lord,* and to offer

the sacrifice of *a pair of turtledoves or two young pigeons,* in accordance with the dictate in the law of the Lord.

Now there was a man in Jerusalem whose name was Simeon. This man was righteous and devout, awaiting the consolation of Israel, and the Holy Spirit was upon him. It had been revealed to him by the Holy Spirit that he should not see death before he had seen the Christ of the Lord. He came in the Spirit into the temple; and when the parents brought in the child Jesus to perform the custom of the law in regard to him, he took him into his arms and blessed God, saying:

"Now, Master, you may let your servant go
in peace, according to your word,
for my eyes have seen your salvation,
which you prepared in sight of all the peoples,
a light for revelation to the Gentiles,
and glory for your people Israel."

The child's father and mother were amazed at what was said about him; and Simeon blessed them and said to Mary his mother, "Behold, this child is destined for the fall and rise of many in Israel, and to be a sign that will be contradicted—and **you yourself a sword will pierce**—so that the thoughts of many hearts may be revealed." There was also a prophetess, Anna, the daughter of Phanuel, of the tribe of Asher. She was advanced in years, having lived seven years with her husband after her marriage, and then as a widow until she was eighty-four. She never left the temple, but worshiped night and day with fasting and prayer. And coming forward at that very time, she gave thanks to God and spoke about the child to all who were awaiting the redemption of Jerusalem.]

When they had fulfilled all the prescriptions of the law of the Lord, they returned to Galilee, to their own town of Nazareth. The child grew and became strong, filled with wisdom; and the favor of God was upon him.

The Gospel of the Lord. **Praise to you, Lord Jesus Christ.**

Key Words

Genesis is the first book of the Bible. It tells many stories, including the stories of Creation, Adam and Eve, the Flood, Abraham, and the people's faith in God. These stories help us understand that God loves us and wants our love in return.

Abram had true faith in God. God promised him that he would become the head of a huge family. God then gave him a new name: Abraham.

Faith is a gift that God gives to all people. Those who accept it grow to trust God more. Through faith we can know things that we can't see or touch, such as God's love. Our faith leads us to help others know God too.

Sterile is used here to mean a woman who can't have children. Abraham and Sarah show us that, even though they thought Sarah was too old to have children, their trust in God was rewarded by the birth of their son, Isaac. All things are possible for God.

The **purification** rite was performed at the temple in Jerusalem 40 days after the birth of Jesus, as was the custom at the time. It involved the whole family—Jesus, Mary, and Joseph.

When Simeon saw Jesus, he understood that this was the Messiah, the long-awaited one. Simeon could also see that Jesus' mission would bring much suffering to Mary, Jesus' mother. When Simeon tells Mary that "**you yourself a sword will pierce**," we recall Jesus' death on the cross.

January 1

Solemnity of Mary, the Holy Mother of God

First Reading (Numbers 6:22-27)

The LORD said to **Moses**: "Speak to **Aaron** and his sons and tell them: This is how you shall bless the Israelites. Say to them:

The LORD bless you and keep you!
The LORD let his face shine upon you, and be gracious to you!
The LORD look upon you kindly and give you peace!

So shall they invoke my name upon the Israelites, and I will bless them."

The word of the Lord. **Thanks be to God.**

Responsorial Psalm (Psalm 67:2-3, 5, 6, 8)

℟. **May God bless us in his mercy.**

May God have pity on us and bless us;
may he let his face shine upon us.
So may your way be known upon earth;
among all nations, your salvation. ℟.

May the nations be glad and exult
because you rule the peoples in **equity**;
the nations on the earth you guide. ℟.

May the peoples praise you, O God;
may all the peoples praise you!
May God bless us,
and may all the ends of the earth fear him! ℟.

Second Reading (Galatians 4:4-7)

Brothers and sisters: When the **fullness of time** had come, God sent his Son, born of a woman, born under the law, to ransom those under the law, so that we might receive adoption as sons. As proof that you are sons, God sent the Spirit of his Son into our hearts, crying out, "**Abba**, Father!" So you are no longer a slave but a son, and if a son then also an heir, through God.

The word of the Lord. **Thanks be to God.**

Gospel (Luke 2:16-21)

A reading from the holy Gospel according to Luke.
Glory to you, O Lord.

The shepherds went in haste to Bethlehem and found Mary and Joseph, and the infant lying in the **manger**. When they saw this, they made known the message that had been told them about this child. All who heard it were amazed by what had been told them by the shepherds. And Mary kept all these things, **reflecting on** them in her heart. Then the shepherds returned, glorifying and praising God for all they had heard and seen, just as it had been told to them.

When eight days were completed for his circumcision, he was named Jesus, the name given him by the angel before he was conceived in the womb.

The Gospel of the Lord. **Praise to you, Lord Jesus Christ.**

Key Words

The **Book of Numbers** is found in the Hebrew Scriptures or Old Testament. It is called "Numbers" because it talks about many numbers and times when the people of Israel were counted. In Hebrew, it is called "In the Desert," because it tells of the travels of the Israelites after they left slavery in Egypt.

Moses was a friend of God who was born in Egypt when the Israelites were slaves there. When God asked him to lead the people to freedom, Moses said yes because he loved God and didn't want the people to suffer any more. The people left Egypt on a journey called the "Exodus" about 1,250 years before the time of Jesus.

Aaron, Moses' older brother, helped him free the Israelites. When Moses went up Mount Sinai to receive God's law, Aaron stayed with the people.

To judge with **equity** is to be fair to everyone. In the psalm, the psalmist is praising God for God's fairness to all people on earth.

Fullness of time means when the time was right for God to send Jesus into the world.

In Aramaic, the language Jesus spoke, **Abba** means Daddy. By calling God "Abba," Jesus shows that we can talk to God with the same trust and love that small children have for their father.

A **manger** is the place in a barn or stable for the animals' food. Its name is from the French word *manger* (to eat).

Reflecting on means to think about something a lot. Like all mothers, Mary remembered all the details surrounding the birth of her child.

January 3

Epiphany of the Lord

Mass During the Day

First Reading (Isaiah 60:1-6)

Rise up in splendor, Jerusalem! Your light has come,
    the glory of the Lord shines upon you.
See, darkness covers the earth,
    and thick clouds cover the peoples;
but upon you the Lord shines,
    and over you appears his glory.
Nations shall walk by your light,
    and kings by your shining radiance.
Raise your eyes and look about;
    they all gather and come to you:
your sons come from afar,
    and your daughters in the arms of their nurses.

Then you shall be radiant at what you see,
    your heart shall throb and overflow,
for the riches of the sea shall be emptied out before you,
    the wealth of nations shall be brought to you.
Caravans of camels shall fill you,
    dromedaries from **Midian** and **Ephah**;
all from **Sheba** shall come
    bearing gold and frankincense,
    and proclaiming the praises of the Lord.

The word of the Lord. **Thanks be to God.**

Responsorial Psalm (Psalm 72:1-2, 7-8, 10-11, 12-13)

℟. **Lord, every nation on earth will adore you.**

O God, with your judgment endow the king,
and with your justice, the king's son;
he shall govern your people with justice
and your afflicted ones with judgment. ℟.

Justice shall flower in his days,
and profound peace, till the moon be no more.
May he rule from sea to sea,
and from the River to the ends of the earth. ℟.

The kings of Tarshish and the Isles shall offer gifts;
the kings of Arabia and Seba shall bring tribute.
All kings shall pay him homage,
all nations shall serve him. ℟.

For he shall rescue the poor when he cries out,
and the afflicted when he has no one to help him.
He shall have pity for the lowly and the poor;
the lives of the poor he shall save. ℟.

Second Reading (Ephesians 3:2-3a, 5-6)

Brothers and sisters: You have heard of the stewardship of God's grace that was given to me for your benefit, namely, that the **mystery** was made known to me by **revelation**. It was not made known to people in other generations as it has now been revealed to his holy apostles and prophets by the Spirit: that the Gentiles are coheirs, members of the same body, and copartners in the promise in Christ Jesus through the gospel.

The word of the Lord. **Thanks be to God.**

Gospel (Matthew 2:1-12)

A reading from the holy Gospel according to Matthew.
Glory to you, O Lord.

When Jesus was born in **Bethlehem of Judea**, in the days of King Herod, behold, magi from the east arrived in Jerusalem, saying, "Where is the newborn king of the Jews? We saw his star at its rising and have come to do him **homage**." When King Herod heard this, he was greatly troubled, and all Jerusalem with him. Assembling all the chief priests and the scribes of the people, he inquired of them where the Christ was to be born. They said to him, "In Bethlehem of Judea, for thus it has been written through the prophet:

And you, Bethlehem, land of Judah,
are by no means least among the rulers of Judah;
since from you shall come a ruler,
who is to shepherd my people Israel."

Then Herod called the magi secretly and ascertained from them the time of the star's appearance. He sent them to Bethlehem and said, "Go and search diligently for the child. When you have found him, bring me word, that I too may go and do him homage." After their audience with the king they set out. And behold, the star that they had seen at its rising preceded them, until it came and stopped over the place where the child was. They were overjoyed at seeing the star, and on entering the house they saw the child with Mary his mother. They prostrated themselves and did him homage. Then they opened their treasures and offered him gifts of **gold, frankincense, and myrrh**. And having been warned in a dream not to return to Herod, they departed for their country by another way.

The Gospel of the Lord. **Praise to you, Lord Jesus Christ.**

Key Words

Epiphany is a Greek word that means "unveiling," where something is revealed. God revealed love for all people by sending his Son, Jesus, into the world.

Midian, Ephah, and Sheba were three ancient kingdoms near Israel. In the book of the Prophet Isaiah in the Bible, they represent all the nations outside Israel.

The **Ephesians** were a group of Christians in the city of Ephesus. A letter Saint Paul wrote to them is now part of the Bible. Ephesus is located in modern-day Turkey.

A **mystery** is something that is very hard to understand. In Saint Paul's letter to the Ephesians, it means God's plan to create a human community in Christ.

To know something by **revelation** means that God has shown or given someone this knowledge.

Bethlehem of Judea is the city of King David, one of Jesus' ancestors. Joseph and Mary went to Bethlehem for a census (an official counting of all the people). Jesus was born during their stay there.

To pay someone **homage** is to show your respect or honor for them in a public way, such as by bowing or bringing gifts.

Gold, frankincense, and myrrh are three very expensive gifts: gold is a precious metal; frankincense and myrrh are rare, sweet-smelling incenses. Myrrh is the main ingredient in holy anointing oil.

January 10

The Baptism of the Lord

These are the readings for Year B. The first reading, responsorial psalm, and second reading from Year A (Isaiah 42:1-4, 6-7; Psalm 29:1-2, 3-4, 3, 9-10; and Acts 10:34-38) may also be used.

First Reading (Isaiah 55:1-11)

Thus says the LORD:
All you who are thirsty,
come to the water!
You who have no money,
come, receive grain and eat;
come, without paying and without cost,
drink wine and milk!
Why spend your money for what is not bread,
your wages for what fails to satisfy?
Heed me, and you shall eat well,
you shall delight in rich fare.
Come to me heedfully,
listen, that you may have life.
I will renew with you the everlasting **covenant**,
the benefits assured to David.
As I made him a witness to the peoples,
a leader and commander of nations,
so shall you summon a nation you knew not,
and nations that knew you not shall run to you,
because of the LORD, your God,
the Holy One of Israel, who has glorified you.

Seek the LORD while he may be found,
call him while he is near.
Let the scoundrel forsake his way,
and the wicked man his thoughts;
let him turn to the LORD for mercy;
to our God, who is generous in forgiving.
For my thoughts are not your thoughts,
nor are your ways my ways, says the LORD.
As high as the heavens are above the earth
so high are my ways above your ways
and my thoughts above your thoughts.

For just as from the heavens
the rain and snow come down
and do not return there
till they have watered the earth,
making it fertile and fruitful,
giving seed to the one who sows
and bread to the one who eats,
so shall my word be
that goes forth from my mouth;
my word shall not return to me void,
but shall do my will,
achieving the end for which I sent it.

The word of the Lord. **Thanks be to God.**

Responsorial Psalm (Isaiah 12:2-3, 4bcd, 5-6)

℟. **You will draw water joyfully from the springs of salvation.**

God indeed is my savior;
I am confident and unafraid.
My strength and my courage is the LORD,
and he has been my savior.
With joy you will draw water
at the fountain of salvation. ℟.

Give thanks to the LORD, acclaim his name;
among the nations make known his deeds,
proclaim how exalted is his name. ℟.

Sing praise to the LORD for his glorious achievement;
let this be known throughout all the earth.
Shout with exultation, O city of Zion,
for great in your midst
is the Holy One of Israel! ℟.

Second Reading (1 John 5:1-9)

Beloved: Everyone who believes that Jesus is the Christ is begotten by God, and everyone who loves the Father loves also the one begotten by him. In this way we know that we love the children of God when we love God and obey his commandments. For the love of God is this, that we keep his commandments. And his commandments are not burdensome, for whoever is begotten by God conquers the world. And the victory that conquers the world is our faith. Who indeed is the victor over the world but the one who believes that Jesus is the Son of God?

This is the one who came **through water and blood**, Jesus Christ, not by water alone, but by water and blood. The Spirit is the one who testifies, and the Spirit is truth. So there are three that testify, the Spirit, the water, and the blood, and the three are of one accord. If we accept human testimony, the testimony of God is surely greater. Now the testimony of God is this, that he has testified on behalf of his Son.

The word of the Lord. **Thanks be to God.**

Gospel (Mark 1:7-11)

A reading from the holy Gospel according to Mark.
Glory to you, O Lord.

This is what John the Baptist proclaimed: "One mightier than I is coming after me. I am not worthy to stoop and **loosen the thongs of his sandals**. I have baptized you with water; he will baptize you with the Holy Spirit."

It happened in those days that Jesus came from Nazareth of Galilee and was baptized in the Jordan by John. On coming up out of the water he saw the heavens being torn open and the Spirit, like a dove, descending upon him. And a voice came from the heavens, "You are my beloved Son; with you I am well pleased."

The Gospel of the Lord. **Praise to you, Lord Jesus Christ.**

Key Words

The Christmas Season ends today with the **Baptism of the Lord**, the last of Jesus' three epiphanies. The first two are: Jesus' revelation as a child to the shepherds; and Jesus' revelation to the Wise Men on the feast of the Epiphany (which we celebrated last Sunday). In today's gospel Jesus is a grown man, and his baptism by John the Baptist marks the beginning of his earthly ministry.

A **covenant** is a promise between two people or groups. In the first covenant, also called the Old Testament, God promised to care for his people and the people agreed to worship only God. In the new covenant through Jesus, also called the New Testament, God renews his promise and we agree to love God and one another.

Saint John tells us in his first Letter that Jesus came **through water and blood**. First, Jesus was baptized in the water of the River Jordan by John the Baptist; when he died on the cross, Jesus shed his blood for us. Both these events in the life of Jesus are signs that "Christ is begotten by God."

When one person was recognized as being much more important than another, the less-important person was not worthy even to **loosen the thongs of his sandals** (a job for a slave to carry out). John the Baptist uses this image to show how great the difference is between himself and Jesus.

January 17

2nd Sunday in Ordinary Time

First Reading (1 Samuel 3:3b-10, 19)

Samuel was sleeping in the temple of the LORD where the **ark of God** was. The LORD called to Samuel, who answered, "Here I am." Samuel ran to Eli and said, "Here I am. You called me." "I did not call you," Eli said. "Go back to sleep." So he went back to sleep. Again the LORD called Samuel, who rose and went to Eli. "Here I am," he said. "You called me." But Eli answered, "I did not call you, my son. Go back to sleep."

At that time Samuel was not familiar with the LORD, because the LORD had not revealed anything to him as yet. The LORD called Samuel again, for the third time. Getting up and going to Eli, he said, "Here I am. You called me." Then Eli understood that the LORD was calling the youth. So he said to Samuel, "Go to sleep, and if you are called, reply, Speak, LORD, for your servant is listening." When Samuel went to sleep in his place, the LORD came and revealed his presence, calling out as before, "Samuel, Samuel!" Samuel answered, "Speak, for your servant is listening."

Samuel grew up, and the LORD was with him, not permitting any word of his to be without effect.

The word of the Lord. **Thanks be to God.**

Responsorial Psalm (Psalm 40:2, 4, 7-8, 8-9, 10)

℟. **Here am I, Lord; I come to do your will.**

I have waited, waited for the LORD,
and he stooped toward me and heard my cry.
And he put a new song into my mouth,
a hymn to our God. ℟.

Sacrifice or offering you wished not,
but ears open to obedience you gave me.
Holocausts or sin-offerings you sought not;
then said I, "Behold I come." ℟.

"In the written scroll it is prescribed for me,
to do your will, O my God, is my delight,
and your law is within my heart!" ℟.

I announced your justice in the vast assembly;
I did not restrain my lips, as you, O LORD, know. R.

Second Reading (1 Corinthians 6:13c-15a, 17-20)

Brothers and sisters: The body is not for immorality, but for the Lord, and the Lord is for the body; God raised the Lord and will also raise us by his power.

Do you not know that your bodies are members of Christ? But whoever is joined to the Lord becomes one Spirit with him. Avoid immorality. Every other sin a person commits is outside the body, but the immoral person sins against his own body. Do you not know that your **body is a temple of the Holy Spirit** within you, whom you have from God, and that you are not your own? For you have been purchased at a **price**. Therefore **glorify** God in your body.

The word of the Lord. **Thanks be to God.**

Gospel (John 1:35-42)

A reading from the holy Gospel according to John.
Glory to you, O Lord.

John was standing with two of his disciples, and as he watched Jesus walk by, he said, "Behold, the Lamb of God." The two disciples heard what he said and followed Jesus. Jesus turned and saw them following him and said to them, "What are you looking for?" They said to him, "Rabbi"—which translated means Teacher—, "where are you staying?" He said to them, "Come, and you will see." So they went and saw where Jesus was staying, and they stayed with him that day. It was about four in the afternoon. Andrew, the brother of Simon Peter, was one of the two who heard John and followed Jesus. He first found his own brother Simon and told him, "We have found the Messiah"—which is translated Christ. Then he brought him to Jesus. Jesus looked at him and said, "You are Simon the son of John; you will be called Cephas"—which is translated Peter.

The Gospel of the Lord. **Praise to you, Lord Jesus Christ.**

Key Words

The **ark of God**, also called the ark of the covenant, was a wooden box in which the Israelites stored important objects that reminded them that God was their savior. It was built to contain the two stone tablets on which the Ten Commandments were written, a golden urn of manna (the miraculous bread that fell from heaven when they were living in the desert), and Aaron's staff.

Saint Paul (first known as Saul) was a man who bullied and terrorized the first Christians. One day, he saw the risen Jesus and the experience changed his whole life. He changed his name to Paul and became a great apostle, traveling to cities all around the Mediterranean Sea and telling people about the love of Jesus. Several letters he wrote are now in the Bible, including today's **First Letter to the Corinthians.**

From the moment of our baptism, our **body is a temple of the Holy Spirit**. Because God lives in us, we should live in a way that honors God.

Jesus paid the **price** for our freedom. He gave the most valuable thing he had—his life—in order to free us all from sin and death. He chose to do this because he loves us.

To **glorify** means to give praise. One way we can praise and glorify God is by respecting and taking care of our bodies.

The **John** mentioned in the gospel today is John the Baptist. He came before Jesus and had his own followers or disciples. There is another John in the Bible: he is the apostle who wrote today's gospel.

January 24

3rd Sunday in Ordinary Time

First Reading (Jonah 3:1-5, 10)

The word of the LORD came to Jonah, saying: "Set out for the great city of Nineveh, and announce to it the message that I will tell you." So Jonah made ready and went to **Nineveh**, according to the LORD's bidding. Now Nineveh was an enormously large city; it took three days to go through it. Jonah began his journey through the city, and had gone but a single day's walk announcing, "Forty days more and Nineveh shall be destroyed," when the people of Nineveh believed God; they proclaimed a **fast** and all of them, great and small, put on **sackcloth**.

When God saw by their actions how they turned from their evil way, he repented of the evil that he had threatened to do to them; he did not carry it out.

The word of the Lord. **Thanks be to God.**

Responsorial Psalm (Psalm 25:4-5, 6-7, 8-9)

℟. **Teach me your ways, O Lord.**

Your ways, O LORD, make known to me;
teach me your paths,
guide me in your truth and teach me,
for you are God my savior. ℟.

Remember that your compassion, O LORD,
and your love are from of old.
In your kindness remember me,
because of your goodness, O LORD. ℟.

Good and upright is the LORD;
thus he shows sinners the way.
He guides the humble to justice
and teaches the humble his way. ℟.

Second Reading (1 Corinthians 7:29-31)

I tell you, brothers and sisters, the time is running out. From now on, let those having wives act as not having them, those weeping as not **weeping**, those rejoicing as not rejoicing, those buying as not owning, those using the world as not using it fully. For the world in its present form is passing away.

The word of the Lord. **Thanks be to God.**

Gospel (Mark 1:14-20)

A reading from the holy Gospel according to Mark.
Glory to you, O Lord.

After John had been arrested, Jesus came to Galilee proclaiming the gospel of God: "This is the time of fulfillment. The kingdom of God is at hand. **Repent**, and believe in the gospel."

As he passed by the Sea of Galilee, he saw Simon and his brother Andrew casting their nets into the sea; they were fishermen. Jesus said to them, "Come after me, and I will make you fishers of men." Then they abandoned their nets and followed him. He walked along a little farther and saw James, the son of Zebedee, and his brother John. They too were in a boat mending their nets. Then he called them. So they left their father Zebedee in the boat along with the hired men and followed him.

The Gospel of the Lord. **Praise to you, Lord Jesus Christ.**

Key Words

The **book of the Prophet Jonah** is the story of a man who lived about 800 years before Jesus. God wants Jonah to be his prophet but Jonah runs away instead. He famously spends three days in the belly of a fish before finally accepting God's word. This story was written to help people understand that God is loving and merciful and never gives up on us.

Nineveh was the capital of Assyria (today's northern Iraq) in Jonah's time. The people of Israel saw it as a dangerous and evil city because the people there didn't follow God's laws.

To **fast** means to abstain from all or some kinds of food or drink. To put on **sackcloth** means to wear very rough cloth, which irritates the skin. Fasting and putting on sackcloth were signs that people were sorry for their sins and wanted to make their lives better.

When Saint Paul wrote this **letter to the Corinthians**, Christians thought the world was about to end. Saint Paul says we must change our ways and live as though that day were here—the day we will be with Jesus forever.

Weeping means to cry and feel sad because someone we love has died or something important is lost. Saint Paul reminds us that a new world is coming very soon, where everything will be good and wonderful, and no one will ever be sad.

To **repent** means to be sorry for doing something wrong, and to change our way of thinking and living for the better. Jesus calls us to repent and to believe in the good news of God's love.

January 31

4th Sunday in Ordinary Time

First Reading (Deuteronomy 18:15-20)

Moses spoke to all **the people**, saying: "A prophet like me will the LORD, your God, raise up for you from among your own kin; to him you shall listen. This is exactly what you requested of the LORD, your God, at Horeb on the day of the assembly, when you said, 'Let us not again hear the voice of the LORD, our God, nor see this great fire any more, lest we die.' And the LORD said to me, 'This was well said. I will raise up for them a prophet like you from among their kin, and will put my words into his mouth; he shall tell them all that I command him. Whoever will not listen to my words which he speaks in my name, I myself will make him answer for it. But if a prophet presumes to speak in my name an oracle that I have not commanded him to speak, or speaks in the name of other gods, he shall die.'"

The word of the Lord. **Thanks be to God.**

Responsorial Psalm (Psalm 95:1-2, 6-7, 7-9)

℟. **If today you hear his voice, harden not your hearts.**

Come, let us sing joyfully to the LORD;
let us acclaim the rock of our salvation.
Let us come into his presence with **thanksgiving**;
let us joyfully sing psalms to him. ℟.

Come, let us bow down in worship;
let us kneel before the LORD who made us.
For he is our God,
and we are the people he shepherds, the **flock**
he guides. ℟.

Oh, that today you would hear his voice:
"Harden not your hearts as at Meribah,
as in the day of Massah in the desert,
Where your fathers tempted me;
they tested me though they had seen my works." ℟.

Second Reading (1 Corinthians 7:32-35)

Brothers and sisters: I should like you to be free of anxieties. An unmarried man is anxious about the things of the Lord, how he may please the Lord. But a married man is anxious about the things of the world, how he may please his wife, and he is divided. An unmarried woman or a virgin is anxious about the things of the Lord, so that she may be holy in both body and spirit. A married woman, on the other hand, is anxious about the things of the world, how she may please her husband. I am telling you this for your own benefit, not to impose a restraint upon you, but for the sake of propriety and adherence to the Lord without distraction.

The word of the Lord. **Thanks be to God.**

Gospel (Mark 1:21-28)

A reading from the holy Gospel according to Mark.
Glory to you, O Lord.

Then they came to Capernaum, and on the **sabbath** Jesus entered the synagogue and taught. The people were astonished at his teaching, for he taught them as one having **authority** and not as the **scribes**. In their synagogue was a man with an unclean spirit; he cried out, "What have you to do with us, Jesus of Nazareth? Have you come to destroy us? I know who you are—the Holy One of God!" Jesus rebuked him and said, "Quiet! Come out of him!" The unclean spirit convulsed him and with a loud cry came out of him. All were amazed and asked one another, "What is this? A new teaching with authority. He commands even the unclean spirits and they obey him." His fame spread everywhere throughout the whole region of Galilee.

The Gospel of the Lord. **Praise to you, Lord Jesus Christ.**

Key Words

The people Moses spoke to were the Israelites. He had led them out of slavery in Egypt. At first they did not know how to listen to God and follow God's ways. Over time, after many hardships, they learned what it means to be chosen by God and to do God's will.

Thanksgiving means to say thanks. We give thanks to God for every good thing in the world, which comes from God. "Eucharist" is the Greek word for thanksgiving.

Having a **flock** of sheep was very important for the people of Israel: sheep gave them milk, wool, and meat. The shepherd had the crucial job of protecting and feeding the sheep; he called them by name and they would follow him. God cares for us like a shepherd cares for his sheep because God loves us. God's powerful hand protects us from harm. We hear God's voice and we follow.

The **sabbath** is the day of the week when human beings rest as God did on the seventh day of creation. It is a chance for us to spend time praising God and enjoying creation.

Authority is the power to both say something and do something. Jesus receives his authority from God, his Father. When Jesus tells the unclean spirit to be quiet and come out of the man, it does.

The word "scribe" comes from the Latin word *scribere*, to write. In Jesus' time, **scribes** wrote letters and kept records for the community. They also studied the Law of Moses. In the gospels, scribes often asked Jesus hard questions. This was how they learned and tested their knowledge of the Law.

February 7

5th Sunday in Ordinary Time

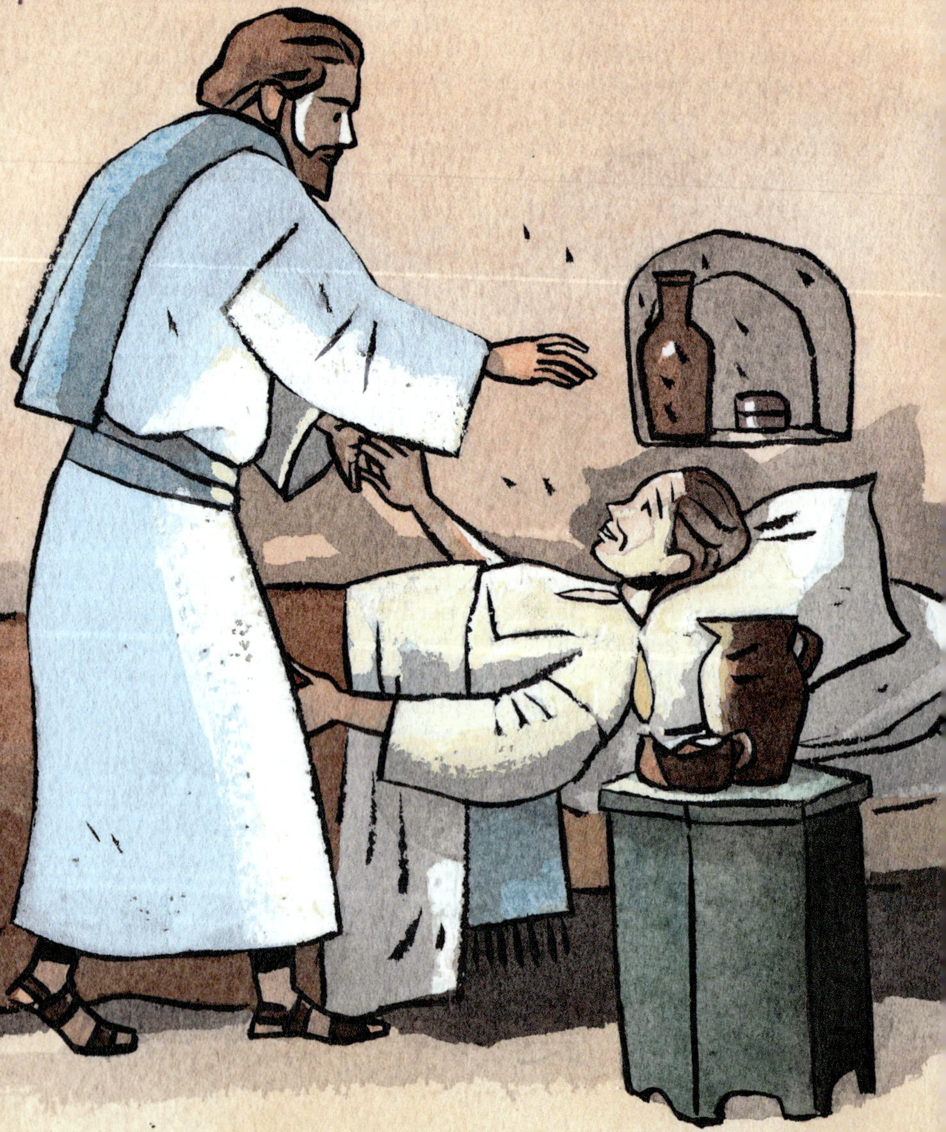

First Reading (Job 7:1-4, 6-7)

Job spoke, saying:
Is not man's life on earth a drudgery?
Are not his days those of hirelings?
He is a slave who longs for the shade,
a hireling who waits for his wages.
So I have been assigned months of misery,
and troubled nights have been allotted to me.
If in bed I say, "When shall I arise?"
then the night drags on;
I am filled with restlessness until the dawn.
My days are swifter than a **weaver's shuttle**;
they come to an end without hope.
Remember that my life is like the wind;
I shall not see happiness again.

The word of the Lord. **Thanks be to God.**

Responsorial Psalm (Psalm 147:1-2, 3-4, 5-6)

℟. **Praise the Lord, who heals the brokenhearted.**
Or **Alleluia.**

Praise the LORD, for he is good;
sing praise to our God, for he is gracious;
it is fitting to praise him.
The LORD rebuilds Jerusalem;
the dispersed of Israel he gathers. ℟.

He heals the brokenhearted
and binds up their wounds.
He tells the number of the stars;
he calls each by name. ℟.

Great is our Lord and mighty in power;
to his wisdom there is no limit.
The LORD sustains the lowly;
the wicked he casts to the ground. ℟.

Second Reading (1 Corinthians 9:16-19, 22-23)

Brothers and sisters: If I preach the gospel, this is no reason for me to boast, for an obligation has been imposed on me, and woe to me if I do not preach it! If I do so willingly, I have a recompense, but if unwillingly, then I have been entrusted with a stewardship. What then is my recompense? That, when I preach, I offer the gospel free of charge so as not to make full use of my right in the gospel.

Although I am free in regard to all, I have made myself a slave to all so as to win over as many as possible. To the weak I became weak, to win over the weak. I have become all things to all, to save at least some. All this I do for the sake of the gospel, so that I too may have a share in it.

The word of the Lord. **Thanks be to God.**

Gospel (Mark 1:29-39)

A reading from the holy Gospel according to Mark.
Glory to you, O Lord.

On leaving the synagogue Jesus entered the house of Simon and Andrew with James and John. Simon's mother-in-law lay sick with a fever. They immediately told him about her. He approached, grasped her hand, and helped her up. Then the fever left her and she waited on them.

When it was evening, after sunset, they brought to him all who were ill or **possessed by demons**. The whole town was gathered at the door. He cured many who were sick with various diseases, and he drove out many demons, not permitting them to speak because they knew him.

Rising very early before dawn, he left and went off to a deserted place, where he **prayed**. Simon and those who were with him pursued him and on finding him said, "Everyone is looking for you." He told them, "Let us go on to the nearby villages that I may preach there also. For this purpose have I come." So he went into their **synagogues**, preaching and driving out demons throughout the whole of **Galilee**.

The Gospel of the Lord. **Praise to you, Lord Jesus Christ.**

Key Words

The **Book of Job** is well known because it talks a lot about why people suffer and where God is when people suffer. It reminds us that even when bad things happen, God is always with us.

A **weaver's shuttle** is a piece of wood that goes back and forth on a loom, weaving the thread and forming a piece of cloth. An expert weaver can work so fast that sometimes it is hard to see the shuttle. Job says that, like a shuttle, life goes by very quickly.

Long ago, people thought those who acted in strange ways were **possessed by demons**. By casting out demons, Jesus showed that he had power over what was evil.

To **pray** is to place ourselves in the presence of God and to listen with our hearts to what God says. Jesus spent many hours praying and he taught his disciples how to pray (the Lord's Prayer). All Christians should take time to pray, alone and with others.

The **synagogue** is a place where Jews gather to read the Scriptures and pray.

Galilee is a province in the north of Palestine. Nazareth, the town where Jesus lived with his parents, is in Galilee, as is the Sea of Galilee, where some of Jesus' disciples worked as fishermen. In Jerusalem, Jesus was known as a Galilean because of his northern accent.

February 10

Ash Wednesday

First Reading (Joel 2:12-18)

Even now, says the LORD,
return to me with your whole heart,
with fasting, and weeping, and mourning;
Rend your hearts, not your garments,
and return to the LORD, your God.
For gracious and merciful is he,
slow to anger, rich in kindness,
and relenting in punishment.
Perhaps he will again relent
and leave behind him a blessing,
Offerings and libations
for the LORD, your God.

Blow the trumpet in Zion!
proclaim a fast,
call an assembly;
Gather the people,
notify the **congregation**;
Assemble the elders,
gather the children
and the infants at the breast;
Let the bridegroom quit his room
and the bride her chamber.
Between the porch and the altar
let the priests, the ministers of the LORD, weep,
And say, "Spare, O LORD, your people,
and make not your heritage a reproach,
with the nations ruling over them!
Why should they say among the peoples,
'Where is their God?' "

Then the LORD was stirred to concern for his land
and took pity on his people.

The word of the Lord. **Thanks be to God.**

Responsorial Psalm (Psalm 51:3-4, 5-6ab, 12-13, 14, 17)

℟. **Be merciful, O Lord, for we have sinned.**

Have mercy on me, O God, in your goodness;
in the greatness of your compassion wipe out my offense.
Thoroughly wash me from my guilt
and of my sin cleanse me. ℟.

For I acknowledge my offense,
and my sin is before me always:
"Against you only have I sinned,
and done what is evil in your sight." ℟.

A clean heart create for me, O God,
and a steadfast spirit renew within me.
Cast me not out from your presence,
and your Holy Spirit take not from me. ℟.

Give me back the joy of your salvation,
and a willing spirit sustain in me.
O Lord, open my lips,
and my mouth shall proclaim your praise. ℟.

Second Reading (2 Corinthians 5:20–6:2)

Brothers and sisters: We are **ambassadors** for Christ, as if God were appealing through us. We implore you on behalf of Christ, be **reconciled** to God. For our sake he made him to be sin who did not know sin, so that we might become the righteousness of God in him.

Working together, then, we appeal to you not to receive the grace of God in vain. For he says:
In an acceptable time I heard you,
and on the day of salvation I helped you.
Behold, now is a very acceptable time; behold, now is the day of salvation.

The word of the Lord. **Thanks be to God.**

Gospel (Matthew 6:1-6, 16-18)

A reading from the holy Gospel according to Matthew.
Glory to you, O Lord.

Jesus said to his disciples: "Take care not to perform righteous deeds in order that people may see them; otherwise, you will have no recompense from your heavenly Father. When you give **alms**, do not blow a trumpet before you, as the **hypocrites** do in the synagogues and in the streets to win the praise of others. Amen, I say to you, they have received their reward. But when you give alms, do not let your left hand know what your right is doing, so that your almsgiving may be secret. And your Father who sees in secret will repay you.

"When you pray, do not be like the hypocrites, who love to stand and pray in the synagogues and on street corners so that others may see them. Amen, I say to you, they have received their reward. But when you pray, go to your inner room, close the door, and pray to your Father in secret. And your Father who sees in secret will repay you.

"When you fast, do not look gloomy like the hypocrites. They neglect their appearance, so that they may appear to others to be fasting. Amen, I say to you, they have received their reward. But when you fast, anoint your head and wash your face, so that you may not appear to be fasting, except to your Father who is hidden. And your Father who sees what is hidden will repay you."

The Gospel of the Lord.
Praise to you, Lord Jesus Christ.

Key Words

Ash Wednesday marks the beginning of Lent. Ashes are used as a sign of our sorrow for having turned away from God; they are placed on our forehead in the sign of the cross and we keep them until they wear off. The ashes are often produced by burning palms from the previous year's Palm Sunday celebration.

To **rend** something is to tear it apart forcefully. In biblical times, people would tear their clothing and cover themselves with ashes as signs of their repentance or sorrow. The Prophet Joel is saying that God would rather we rend, or open, our hearts as a sign of our willingness to return to God.

A **congregation** is a gathering of people, usually for worship. In the Hebrew Scriptures, it can also mean the whole people of God.

Ambassadors are messengers who have special authority to deliver a message or speak on someone else's behalf. Saint Paul is telling us that we have a role to play as followers of Christ: we are chosen to spread the good news. If we are to be faithful messengers, then we must open our hearts and be reconciled to God.

To be **reconciled** means to be "at-one" with someone, by making up for something wrong we may have done. Through his death, Jesus makes up for our sins and we are reconciled with God.

The three traditional Lenten practices are prayer, fasting, and almsgiving. To give **alms** is to give money to the poor. The word comes from the Greek word for compassion or pity. During Lent, we not only focus on our own spiritual life, we also make a special effort to help those around us who are in need.

Hypocrites are people whose actions don't match their words. They may say they love God, but they don't act in a loving way. Such behavior hurts that person, those around them, and God.

February 14

1st Sunday of Lent

First Reading (Genesis 9:8-15)

God said to **Noah** and to his sons with him: "See, I am now establishing my **covenant** with you and your descendants after you and with every living creature that was with you: all the birds, and the various tame and wild animals that were with you and came out of the ark. I will establish my covenant with you, that never again shall all bodily creatures be destroyed by the waters of a flood; there shall not be another flood to devastate the earth." God added: "This is the sign that I am giving for all ages to come, of the covenant between me and you and every living creature with you: I set my bow in the clouds to serve as a sign of the covenant between me and the earth. When I bring clouds over the earth, and the **bow** appears in the clouds, I will recall the covenant I have made between me and you and all living beings, so that the waters shall never again become a flood to destroy all mortal beings."

The word of the Lord. **Thanks be to God.**

Responsorial Psalm (Psalm 25:4-5, 6-7, 8-9)

℟. **Your ways, O Lord, are love and truth to those who keep your covenant.**

Your ways, O LORD, make known to me;
teach me your paths.
Guide me in your truth and teach me,
for you are God my savior. ℟.

Remember that your compassion, O LORD,
and your love are from of old.
In your kindness remember me,
because of your goodness, O LORD. ℟.

Good and upright is the LORD,
thus he shows sinners the way.
He guides the humble to justice,
and he teaches the humble his way. ℟.

Second Reading (1 Peter 3:18-22)

Beloved: Christ suffered for sins once, the righteous for the sake of the unrighteous, that he might lead you to God. Put to death in the flesh, he was brought to life in the Spirit. In it he also went to preach to the spirits in prison, who had once been disobedient while God patiently waited in the days of Noah during the building of the ark, in which a few persons, eight in all, were saved through water. This prefigured baptism, which saves you now. It is not a removal of dirt from the body but an appeal to God for a clear conscience, through the resurrection of Jesus Christ, who has gone into heaven and is at the right hand of God, with angels, authorities, and powers subject to him.

The word of the Lord. **Thanks be to God.**

Gospel (Mark 1:12-15)

A reading from the holy Gospel according to Mark.
Glory to you, O Lord.

The Spirit drove Jesus out into the desert, and he remained in the desert for forty days, tempted by **Satan**. He was among wild beasts, and the angels ministered to him.

After John had been arrested, Jesus came to Galilee proclaiming the gospel of God: "This is the time of fulfillment. The kingdom of God is at hand. Repent, and believe in the gospel."

The Gospel of the Lord. **Praise to you, Lord Jesus Christ.**

Key Words

We are now in the season of **Lent**, which began on Ash Wednesday and lasts approximately 40 days until Easter. During Lent, we pray and reflect on God's great love for us. We prepare our hearts to recall Jesus' suffering and death on the cross. When Lent ends, we celebrate the great feast of Easter, recalling when Jesus rose from the dead.

Genesis is the first book of the Bible. It tells many stories, including the stories of Creation, Adam and Eve, the flood, Abraham, and the people's faith in God. These stories help us understand that God loves us and wants our love in return.

Noah was a good man. God promised to save him, his family, and a pair of each animal on earth from the flood that was coming. Noah built a big boat or ark before the flood came so they could all float safely on the water.

In the book of Genesis, we hear how God made a **covenant**, or promise, with his people. From time to time, the people would stray and forget their covenant with God, but God never forgot. God is ever faithful.

After the flood, God put a **bow** (rainbow) in the sky as a sign of God's promise to love and care for us forever. Every time we see a rainbow, we can remember God's goodness to all creation.

Satan is one of the names given to the enemy of God and our strongest enemy. Satan works against God and tries to lead people away from God's love. Other names for Satan are the Evil One, Lucifer, or the Devil.

February 21

2nd Sunday of Lent

First Reading (Genesis 22:1-2, 9a, 10-13, 15-18)

God put Abraham to the test. He called to him, "Abraham!" "Here I am!" he replied. Then God said: "Take your son **Isaac**, your only one, whom you love, and go to the land of Moriah. There you shall offer him up as a holocaust on a height that I will point out to you."

When they came to the place of which God had told him, Abraham built an altar there and arranged the wood on it. Then he reached out and took the knife to slaughter his son. But the LORD's messenger called to him from heaven, "Abraham, Abraham!" "Here I am!" he answered. "Do not lay your hand on the boy," said the messenger. "Do not do the least thing to him. I know now how devoted you are to God, since you did not **withhold** from me your own beloved son." As Abraham looked about, he spied a ram caught by its horns in the thicket. So he went and took the ram and offered it up as a holocaust in place of his son.

Again the LORD's messenger called to Abraham from heaven and said: "I swear by myself, declares the LORD, that because you acted as you did in not withholding from me your beloved son, I will bless you abundantly and make your **descendants** as countless as the stars of the sky and the sands of the seashore; your descendants shall take possession of the gates of their enemies, and in your descendants all the nations of the earth shall find blessing—all this because you obeyed my command."

The word of the Lord. **Thanks be to God.**

Responsorial Psalm (Psalm 116:10, 15, 16-17, 18-19)

℟. **I will walk before the Lord, in the land of the living.**

I believed, even when I said,
"I am greatly afflicted."
Precious in the eyes of the LORD
is the death of his faithful ones. ℟.

O LORD, I am your servant;
I am your servant, the son of your handmaid;
you have loosed my bonds.

To you will I offer sacrifice of thanksgiving,
and I will call upon the name of the LORD. ℟.

My vows to the LORD I will pay
in the presence of all his people,
in the courts of the house of the LORD,
in your midst, O Jerusalem. ℟.

Second Reading (Romans 8:31b-34)

Brothers and sisters: If God is for us, who can be against us? He who did not spare his own Son but handed him over for us all, how will he not also give us everything else along with him?

Who will bring a charge against **God's chosen ones?** It is God who acquits us. Who will condemn? Christ Jesus it is who died—or, rather, was raised—who also is at the right hand of God, who indeed **intercedes** for us.

The word of the Lord. **Thanks be to God.**

Gospel (Mark 9:2-10)

A reading from the holy Gospel according to Mark.
Glory to you, O Lord.

Jesus took Peter, James, and John and led them up a high mountain apart by themselves. And he was **transfigured** before them, and his clothes became dazzling white, such as no fuller on earth could bleach them. Then **Elijah** appeared to them along with **Moses**, and they were conversing with Jesus. Then Peter said to Jesus in reply, "Rabbi, it is good that we are here! Let us make three tents: one for you, one for Moses, and one for Elijah." He hardly knew what to say, they were so terrified. Then a cloud came, casting a shadow over them; from the cloud came a voice, "This is my beloved Son. Listen to him." Suddenly, looking around, they no longer saw anyone but Jesus alone with them.

As they were coming down from the mountain, he charged them not to relate what they had seen to anyone, except when the Son of Man had risen from the dead. So they kept the matter to themselves, questioning what rising from the dead meant.

The Gospel of the Lord. **Praise to you, Lord Jesus Christ.**

Key Words

God asks Abraham to do something very hard: to sacrifice **Isaac**, his only son. Even though he didn't understand why he had to do this, Abraham trusted God. Seeing Abraham's faith, God let Isaac live. Isaac eventually had children of his own, including Jacob, the father of the twelve tribes of Israel.

To **withhold** means to hold back, to give as little as possible. Abraham did not withhold his only son, Isaac. God is very generous: God never holds back, even when it comes to giving his only Son, Jesus.

Descendants are the children, grandchildren, and great-grandchildren in a family. Because he trusted in God, Abraham was rewarded with many descendants—the whole people of Israel.

God's chosen ones are the people who become God's children by baptism. Every human being is invited to be a child of God.

To **intercede** means to ask for something on behalf of another person. Saint Paul tells us that we can draw strength in difficult times from the knowledge that Jesus intercedes for us with God.

When Jesus was **transfigured**, he looked different somehow. For a moment, his friends saw who Jesus truly is: the Son of God.

Elijah and **Moses** lived long before Jesus and were important leaders for the people of Israel. By appearing with them, Jesus is showing that he is the fulfillment both of the prophets (Elijah) and the Law (Moses).

February 28

3rd Sunday of Lent

These are the readings for Year B. The readings for Year A may also be used (Exodus 17:3-7; Psalm 95:1-2, 6-7, 8-9; Romans 5:1-2, 5-8; John 4:5-42 or John 4:5-15, 19b-26, 39a, 40-42).

First Reading (Exodus 20:1–17 or 20:1-3, 7-8, 12-17)

For the shorter version, omit the indented parts in brackets.

In those days, God delivered all these commandments: "I, the LORD, am your God, who brought you out of the land of Egypt, that place of slavery. You shall not have other gods besides me.

> [You shall not carve idols for yourselves in the shape of anything in the sky above or on the earth below or in the waters beneath the earth; you shall not bow down before them or worship them. For I, the LORD, your God, am a jealous God, inflicting punishment for their fathers' wickedness on the children of those who hate me, down to the third and fourth generation; but bestowing mercy down to the thousandth generation on the children of those who love me and keep my commandments.]

"You shall not take the name of the LORD, your God, in vain. For the LORD will not leave unpunished the one who takes his name in vain.

"Remember to keep holy the **sabbath** day.

> [Six days you may labor and do all your work, but the seventh day is the sabbath of the LORD, your God. No work may be done then either by you, or your son or daughter, or your male or female slave, or your beast, or by the alien who lives with you. In six days the LORD made the heavens and the earth, the sea and all that is in them; but on the seventh day he rested. That is why the LORD has blessed the sabbath day and made it holy.]

"Honor your father and your mother, that you may have a long life in the land which the LORD, your God, is giving you. You shall not kill. You shall not commit **adultery**. You shall not steal. You shall not bear false witness against your neighbor. You shall not covet your neighbor's house. You shall not covet your neighbor's wife, nor his male or female slave, nor his ox or ass, nor anything else that belongs to him."

The word of the Lord. **Thanks be to God.**

Responsorial Psalm (Psalm 19:8, 9, 10, 11)

℟. **Lord, you have the words of everlasting life.**

The law of the LORD is perfect,
refreshing the soul;
the decree of the LORD is trustworthy,
giving wisdom to the simple. ℟.

The precepts of the LORD are right,
rejoicing the heart;
the command of the LORD is clear,
enlightening the eye. ℟.

The fear of the LORD is pure,
enduring forever;
the ordinances of the LORD are true,
all of them just. ℟.

They are more precious than gold,
than a heap of purest gold;
sweeter also than syrup
or honey from the comb. ℟.

Second Reading (1 Corinthians 1:22-25)

Brothers and sisters: Jews demand signs and Greeks look for wisdom, but we proclaim **Christ** crucified, a stumbling block to Jews and foolishness to **Gentiles**, but to those who are called, Jews and Greeks alike, Christ the power of God and the wisdom of God. For the foolishness of God is wiser than human wisdom, and the weakness of God is stronger than human strength.

The word of the Lord. **Thanks be to God.**

Gospel (John 2:13-25)

A reading from the holy Gospel according to John.
Glory to you, O Lord.

Since the **Passover** of the Jews was near, Jesus went up to Jerusalem. He found in the temple area those who sold oxen, sheep, and doves, as well as the money changers seated there. He made a whip out of cords and drove them all out of the temple area, with the sheep and oxen, and spilled the coins of the money changers and overturned their tables, and to those who sold doves he said, "Take these out of here, and stop making my Father's house a marketplace." His disciples recalled the words of Scripture, *Zeal for your house will consume me*. At this the Jews answered and said to him, "What sign can you show us for doing this?" Jesus answered and said to them, "Destroy this temple and in three days I will raise it up." The Jews said, "This temple has been under construction for forty-six years, and you will raise it up in three days?" But he was speaking about the temple of his body. Therefore, when he was raised from the dead, his disciples remembered that he had said this, and they came to believe the Scripture and the word Jesus had spoken.

While he was in Jerusalem for the feast of Passover, many began to believe in his name when they saw the signs he was doing. But Jesus would not trust himself to them because he knew them all, and did not need anyone to testify about human nature. He himself understood it well.

The Gospel of the Lord. **Praise to you, Lord Jesus Christ.**

Key Words

The **Book of Exodus** is the second book of the Bible. It tells the story of how God, through Moses, freed his people from slavery in Egypt. God made a promise, or covenant, with them and gave them the Ten Commandments to show them how to live well.

The **sabbath** is the day of the week when human beings rest like God did on the seventh day of Creation. It is a chance for us to spend time praising God and enjoying creation.

"You shall not commit **adultery**" reminds husbands and wives to always be faithful to each other.

Christ is a Greek word that means "anointed." The chosen person was blessed with holy oil and given a special mission. The Aramaic word for "anointed" is Messiah.

The word **Gentiles** referred to those who were not Jewish. Saint Paul is called the Apostle to the Gentiles because he taught about Jesus to people who were not Jewish.

The **Gospel of John** tells us about the life, death, and resurrection of Jesus. It was written about 70 years after Jesus died. John's gospel includes some stories and sayings of Jesus that are not in the other three gospels (Matthew, Mark, and Luke).

Passover is a week-long festival when the Jewish people remember and celebrate that God freed their ancestors from slavery in Egypt. Jesus celebrated the Passover with his friends.

March 7

4th Sunday of Lent

These are the readings for Year B. The readings for Year A may also be used (1 Samuel 16:1b, 6-7, 10-13a; Psalm 23:1-3a. 3b-4, 5, 6; Ephesians 5:8-14; John 9:1-41 or John 9:1, 6-9, 13-17, 34-38).

First Reading (2 Chronicles 36:14-16, 19-23)

In those days, all the princes of Judah, the priests, and the people added infidelity to infidelity, practicing all the **abominations** of the nations and polluting the LORD's temple which he had consecrated in Jerusalem.

Early and often did the LORD, the God of their fathers, send his messengers to them, for he had compassion on his people and his dwelling place. But they mocked the messengers of God, despised his warnings, and scoffed at his prophets, until the anger of the LORD against his people was so inflamed that there was no remedy. Their enemies burnt the house of God, tore down the walls of Jerusalem, set all its palaces afire, and destroyed all its precious objects. Those who escaped the sword were carried captive to Babylon, where they became servants of the king of the Chaldeans and his sons until the kingdom of the Persians came to power. All this was to fulfill the word of the LORD spoken by Jeremiah: "Until the land has retrieved its lost sabbaths, during all the time it lies waste it shall have rest while seventy years are fulfilled."

In the first year of Cyrus, king of Persia, in order to fulfill the word of the LORD spoken by Jeremiah, the LORD inspired King Cyrus of Persia to issue this proclamation throughout his kingdom, both by word of mouth and in writing: "Thus says Cyrus, king of Persia: All the kingdoms of the earth the LORD, the God of heaven, has given to me, and he has also charged me to build him a house in Jerusalem, which is in Judah. Whoever, therefore, among you belongs to any part of his people, let him go up, and may his God be with him!"

The word of the Lord. **Thanks be to God.**

Responsorial Psalm (Psalm 137:1-2, 3, 4-5, 6)

℟. **Let my tongue be silenced, if I ever forget you!**

By the streams of Babylon
we sat and wept
when we remembered Zion.
On the aspens of that land
we hung up our harps. ℟.

For there our captors asked of us
the lyrics of our songs,
and our despoilers urged us to be joyous:
"Sing for us the songs of Zion!" ℟.

How could we sing a song of the LORD
in a foreign land?
If I forget you, Jerusalem,
may my right hand be forgotten! ℟.

May my tongue cleave to my palate
if I remember you not,
if I place not Jerusalem
ahead of my joy. ℟.

Second Reading (Ephesians 2:4-10)

Brothers and sisters: God, who is rich in mercy, because of the great love he had for us, even when we were dead in our transgressions, brought us to life with Christ—by **grace** you have been saved—, raised us up with him, and seated us with him in the heavens in Christ Jesus, that in the ages to come he might show the immeasurable riches of his grace in his kindness to us in Christ Jesus. For by grace you have been saved through faith, and this is not from you; it is the gift of God; it is not from works, so no one may boast. For we are his handiwork, created in Christ Jesus for the good works that God has prepared in advance, that we should live in them.

The word of the Lord. **Thanks be to God.**

Gospel (John 3:14-21)

A reading from the holy Gospel according to John.
Glory to you, O Lord.

Jesus said to Nicodemus: "Just as Moses lifted up the **serpent** in the desert, so must the Son of Man be lifted up, so that everyone who believes in him may have eternal life."

For God so loved the world that he gave his only Son, so that everyone who believes in him might not perish but might have eternal life. For God did not send his Son into the world to condemn the world, but that the world might be saved through him. Whoever believes in him will not be condemned, but whoever does not believe has already been condemned, because he has not believed in the name of the only Son of God. And this is the verdict, that the **light** came into the world, but people preferred **darkness** to light, because their works were evil. For everyone who does wicked things hates the light and does not come toward the light, so that his works might not be exposed. But whoever lives the truth comes to the light, so that his works may be clearly seen as done in God.

The Gospel of the Lord. **Praise to you, Lord Jesus Christ.**

Key Words

The first and second books of **Chronicles** are part of the Old Testament or Hebrew Scriptures. They focus on the importance of Jerusalem and the temple for the Jewish religion. They tell the story of David, the king of Israel who conquered Jerusalem and made it the center of the nation.

The **abominations** of the nations are the actions of non-Jewish people that go against God's law. The worst thing of all is to worship false gods, yet this is what some of God's people did.

The **Ephesians** were a group of Christians in the city of Ephesus. A letter Saint Paul wrote to them is now part of the Bible. Ephesus is located in modern-day Turkey.

Grace means a gift from God. God gives us the gift of eternal salvation so we can live as God's children.

When the Israelites wandered through the desert, they encountered poisonous snakes. God told Moses to make a bronze **serpent** and lift it up on a pole, like a flag. Anyone who was bitten by a snake and looked at the bronze serpent was healed. In today's gospel, Jesus tells Nicodemus that when he, Jesus, is lifted up on the cross and then raised from the dead, he will bring eternal life to all people who believe in him.

Light is a symbol of everything good and especially of Jesus, who is the Light of the World. **Darkness** represents evil, especially turning away from God.

March 14

5th Sunday of Lent

These are the readings for Year B. The readings for Year A may also be used (Ezekiel 37:12-14; Psalm 130:1-2, 3-4, 5-6, 7-8; Romans 8:8-11; John 11:1-45 or John 11:3-7, 17, 20-27, 33b-45).

First Reading (Jeremiah 31:31-34)

The days are coming, says the LORD, when I will make a new **covenant** with the **house of Israel** and the **house of Judah**. It will not be like the covenant I made with their fathers the day I took them by the hand to lead them forth from the land of Egypt; for they broke my covenant, and I had to show myself their master, says the LORD. But this is the covenant that I will make with the house of Israel after those days, says the LORD. I will place my law within them and write it upon their hearts; I will be their God, and they shall be my people. No longer will they have need to teach their friends and relatives how to know the LORD. All, from least to greatest, shall know me, says the LORD, for I will forgive their evildoing and remember their sin no more.

The word of the Lord. **Thanks be to God.**

Responsorial Psalm (Psalm 51:3-4, 12-13, 14-15)

℟. **Create a clean heart in me, O God.**

Have mercy on me, O God, in your goodness;
in the greatness of your compassion wipe out
my offense.
Thoroughly wash me from my guilt
and of my sin cleanse me. ℟.

A clean heart create for me, O God,
and a steadfast spirit renew within me.
Cast me not out from your presence,
and your Holy Spirit take not from me. ℟.

Give me back the joy of your salvation,
and a willing spirit sustain in me.
I will teach transgressors your ways,
and sinners shall return to you. ℟.

Second Reading (Hebrews 5:7-9)

In the days when Christ Jesus was in the flesh, he offered prayers and supplications with loud cries and tears to the one who was able to save him from death, and he was heard because of his reverence. Son though he was, he learned obedience from what he suffered; and when he was made perfect, he became the source of eternal salvation for all who obey him.

The word of the Lord. **Thanks be to God.**

Gospel (John 12:20-33)

A reading from the holy Gospel according to John.
Glory to you, O Lord.

Some Greeks who had come to worship at the Passover Feast came to Philip, who was from Bethsaida in Galilee, and asked him, "Sir, we would like to see Jesus." Philip went and told Andrew; then Andrew and Philip went and told Jesus. Jesus answered them, "The hour has come for the Son of Man **to be glorified**. Amen, amen, I say to you, unless a grain of wheat falls to the ground and dies, it remains just a grain of wheat; but if it dies, it produces much fruit. Whoever loves his life loses it, and whoever hates his life in this world will preserve it for eternal life. Whoever serves me must follow me, and where I am, there also will my servant be. The Father will honor whoever serves me.

"I am troubled now. Yet what should I say? 'Father, save me from this hour'? But it was for this purpose that I came to this hour. Father, glorify your name." Then a voice came from heaven, "I have glorified it and will glorify it again." The crowd there heard it and said it was thunder; but others said, "An angel has spoken to him." Jesus answered and said, "This voice did not come for my sake but for yours. Now is the time of judgment on this world; now the **ruler of this world** will be driven out. And when I am **lifted up from the earth**, I will draw everyone to myself." He said this indicating the kind of death he would die.

The Gospel of the Lord. **Praise to you, Lord Jesus Christ.**

Key Words

Jeremiah lived about 600 years before Jesus. When he was still very young, God called him to guide the people of Israel back to God. Many people ignored Jeremiah at first and sent him away. But when the people of Israel feared that God had stopped loving them, Jeremiah gave them hope that God would not abandon them.

A **covenant** is a promise between two people or groups. Although God's people often forgot their covenant, God continued to renew the covenant promise over and over again. In the new covenant through Jesus, God renews this promise to us yet again, and we agree to love one another and God.

At the time of Jeremiah, God's people were divided into two kingdoms: the **house of Israel** in the north and the **house of Judah** in the south. Jeremiah announces God's wish for both kingdoms to be united into one nation, under one covenant.

When Jesus says that the time has come for him **to be glorified**, he is talking about his death. Jesus knows that his path to glory is through a painful death on the cross.

The **ruler of this world** here means Satan—the enemy of God and all people. Satan tries to turn us away from God, but Jesus promises to draw all people to himself and God.

When Jesus says he will be **lifted up from the earth**, he is talking about when he will rise from the dead to be with God in heaven.

March 21

Palm Sunday of the Passion of the Lord

An alternate reading follows.

Gospel (Mark 11:1-10)

A reading from the holy Gospel according to Mark.
Glory to you, O Lord.

When Jesus and his disciples drew near to Jerusalem, to Bethphage and Bethany at the Mount of Olives, he sent two of his disciples and said to them, "Go into the village opposite you, and immediately on entering it, you will find a colt tethered on which no one has ever sat. Untie it and bring it here. If anyone should say to you, 'Why are you doing this?' reply, 'The Master has need of it and will send it back here at once.'" So they went off and found a colt tethered at a gate outside on the street, and they untied it. Some of the bystanders said to them, "What are you doing, untying the colt?" They answered them just as Jesus had told them to, and they permitted them to do it. So they brought the colt to Jesus and put their cloaks over it. And he sat on it. Many people spread their cloaks on the road, and others spread leafy branches that they had cut from the fields. Those preceding him as well as those following kept crying out:

"Hosanna!
Blessed is he who comes in the name of the Lord!
Blessed is the kingdom of our father David that is to come!
Hosanna in the highest!"

The Gospel of the Lord. **Praise to you, Lord Jesus Christ.**

Or

Gospel (John 12:12-16)

A reading from the holy Gospel according to John.
Glory to you, O Lord.

When the great crowd that had come to the feast heard that Jesus was coming to Jerusalem, they took palm branches and went out to meet him, and cried out:

"Hosanna!
"Blessed is he who comes in the name of the Lord,
the king of Israel."

Jesus found an ass and sat upon it, as is written:
Fear no more, O daughter Zion;
see, your king comes, seated upon an ass's colt.
His disciples did not understand this at first, but when Jesus had been glorified they remembered that these things were written about him and that they had done this for him.

The Gospel of the Lord. **Praise to you, Lord Jesus Christ.**

First Reading (Isaiah 50:4-7)

The Lord GOD has given me
a well-trained tongue,
that I might know how to speak to the weary
a word that will rouse them.
Morning after morning
he opens my ear that I may hear;
and I have not rebelled,
have not turned back.
I gave my back to those who beat me,
my cheeks to those who plucked my beard;
my face I did not shield
from buffets and spitting.

The Lord GOD is my help,
therefore I am not disgraced;
I have set my face like flint,
knowing that I shall not be put to shame.

The word of the Lord. **Thanks be to God.**

Responsorial Psalm (Psalm 22:8-9, 17-18, 19-20, 23-24)

℟. **My God, my God, why have you abandoned me?**

All who see me scoff at me;
they mock me with parted lips, they wag
their heads:
"He relied on the LORD; let him deliver him,
let him rescue him, if he loves him." ℟.

Indeed, many dogs surround me,
a pack of evildoers closes in upon me;
they have pierced my hands and my feet;
I can count all my bones. R.

They divide my garments among them,
and for my vesture they cast lots.
But you, O LORD, be not far from me;
O my help, hasten to aid me. R.

I will proclaim your name to my brethren;
in the midst of the assembly I will praise you:
"You who fear the LORD, praise him;
all you descendants of Jacob, give glory to him;
revere him, all you descendants of Israel!" R.

Second Reading (Philippians 2:6-11)

Christ Jesus, though he was in the form of God,
did not regard equality with God
something to be grasped.
Rather, he emptied himself,
taking the form of a slave,
coming in human likeness;
and found human in appearance,
he humbled himself,
becoming obedient to the point of death,
even death on a cross.
Because of this, God greatly exalted him
and bestowed on him the name
which is above every name,
that at the name of Jesus
every knee should bend,
of those in heaven and on earth and under the earth,
and every tongue confess that
Jesus Christ is Lord,
to the glory of God the Father.

The word of the Lord. **Thanks be to God.**

Gospel (Mark 14:1–15:47 or 15:1-39)

Several readers may proclaim the passion narrative today. (N) indicates the narrator, (†) the words of Jesus, (V) a voice, and (C) the crowd. The shorter version begins (page 152) and ends (page 154) at the asterisks.

N The **Passion** of our Lord Jesus Christ according to Mark.

The Passover and the **Feast of Unleavened Bread** were to take place in two days' time. So the chief priests and the scribes were seeking a way to arrest him by treachery and put him to death. They said,

C **"Not during the festival, for fear that there may be a riot among the people."**

N When he was in Bethany reclining at table in the house of Simon the leper, a woman came with an alabaster jar of perfumed oil, costly genuine spikenard. She broke the alabaster jar and poured it on his head. There were some who were indignant.

C **"Why has there been this waste of perfumed oil? It could have been sold for more than three hundred days' wages and the money given to the poor."**

N They were infuriated with her. Jesus said,

† "Let her alone. Why do you make trouble for her? She has done a good thing for me. The poor you will always have with you, and whenever you wish you can do good to them, but you will not always have me. She has done what she could. She has anticipated anointing my body for burial. Amen, I say to you, wherever the gospel is proclaimed to the whole world, what she has done will be told in memory of her."

N Then Judas Iscariot, one of the Twelve, went off to the chief priests to hand him over to them. When they heard him they were pleased and promised to pay him money. Then he looked for an opportunity to hand him over.

On the first day of the Feast of Unleavened Bread, when they sacrificed the **Passover lamb**, his disciples said to him,

C **"Where do you want us to go and prepare for you to eat the Passover?"**

N He sent two of his disciples and said to them,

† "Go into the city and a man will meet you, carrying a jar of water. Follow him. Wherever he enters, say to the master of the house, 'The Teacher says, "Where is my guest room where I may eat the Passover with my disciples?" ' Then he will show you a large upper room furnished and ready. Make the preparations for us there."

N The disciples then went off, entered the city, and found it just as he had told them; and they prepared the Passover.

When it was evening, he came with the Twelve. And as they reclined at table and were eating, Jesus said,

† "Amen, I say to you, one of you will betray me, one who is eating with me."

N They began to be distressed and to say to him, one by one,

V "Surely it is not I?"

N He said to them,

† "One of the Twelve, the one who dips with me into the dish. For the Son of Man indeed goes, as it is written of him, but woe to that man by whom the Son of Man is betrayed. It would be better for that man if he had never been born."

N While they were eating, he took bread, said the blessing, broke it, and gave it to them, and said,

† "Take it; this is my body."

N Then he took a cup, gave thanks, and gave it to them, and they all drank from it. He said to them,

† "This is my blood of the covenant, which will be shed for many. Amen, I say to you, I shall not drink again the fruit of the vine until the day when I drink it new in the kingdom of God."

N Then, after singing a hymn, they went out to the Mount of Olives.

Then Jesus said to them,

† "All of you will have your faith shaken, for it is written:

I will strike the shepherd,
and the sheep will be dispersed.

But after I have been raised up, I shall go before you to Galilee."

N Peter said to him,

V "Even though all should have their faith shaken, mine will not be."

N Then Jesus said to him,

† "Amen, I say to you, this very night before the cock crows twice you will deny me three times."

N But he vehemently replied,

V "Even though I should have to die with you, I will not deny you."

N And they all spoke similarly.

Then they came to a place named Gethsemane, and he said to his disciples,

† "Sit here while I pray."

N He took with him Peter, James, and John, and began to be troubled and distressed. Then he said to them,

† "My soul is sorrowful even to death. Remain here and keep watch."

N He advanced a little and fell to the ground and prayed that if it were possible the hour might pass by him; he said,

† "Abba, Father, all things are possible to you. Take this cup away from me, but not what I will but what you will."

N When he returned he found them asleep. He said to Peter,

† "Simon, are you asleep? Could you not keep watch for one hour? Watch and pray that you may not undergo the test. The spirit is willing but the flesh is weak."

N Withdrawing again, he prayed, saying the same thing. Then he returned once more and found them asleep, for they could not keep their eyes open and did not know what to answer him. He returned a third time and said to them,

† "Are you still sleeping and taking your rest? It is enough. The hour has come. Behold, the Son of Man is to be handed over to sinners. Get up, let us go. See, my betrayer is at hand."

N Then, while he was still speaking, Judas, one of the Twelve, arrived, accompanied by a crowd with swords and clubs who had come from the chief priests, the scribes, and the elders. His betrayer had arranged a signal with them, saying,

V "The man I shall kiss is the one; arrest him and lead him away securely."

N He came and immediately went over to him and said,

V "Rabbi."

N And he kissed him. At this they laid hands on him and arrested him. One of the bystanders drew his sword, struck the high priest's servant, and cut off his ear. Jesus said to them in reply,

† "Have you come out as against a robber, with swords and clubs, to seize me? Day after day I was with you teaching in the temple area, yet you did not arrest me; but that the Scriptures may be fulfilled."

N And they all left him and fled. Now a young man followed him wearing nothing but a linen cloth about his body. They seized him, but he left the cloth behind and ran off naked.

They led Jesus away to the **high priest**, and all the chief priests and the elders and the scribes came together. Peter followed him at a distance into the high priest's courtyard and was seated with the guards, warming himself at the fire. The chief priests and the entire Sanhedrin kept trying to obtain testimony against Jesus in order to put him to death, but they found none. Many gave false witness against him, but their testimony did not agree. Some took the stand and testified falsely against him, alleging,

C **"We heard him say, 'I will destroy this temple made with hands and within three days I will build another not made with hands.'"**

N Even so their testimony did not agree. The high priest rose before the assembly and questioned Jesus, saying,

V "Have you no answer? What are these men testifying against you?"

N But he was silent and answered nothing. Again the high priest asked him and said to him,

V "Are you the Christ, the son of the Blessed One?"

N Then Jesus answered,

† "I am;
    and 'you will see the Son of Man
        seated at the right hand of the Power
        and coming with the clouds of heaven.'"

N At that the high priest tore his garments and said,

V "What further need have we of witnesses? You have heard the blasphemy. What do you think?"

N They all condemned him as deserving to die. Some began to spit on him. They blindfolded him and struck him and said to him,

C **"Prophesy!"**

N And the guards greeted him with blows.

While Peter was below in the courtyard, one of the high priest's maids came along. Seeing Peter warming himself, she looked intently at him and said,

C **"You too were with the Nazarene, Jesus."**

N But he denied it saying,

V "I neither know nor understand what you are talking about."

N So he went out into the outer court. Then the cock crowed. The maid saw him and began again to say to the bystanders,

C **"This man is one of them."**

N Once again he denied it. A little later the bystanders said to Peter once more,

C **"Surely you are one of them; for you too are a Galilean."**

N He began to curse and to swear,

V "I do not know this man about whom you are talking."

N And immediately a cock crowed a second time. Then Peter remembered the word that Jesus had said to him, "Before the cock crows twice you will deny me three times." He broke down and wept.

* * *

N As soon as morning came, the chief priests with the elders and the scribes, that is, the whole Sanhedrin, held a council. They bound Jesus, led him away, and handed him over to Pilate. Pilate questioned him,

V "Are you the king of the Jews?"

N He said to him in reply,

† "You say so."

N The chief priests accused him of many things. Again Pilate questioned him,

V "Have you no answer? See how many things they accuse you of."

N Jesus gave him no further answer, so that Pilate was amazed.

Now on the occasion of the feast he used to release to them one prisoner whom they requested. A man called Barabbas was then in prison along with the rebels who had committed murder in a rebellion. The crowd came forward and began to ask him to do for them as he was accustomed. Pilate answered,

V "Do you want me to release to you the king of the Jews?"

N For he knew that it was out of envy that the chief priests had handed him over. But the chief priests stirred up the crowd to have him release Barabbas for them instead. Pilate again said to them in reply,

V "Then what do you want me to do with the man you call the king of the Jews?"

N They shouted again,

C **"Crucify him."**

N Pilate said to them,

V "Why? What evil has he done?"

N They only shouted the louder,

C **"Crucify him."**

N So Pilate, wishing to satisfy the crowd, released Barabbas to them and, after he had Jesus scourged, handed him over to be crucified.

The soldiers led him away inside the palace, that is, the praetorium, and assembled the whole cohort. They clothed him in purple and, weaving a crown of thorns, placed it on him. They began to salute him with,

C **"Hail, King of the Jews!"**

N and kept striking his head with a reed and spitting upon him. They knelt before him in homage. And when they had mocked him, they stripped him of the purple cloak, dressed him in his own clothes, and led him out to crucify him.

They pressed into service a passer-by, Simon, a Cyrenian, who was coming in from the country, the father of Alexander and Rufus, to carry his cross.

They brought him to the place of Golgotha—which is translated Place of the Skull—. They gave him wine drugged with myrrh, but he did not take it. Then they crucified him and divided his garments by casting lots for them to see what each should take. It was nine o'clock in the morning when they crucified him. The inscription of the charge against him read, "The King of the Jews." With him they crucified two revolutionaries, one on his right and one on his left. Those passing by reviled him, shaking their heads and saying,

C **"Aha! You who would destroy the temple and rebuild it in three days, save yourself by coming down from the cross."**

N Likewise the chief priests, with the scribes, mocked him among themselves and said,

C **"He saved others; he cannot save himself. Let the Christ, the King of Israel, come down now from the cross that we may see and believe."**

N Those who were crucified with him also kept abusing him.

At noon darkness came over the whole land until three in the afternoon. And at three o'clock Jesus cried out in a loud voice,

† *"Eloi, Eloi, lema sabachthani?"*

N which is translated,

† "My God, my God, why have you forsaken me?"

N Some of the bystanders who heard it said,

C **"Look, he is calling Elijah."**

N One of them ran, soaked a sponge with wine, put it on a reed and gave it to him to drink saying,

V "Wait, let us see if Elijah comes to take him down."

N Jesus gave a loud cry and breathed his last.

(Here all kneel and pause for a short time.)

N The veil of the sanctuary was torn in two from top to bottom. When the centurion who stood facing him saw how he breathed his last he said,

V "Truly this man was the Son of God!"

* * *

N There were also women looking on from a distance. Among them were Mary Magdalene, Mary the mother of the younger James and of Joses, and Salome. These women had followed him when he was in Galilee and ministered to him. There were also many other women who had come up with him to Jerusalem.

When it was already evening, since it was the day of preparation, the day before the sabbath, Joseph of Arimathea, a distinguished member of the council, who was himself awaiting the kingdom of God, came and courageously went to Pilate and asked for the body of Jesus. Pilate was amazed that he was already dead. He summoned the centurion and asked him if Jesus had already died. And when he learned of it from the centurion, he gave the body to Joseph. Having bought a linen cloth, he took him down, wrapped him in the linen cloth, and laid him in a tomb that had been hewn out of the rock. Then he rolled a stone against the entrance to the tomb. Mary Magdalene and Mary the mother of Joses watched where he was laid.

The Gospel of the Lord. **Praise to you, Lord Jesus Christ.**

Key Words

Holy Week begins with **Palm Sunday**, which is also called Passion Sunday. On this day we recall Jesus' arrival in Jerusalem, where people greeted him in the streets, shouting and waving palm branches. The gospel today tells the whole story of Jesus' last days on earth.

Saint Paul wrote to the **Philippians**, a community of Christians in Philippi in Greece, when he was in prison. He thanked them for their help and encouraged them to keep their faith in Jesus strong.

The name **Christ Jesus** or **Jesus Christ** brings together two words: **Jesus** which means "God saves," the name that his parents gave him; and **Christ** which means "anointed," the one chosen by God to be a true prophet, priest, and king.

The **Passion** of Jesus is the story of the last hours of his life. It begins with the Last Supper and ends when his body is placed in the tomb. Passion is a fitting word, for it originally means "suffering."

The **Feast of Unleavened Bread** is part of the Passover feast. For seven days, Jews eat only unleavened bread with their meals. The bread is baked without leaven, also called yeast, and it comes out flat. Jesus used this kind of bread at the Last Supper.

Each Jewish family prepares a **Passover lamb** for the festival dinner, when they gather to recall how God freed their ancestors from slavery in Egypt. This follows the instructions that the angel of God gave to the Israelites to sacrifice a spring lamb as they prepared to flee Egypt.

The **high priest** was in charge of the temple in Jerusalem. He and the chief priests could decide if Jesus had broken any of God's laws.

March 28

Easter Sunday of the Resurrection of the Lord

*For the **Mass During the Day**, turn to page 173.*

Vigil Mass

First Reading (Genesis 1:1–2:2 or 1:1, 26-31a)

For the shorter version, omit the indented parts in brackets.

In the beginning, when God created the heavens and the earth,

[the earth was a formless wasteland, and darkness covered the abyss, while a mighty wind swept over the waters.

Then God said, "Let there be light," and there was light. God saw how good the light was. God then separated the light from the darkness. God called the light "day," and the darkness he called "night." Thus evening came, and morning followed—the first day.

Then God said, "Let there be a dome in the middle of the waters, to separate one body of water from the other." And so it happened: God made the dome, and it separated the water above the dome from the water below it. God called the dome "the sky." Evening came, and morning followed—the second day.

Then God said, "Let the water under the sky be gathered into a single basin, so that the dry land may appear." And so it happened: the water under the sky was gathered into its basin, and the dry land appeared. God called the dry land "the earth," and the basin of the water he called "the sea." God saw how good it was. Then God said, "Let the earth bring forth vegetation: every kind of plant that bears seed and every kind of fruit tree on earth that bears fruit with its seed in it." And so it happened: the earth brought forth every kind of plant that bears seed and every kind of fruit tree on earth that bears fruit with its seed in it. God saw how good it was. Evening came, and morning followed—the third day.

Then God said: "Let there be lights in the dome of the sky, to separate day from night. Let them mark the fixed times, the days and the years, and serve as luminaries in the dome of the sky, to shed light upon the earth." And so it happened: God made the two great lights, the greater one to govern the day, and the lesser one to govern the night; and he made the stars. God set them in the dome of the sky, to shed light upon the earth, to govern the day and the night, and to separate the light from the darkness. God saw how good it was. Evening came, and morning followed—the fourth day.

Then God said, "Let the water teem with an abundance of living creatures, and on the earth let birds fly beneath the dome of the sky." And so it happened: God created the great sea monsters and all kinds of swimming creatures with which the water teems, and all kinds of winged birds. God saw how good it was, and God blessed them, saying, "Be fertile, multiply, and fill the water of the seas; and let the birds multiply on the earth." Evening came, and morning followed—the fifth day.

Then God said, "Let the earth bring forth all kinds of living creatures: cattle, creeping things, and wild animals of all kinds." And so it happened: God made all kinds of wild animals, all kinds of cattle, and all kinds of creeping things of the earth. God saw how good it was. Then]

God said: "Let us make man in our image, after our likeness. Let them have dominion over the fish of the sea, the birds of the air, and the cattle, and over all the wild animals and all the creatures that crawl on the ground."

God created man in his image;
in the image of God he created him;
male and female he created them.

God blessed them, saying: "Be fertile and multiply; fill the earth and subdue it. Have dominion over the fish of the sea, the birds of the air, and all the living things that move on the earth." God also said: "See, I give you every seed-bearing plant all over the earth and every tree that has seed-bearing fruit on it to be your food; and to all the animals of the land, all the birds of the air, and all the living creatures that crawl on the ground, I give all the green plants for food." And so it happened. God looked at everything he had made, and he found it very good.

[Evening came, and morning followed—the sixth day.

Thus the heavens and the earth and all their array were completed. Since on the seventh day God was finished with

the work he had been doing, he rested on the seventh day
from all the work he had undertaken.]

The word of the Lord. **Thanks be to God.**

An alternate psalm follows.

Responsorial Psalm

(Psalm 104:1-2, 5-6, 10, 12, 13-14, 24, 35)

℟. **Lord, send out your Spirit,**
and renew the face of the earth.

Bless the LORD, O my soul!
O LORD, my God, you are great indeed!
You are clothed with majesty and glory,
robed in light as with a cloak. ℟.

You fixed the earth upon its foundation,
not to be moved forever;
with the ocean, as with a garment, you covered it;
above the mountains the waters stood. ℟.

You send forth springs into the watercourses
that wind among the mountains.
Beside them the birds of heaven dwell;
from among the branches they send forth
their song. ℟.

You water the mountains from your palace;
the earth is replete with the fruit of your works.
You raise grass for the cattle,
and vegetation for man's use,
producing bread from the earth. ℟.

How manifold are your works, O LORD!
In wisdom you have wrought them all—
the earth is full of your creatures.
Bless the LORD, O my soul! ℟.

Or

Responsorial Psalm (Psalm 33:4-5, 6-7, 12-13, 20 and 22)

℟. The earth is full of the goodness of the Lord.

Upright is the word of the LORD,
 and all his works are trustworthy.
He loves justice and right;
 of the kindness of the LORD the earth is full. ℟.

By the word of the LORD the heavens were made;
 by the breath of his mouth all their host.
He gathers the waters of the sea as in a flask;
 in cellars he confines the deep. ℟.

Blessed the nation whose God is the LORD,
 the people he has chosen for his own inheritance.
From heaven the LORD looks down;
 he sees all mankind. ℟.

Our soul waits for the LORD,
 who is our help and our shield.
May your kindness, O LORD, be upon us
 who have put our hope in you. ℟.

Second Reading (Genesis 22:1-18 or 22:1-2, 9a, 10-13, 15-18)

For the shorter version, omit the indented parts in brackets.

God put Abraham to the test. He called to him, "Abraham!" "Here I am," he replied. Then God said: "Take your son Isaac, your only one, whom you love, and go to the land of Moriah. There you shall offer him up as a holocaust on a height that I will point out to you."

> [Early the next morning Abraham saddled his donkey, took with him his son Isaac and two of his servants as well, and with the wood that he had cut for the holocaust, set out for the place of which God had told him.

On the third day Abraham got sight of the place from afar. Then he said to his servants: "Both of you stay here with the donkey, while the boy and I go on over yonder. We will worship and then come back to you." Thereupon Abraham took the wood for the holocaust and laid it on his son Isaac's shoulders, while he himself carried the fire and the knife. As the two walked on together, Isaac spoke to his father Abraham: "Father!" Isaac said. "Yes, son," he replied. Isaac continued, "Here are the fire and the wood, but where is the sheep for the holocaust?" "Son," Abraham answered, "God himself will provide the sheep for the holocaust." Then the two continued going forward.]

When they came to the place of which God had told him, Abraham built an altar there and arranged the wood on it.

[Next he tied up his son Isaac, and put him on top of the wood on the altar.]

Then he reached out and took the knife to slaughter his son. But the LORD's messenger called to him from heaven, "Abraham, Abraham!" "Here I am," he answered. "Do not lay your hand on the boy," said the messenger. "Do not do the least thing to him. I know now how devoted you are to God, since you did not withhold from me your own beloved son." As Abraham looked about, he spied a ram caught by its horns in the thicket. So he went and took the ram and offered it up as a holocaust in place of his son.

[Abraham named the site Yahweh-yireh; hence people now say, "On the mountain the LORD will see."]

Again the LORD's messenger called to Abraham from heaven and said: "I swear by myself, declares the LORD, that because you acted as you did in not withholding from me your beloved son, I will bless you abundantly and make your descendants as countless as the stars of the sky and the sands of the seashore; your descendants shall take possession of the gates of their enemies, and in your descendants all the nations of the earth shall find blessing—all this because you obeyed my command."

The word of the Lord. **Thanks be to God.**

Responsorial Psalm (Psalm 16:5, 8, 9-10, 11)

℟. **You are my inheritance, O Lord.**

O Lord, my allotted portion and my cup,
you it is who hold fast my lot.
I set the Lord ever before me;
with him at my right hand I shall not be disturbed. ℟.

Therefore my heart is glad and my soul rejoices,
my body, too, abides in confidence;
because you will not abandon my soul
to the netherworld,
nor will you suffer your faithful one
to undergo corruption. ℟.

You will show me the path to life,
fullness of joys in your presence,
the delights at your right hand forever. ℟.

Third Reading (Exodus 14:15–15:1)

The Lord said to Moses, "Why are you crying out to me? Tell the Israelites to go forward. And you, lift up your staff and, with hand outstretched over the sea, split the sea in two, that the Israelites may pass through it on dry land. But I will make the Egyptians so obstinate that they will go in after them. Then I will receive glory through Pharaoh and all his army, his chariots and charioteers. The Egyptians shall know that I am the Lord, when I receive glory through Pharaoh and his chariots and charioteers."

The angel of God, who had been leading Israel's camp, now moved and went around behind them. The column of cloud also, leaving the front, took up its place behind them, so that it came between the camp of the Egyptians and that of Israel. But the cloud now became dark, and thus the night passed without the rival camps coming any closer together all night long. Then Moses stretched out his hand over the sea, and the Lord swept the sea with a strong east wind throughout the night and so turned it into dry land. When the water was thus divided, the Israelites marched into the midst of the sea on dry land, with the water like a wall to their right and to their left.

The Egyptians followed in pursuit; all Pharaoh's horses and chariots and charioteers went after them right into the midst of the sea. In the night watch just before dawn the LORD cast through the column of the fiery cloud upon the Egyptian force a glance that threw it into a panic; and he so clogged their chariot wheels that they could hardly drive. With that the Egyptians sounded the retreat before Israel, because the LORD was fighting for them against the Egyptians.

Then the LORD told Moses, "Stretch out your hand over the sea, that the water may flow back upon the Egyptians, upon their chariots and their charioteers." So Moses stretched out his hand over the sea, and at dawn the sea flowed back to its normal depth. The Egyptians were fleeing head on toward the sea, when the LORD hurled them into its midst. As the water flowed back, it covered the chariots and the charioteers of Pharaoh's whole army which had followed the Israelites into the sea. Not a single one of them escaped. But the Israelites had marched on dry land through the midst of the sea, with the water like a wall to their right and to their left. Thus the LORD saved Israel on that day from the power of the Egyptians. When Israel saw the Egyptians lying dead on the seashore and beheld the great power that the LORD had shown against the Egyptians, they feared the LORD and believed in him and in his servant Moses.

Then Moses and the Israelites sang this song to the LORD:
   I will sing to the LORD, for he is gloriously triumphant;
   horse and chariot he has cast into the sea.

The word of the Lord. **Thanks be to God.**

Responsorial Canticle (Exodus 15:1-2, 3-4, 5-6, 17-18)

℟. **Let us sing to the Lord; he has covered himself in glory.**

I will sing to the LORD, for he is gloriously triumphant;
horse and chariot he has cast into the sea.
My strength and my courage is the LORD,
and he has been my savior.
He is my God, I praise him;
the God of my father, I extol him. ℟.

The LORD is a warrior,
LORD is his name!
Pharaoh's chariots and army he hurled into the sea;
the elite of his officers were submerged
in the Red Sea. ℟.

The flood waters covered them,
they sank into the depths like a stone.
Your right hand, O LORD, magnificent in power,
your right hand, O LORD, has shattered
the enemy. ℟.

You brought in the people you redeemed
and planted them on the mountain
of your inheritance—
the place where you made your seat, O LORD,
the sanctuary, LORD, which your hands established.
The LORD shall reign forever and ever. ℟.

Fourth Reading (Isaiah 54:5-14)

The One who has become your husband is your Maker;
his name is the LORD of hosts;
your redeemer is the Holy One of Israel,
called God of all the earth.
The LORD calls you back,
like a wife forsaken and grieved in spirit,
a wife married in youth and then cast off,
says your God.
For a brief moment I abandoned you,

but with great tenderness I will take you back.
In an outburst of wrath, for a moment
I hid my face from you;
but with enduring love I take pity on you,
says the LORD, your redeemer.
This is for me like the days of Noah,
when I swore that the waters of Noah
should never again deluge the earth;
so I have sworn not to be angry with you,
or to rebuke you.
Though the mountains leave their place
and the hills be shaken,
my love shall never leave you
nor my covenant of peace be shaken,
says the LORD, who has mercy on you.
O afflicted one, storm-battered and unconsoled,
I lay your pavements in carnelians,
and your foundations in sapphires;
I will make your battlements of rubies,
your gates of carbuncles,
and all your walls of precious stones.
All your children shall be taught by the LORD,
and great shall be the peace of your children.
In justice shall you be established,
far from the fear of oppression,
where destruction cannot come near you.

The word of the Lord. **Thanks be to God.**

Responsorial Psalm (Psalm 30:2, 4, 5-6, 11-12, 13)

℟. **I will praise you, Lord, for you have rescued me.**

I will extol you, O LORD, for you drew me clear
and did not let my enemies rejoice over me.
O LORD, you brought me up from the netherworld;
you preserved me from among those going down
into the pit. ℟.

Sing praise to the LORD, you his faithful ones,
  and give thanks to his holy name.
For his anger lasts but a moment;
  a lifetime, his good will.
At nightfall, weeping enters in,
  but with the dawn, rejoicing. ℟.

Hear, O LORD, and have pity on me;
  O LORD, be my helper.
You changed my mourning into dancing;
  O LORD, my God, forever will I give you thanks. ℟.

Fifth Reading (Isaiah 55:1-11)

Thus says the LORD:
All you who are thirsty,
  come to the water!
You who have no money,
  come, receive grain and eat;
come, without paying and without cost,
  drink wine and milk!
Why spend your money for what is not bread,
  your wages for what fails to satisfy?
Heed me, and you shall eat well,
  you shall delight in rich fare.
Come to me heedfully,
  listen, that you may have life.
I will renew with you the everlasting covenant,
  the benefits assured to David.
As I made him a witness to the peoples,
  a leader and commander of nations,
so shall you summon a nation you knew not,
  and nations that knew you not shall run to you,
because of the LORD, your God,
  the Holy One of Israel, who has glorified you.

Seek the LORD while he may be found,
  call him while he is near.
Let the scoundrel forsake his way,
  and the wicked man his thoughts;
let him turn to the LORD for mercy;
  to our God, who is generous in forgiving.

For my thoughts are not your thoughts,
    nor are your ways my ways, says the LORD.
As high as the heavens are above the earth,
    so high are my ways above your ways
    and my thoughts above your thoughts.

For just as from the heavens
    the rain and snow come down
and do not return there
    till they have watered the earth,
    making it fertile and fruitful,
giving seed to the one who sows
    and bread to the one who eats,
so shall my word be
    that goes forth from my mouth;
my word shall not return to me void,
    but shall do my will,
    achieving the end for which I sent it.

The word of the Lord. **Thanks be to God.**

Responsorial Canticle (Isaiah 12:2-3, 4, 5-6)

℟. **You will draw water joyfully from the springs of salvation.**

God indeed is my savior;
    I am confident and unafraid.
My strength and my courage is the LORD,
    and he has been my savior.
With joy you will draw water
    at the fountain of salvation. ℟.

Give thanks to the LORD, acclaim his name;
    among the nations make known his deeds,
    proclaim how exalted is his name. ℟.

Sing praise to the LORD for his glorious achievement;
    let this be known throughout all the earth.
Shout with exultation, O city of Zion,
    for great in your midst
    is the Holy One of Israel! ℟.

Sixth Reading (Baruch 3:9-15, 32–4:4)

Hear, O Israel, the commandments of life:
listen, and know prudence!
How is it, Israel,
that you are in the land of your foes,
grown old in a foreign land,
defiled with the dead,
accounted with those destined for the netherworld?
You have forsaken the fountain of wisdom!
Had you walked in the way of God,
you would have dwelt in enduring peace.
Learn where prudence is,
where strength, where understanding;
that you may know also
where are length of days, and life,
where light of the eyes, and peace.
Who has found the place of wisdom,
who has entered into her treasuries?

The One who knows all things knows her;
he has probed her by his knowledge—
the One who established the earth for all time,
and filled it with four-footed beasts;
he who dismisses the light, and it departs,
calls it, and it obeys him trembling;
before whom the stars at their posts
shine and rejoice;
when he calls them, they answer, "Here we are!"
shining with joy for their Maker.
Such is our God;
no other is to be compared to him:
he has traced out the whole way of understanding,
and has given her to Jacob, his servant,
to Israel, his beloved son.

Since then she has appeared on earth,
and moved among people.
She is the book of the precepts of God,
the law that endures forever;
all who cling to her will live,
but those will die who forsake her.
Turn, O Jacob, and receive her:
walk by her light toward splendor.

Give not your glory to another,
your privileges to an alien race.
Blessed are we, O Israel;
for what pleases God is known to us!

The word of the Lord. **Thanks be to God.**

Responsorial Psalm (Psalm 19:8, 9, 10, 11)

℟. **Lord, you have the words of everlasting life.**

The law of the LORD is perfect,
refreshing the soul;
the decree of the LORD is trustworthy,
giving wisdom to the simple. ℟.

The precepts of the LORD are right,
rejoicing the heart;
the command of the LORD is clear,
enlightening the eye. ℟.

The fear of the LORD is pure,
enduring forever;
the ordinances of the LORD are true,
all of them just. ℟.

They are more precious than gold,
than a heap of purest gold;
sweeter also than syrup
or honey from the comb. ℟.

Seventh Reading (Ezekiel 36:16-17a, 18-28)

The word of the LORD came to me, saying: Son of man, when the house of Israel lived in their land, they defiled it by their conduct and deeds. Therefore I poured out my fury upon them because of the blood that they poured out on the ground, and because they defiled it with idols. I scattered them among the nations, dispersing them over foreign lands; according to their conduct and deeds I judged them. But when they came among the nations wherever they came, they served to profane my holy name, because it was said of them: "These are the people of the LORD, yet they had to leave their land." So I have relented because of my holy name which the house of Israel profaned among the nations where they came. Therefore say to the house of Israel: Thus says the Lord GOD: Not for your sakes do I act, house of Israel, but for the sake of my holy name, which you profaned among the nations to which you came. I will prove the holiness of my great name, profaned among the nations, in whose midst you have profaned it. Thus the nations shall know that I am the LORD, says the Lord GOD, when in their sight I prove my holiness through you. For I will take you away from among the nations, gather you from all the foreign lands, and bring you back to your own land. I will sprinkle clean water upon you to cleanse you from all your impurities, and from all your idols I will cleanse you. I will give you a new heart and place a new spirit within you, taking from your bodies your stony hearts and giving you natural hearts. I will put my spirit within you and make you live by my statutes, careful to observe my decrees. You shall live in the land I gave your fathers; you shall be my people, and I will be your God.

The word of the Lord. **Thanks be to God.**

When baptism is celebrated, sing Psalm 42/43 (below); when baptism is not celebrated, sing Isaiah 12 (page 167) or Psalm 51 (page 171).

Responsorial Psalm (Psalm 42:3, 5; 43:3, 4)

℟. **Like a deer that longs for running streams,**
my soul longs for you, my God.

Athirst is my soul for God, the living God.
When shall I go and behold the face of God? ℟.

I went with the throng
and led them in procession to the house of God,
amid loud cries of joy and thanksgiving,
with the multitude keeping festival. ℟.

Send forth your light and your fidelity;
they shall lead me on
and bring me to your holy mountain,
to your dwelling-place. ℟.

Then will I go in to the altar of God,
the God of my gladness and joy;
then will I give you thanks upon the harp,
O God, my God! ℟.

Or

Responsorial Psalm (Psalm 51:12-13, 14-15, 18-19)

℟. **Create a clean heart in me, O God.**

A clean heart create for me, O God,
and a steadfast spirit renew within me.
Cast me not out from your presence,
and your Holy Spirit take not from me. ℟.

Give me back the joy of your salvation,
and a willing spirit sustain in me.
I will teach transgressors your ways,
and sinners shall return to you. ℟.

For you are not pleased with sacrifices;
should I offer a holocaust, you would not accept it.
My sacrifice, O God, is a contrite spirit;
a heart contrite and humbled, O God,
you will not spurn. ℟.

Epistle (Romans 6:3-11)

Brothers and sisters: Are you unaware that we who were baptized into Christ Jesus were baptized into his death? We were indeed buried with him through baptism into death, so that, just as Christ was raised from the dead by the glory of the Father, we too might live in newness of life.

For if we have grown into union with him through a death like his, we shall also be united with him in the resurrection. We know that our old self was crucified with him, so that our sinful body might be done away with, that we might no longer be in slavery to sin. For a dead person has been absolved from sin. If, then, we have died with Christ, we believe that we shall also live with him. We know that Christ, raised from the dead, dies no more; death no longer has power over him. As to his death, he died to sin once and for all; as to his life, he lives for God. Consequently, you too must think of yourselves as being dead to sin and living for God in Christ Jesus.

The word of the Lord. **Thanks be to God.**

Responsorial Psalm (Psalm 118:1-2, 16-17, 22-23)

℟. **Alleluia, alleluia, alleluia.**

Give thanks to the LORD, for he is good,
for his mercy endures forever.
Let the house of Israel say,
"His mercy endures forever." ℟.

The right hand of the LORD has struck with power;
the right hand of the LORD is exalted.
I shall not die, but live,
and declare the works of the LORD. ℟.

The stone which the builders rejected
has become the cornerstone.
By the LORD has this been done;
it is wonderful in our eyes. ℟.

Gospel (Mark 16:1-7)

A reading from the holy Gospel according to Mark.
Glory to you, O Lord.

When the sabbath was over, Mary Magdalene, Mary, the mother of James, and Salome bought spices so that they might go and anoint him. Very early when the sun had risen, on the first day of the week, they came to the tomb. They were saying to one another, "Who will roll back the stone for us from the entrance to the tomb?" When they looked up, they saw that the stone had been rolled back; it was very large. On entering the tomb they saw a young man sitting on the right side, clothed in a white robe, and they were utterly amazed. He said to them, "Do not be amazed! You seek Jesus of Nazareth, the crucified. He has been raised; he is not here. Behold the place where they laid him. But go and tell his disciples and Peter, 'He is going before you to Galilee; there you will see him, as he told you.' "

The Gospel of the Lord. **Praise to you, Lord Jesus Christ.**

Mass During the Day

First Reading (Acts 10:34a, 37-43)

Peter proceeded to speak and said: "You know what has happened all over Judea, beginning in Galilee after the baptism that John preached, how God **anointed** Jesus of Nazareth with the Holy Spirit and power. He went about doing good and healing all those oppressed by the devil, for God was with him. We are witnesses of all that he did both in the country of the Jews and in Jerusalem. They put him to death by hanging him on a tree. **This man God raised** on the third day and granted that he be visible, not to all the people, but to us, the witnesses chosen by God in advance, who ate and drank with him after he rose from the dead. He commissioned us to preach to the people and testify that he is the one appointed by God as judge of the living and the dead. To him all the **prophets** bear witness, that everyone who believes in him will receive forgiveness of sins through his name."

The word of the Lord. **Thanks be to God.**

Responsorial Psalm (Psalm 118:1-2, 16-17, 22-23)

℟. **This is the day the Lord has made;**
let us rejoice and be glad. *Or* **Alleluia.**

Give thanks to the LORD, for he is good,
for his mercy endures forever.
Let the house of Israel say,
"His mercy endures forever." ℟.

"The right hand of the LORD has struck with power;
the right hand of the LORD is exalted.
I shall not die, but live,
and declare the works of the LORD." ℟.

The stone which the builders rejected
has become the cornerstone.
By the LORD has this been done;
it is wonderful in our eyes. ℟.

An alternate reading follows.

Second Reading (Colossians 3:1-4)

Brothers and sisters: If then you were raised with Christ, seek **what is above**, where Christ is seated at the right hand of God. Think of what is above, not of what is on earth. For you have died, and your life is hidden with Christ in God. When Christ your life appears, then you too will appear with him in glory.

The word of the Lord. **Thanks be to God.**

Or

Second Reading (1 Corinthians 5:6b-8)

Brothers and sisters: Do you not know that a little yeast leavens all the dough? Clear out the old yeast, so that you may become a fresh batch of dough, inasmuch as you are unleavened. For our paschal lamb, Christ, has been sacrificed. Therefore, let us celebrate the feast, not with the old yeast, the yeast of malice and wickedness, but with the unleavened bread of sincerity and truth.

The word of the Lord. **Thanks be to God.**

Sequence

Christians, to the Paschal Victim
Offer your thankful praises!
A Lamb the sheep redeems;
Christ, who only is sinless,
Reconciles sinners to the Father.

Death and life have contended in that combat stupendous:
The Prince of life, who died, reigns immortal.
Speak, Mary, declaring
What you saw, wayfaring.
"The tomb of Christ, who is living,
The glory of Jesus' resurrection;
Bright angels attesting,
The shroud and napkin resting.
Yes, Christ my hope is arisen;
To Galilee he goes before you."
Christ indeed from death is risen, our new life obtaining.
Have mercy, victor King, ever reigning!
Amen. Alleluia.

The gospel from the Easter Vigil (page 172) may also be used.
For an afternoon or evening Mass, Luke 24:13-35 may be used.

Gospel (John 20:1-9)

A reading from the holy Gospel according to John.
Glory to you, O Lord.

On the first day of the week, Mary of Magdala came to the tomb early in the morning, while it was still dark, and saw the stone removed from the tomb. So she ran and went to Simon Peter and to the other disciple whom Jesus loved, and told them, "They have taken the Lord from the tomb, and we don't know where they put him." So Peter and the other disciple went out and came to the tomb. They both ran, but the other disciple ran faster than Peter and arrived at the tomb first; he bent down and saw the burial cloths there, but did not go in. When Simon Peter arrived after him, he went into the tomb and saw the **burial cloths** there, and the cloth that had covered his head, not with the burial cloths but rolled up in a separate place. Then the other disciple also went in, the one who had arrived at the tomb first, and he saw and believed. For they did not yet understand the Scripture that he had to rise from the dead.

The Gospel of the Lord. **Praise to you, Lord Jesus Christ.**

Key Words

The **Acts of the Apostles** is a book in the New Testament that describes how the Church grew after Jesus rose from the dead. It was written by Saint Luke, who also wrote a gospel.

To **anoint** means to bless with oil. In the Bible it can also mean to give someone a mission, an important job. God anoints Jesus with the Holy Spirit to show that God was giving Jesus his mission. Christians are anointed at baptism and confirmation: our mission is to live as Jesus taught us.

This man God raised: Jesus' resurrection, his passing through death to eternal life, is the most important element of the Christian faith. We believe that Jesus did not remain dead in the tomb, but overcame death, suffering, and sin. We want to live as he taught, in order to be united with him now and in the next life.

The **prophets** were good men and women who spoke for God. Sometimes their message was harsh: they asked people to make big changes in their lives and attitudes in order to grow closer to God. At other times, they brought words of comfort.

Saint Paul wrote to the **Colossians**, a Christian community at Colossae (in what is now modern-day Turkey), to help them to understand that Jesus Christ is above everything. No powers are greater than he is.

What is above, that is, in heaven, is what Jesus teaches about: finding the truth, living simply, trusting in God, and caring for those in need. The things of earth distract us from Jesus: being selfish, hurting others, and ignoring the poor.

The **burial cloths** were the pieces of fabric that covered the body of a dead person in the tomb. Joseph of Arimathea and Nicodemus made sure that Jesus' body was treated with dignity and buried properly: they covered his face and then wrapped his body with burial cloths.

April 4

2nd Sunday of Easter
(Sunday of Divine Mercy)

First Reading (Acts 4:32-35)

The community of believers was of one heart and mind, and no one claimed that any of his possessions was his own, but they **had everything in common**. With great power the **apostles** bore witness to the resurrection of the Lord Jesus, and great favor was accorded them all. There was no needy person among them, for those who owned property or houses would sell them, bring the proceeds of the sale, and put them at the feet of the apostles, and they were distributed to each according to need.

The word of the Lord. **Thanks be to God.**

Responsorial Psalm (Psalm 118:2-4, 13-15, 22-24)

℟. **Give thanks to the Lord for he is good,
his love is everlasting.** *Or* **Alleluia.**

Let the house of Israel say,
"His mercy endures forever."
Let the house of Aaron say,
"His mercy endures forever."
Let those who fear the LORD say,
"His mercy endures forever." ℟.

I was hard pressed and was falling,
but the LORD helped me.
My strength and my courage is the LORD,
and he has been my savior.
The joyful shout of victory
in the tents of the just. ℟.

The stone which the builders rejected
has become the cornerstone.
By the LORD has this been done;
it is wonderful in our eyes.
This is the day the LORD has made;
let us be glad and rejoice in it. ℟.

Second Reading (1 John 5:1-6)

Beloved: Everyone who believes that Jesus is the Christ is begotten by God, and everyone who loves the Father loves also the one begotten by him. In this way we know that we love the children of God when we love God and obey his **commandments**. For the love of God is this, that we keep his commandments. And his commandments are not burdensome, for whoever is begotten by God conquers the world. And the victory that conquers the world is our faith. Who indeed is the victor over the world but the one who believes that Jesus is the Son of God?

This is the one who came through water and blood, Jesus Christ, not by water alone, but by water and blood. The **Spirit** is the one that testifies, and the Spirit is truth.

The word of the Lord. **Thanks be to God.**

Gospel (John 20:19-31)

A reading from the holy Gospel according to John.
Glory to you, O Lord.

On the evening of that first day of the week, when the doors were locked, where the disciples were, for fear of the Jews, Jesus came and stood in their midst and said to them, "Peace be with you." When he had said this, he showed them his hands and his side. The disciples rejoiced when they saw the Lord. Jesus said to them again, "Peace be with you. As the Father has sent me, so I send you." And when he had said this, he **breathed** on them and said to them, "Receive the Holy Spirit. Whose sins you **forgive** are forgiven them, and whose sins you retain are retained."

Thomas, called Didymus, one of the Twelve, was not with them when Jesus came. So the other disciples said to him, "We have seen the Lord." But he said to them, "Unless I see the mark of the nails in his hands and put my finger into the nailmarks and put my hand into his side, I will not believe."

Now a week later his disciples were again inside and Thomas was with them. Jesus came, although the doors were locked, and stood in their midst and said, "Peace be with you." Then he said to Thomas, "Put your finger here and see my hands, and bring your hand and put it into my side, and do not be unbelieving, but believe." Thomas answered and said to him, "My Lord and my God!" Jesus said to him, "Have you come to believe because you have seen me? Blessed are those who have not seen and have believed."

Now Jesus did many other **signs** in the presence of his disciples that are not written in this book. But these are written that you may come to believe that Jesus is the Christ, the Son of God, and that through this belief you may have life in his name.

The Gospel of the Lord. **Praise to you, Lord Jesus Christ.**

Key Words

The first Christians lived in peace together, sharing their goods, so they **had everything in common**. A true Christian shares good things for the benefit of all.

Apostle means "someone who is sent." This word is used for the twelve close friends who went with Jesus when he was teaching people about God. Jesus later sent them to tell others the good news that God loves us.

When Saint John writes of **commandments**, he means more than the Ten Commandments given to Moses. He also means the greatest commandment—given to us by Jesus—to love one another as Jesus has loved us. All the commandments help guide us to love God and everyone we meet.

The Holy **Spirit** is always in our hearts and in the Church, encouraging us to live as children of God. We receive the gifts of the Spirit in the sacraments of baptism and confirmation.

When God created the first humans, he breathed life into them. Our life comes from the depths of God's being. When Jesus appeared to his disciples after his death, he also **breathed** on them, filling them with his Spirit.

Jesus gave his disciples a very important job: to **forgive** sins. Today, in the sacrament of reconciliation, God forgives our sins through the priest we talk to. We must also forgive one another.

In John's gospel, the miracles Jesus performed are called **signs**. Jesus did these miracles to show or signify that he is the Son of God.

April 11

3rd Sunday of Easter

First Reading (Acts 3:13-15, 17-19)

Peter said to the people: "**The God of Abraham, the God of Isaac, and the God of Jacob**, the God of our fathers, has glorified his servant Jesus, whom you handed over and denied in Pilate's presence when he had decided to release him. You denied the Holy and Righteous One and asked that a murderer be released to you. The author of life you put to death, but God raised him from the dead; of this we are witnesses. Now I know, brothers, that you acted out of ignorance, just as your leaders did; but God has thus brought to fulfillment what he had announced beforehand through the mouth of all the prophets, that his Christ would suffer. Repent, therefore, and be converted, that your sins may be wiped away."

The word of the Lord. **Thanks be to God.**

Responsorial Psalm (Psalm 4:2, 4, 7-8, 9)

℟. **Lord, let your face shine on us.** *Or* **Alleluia.**

When I call, answer me, O my just God,
you who relieve me when I am in distress;
have pity on me, and hear my prayer! ℟.

Know that the LORD does wonders for his faithful one;
the LORD will hear me when I call upon him. ℟.

O LORD, let the light of your countenance shine upon us!
You put gladness into my heart. ℟.

As soon as I lie down, I fall peacefully asleep,
for you alone, O LORD,
bring security to my dwelling. ℟.

Second Reading (1 John 2:1-5a)

My children, I am writing this to you so that you may not commit **sin**. But if anyone does sin, we have an Advocate with the Father, Jesus Christ the righteous one. He is expiation for our sins, and not for our sins only but for those of the whole world. The way we may be sure that we know him is to keep his commandments. Those who say, "I know him," but do not keep his commandments are liars, and the truth is not in them. But whoever keeps his word, the love of God is truly perfected in him.

The word of the Lord. **Thanks be to God.**

Gospel (Luke 24:35-48)

A reading from the holy Gospel according to Luke.
Glory to you, O Lord.

The two disciples recounted what had taken place **on the way**, and how Jesus was made known to them in **the breaking of bread**.

While they were still speaking about this, he stood in their midst and said to them, "Peace be with you." But they were startled and terrified and thought that they were seeing a ghost. Then he said to them, "Why are you troubled? And why do questions arise in your hearts? Look at my hands and my feet, that it is I myself. Touch me and see, because a ghost does not have flesh and bones as you can see I have." And as he said this, he showed them his hands and his feet. While they were still incredulous for joy and were amazed, he asked them, "Have you anything here to eat?" They gave him a piece of baked fish; he took it and ate it in front of them.

He said to them, "These are my words that I spoke to you while I was still with you, that everything written about me in the law of Moses and in the prophets and psalms must be fulfilled." Then he opened their minds to understand the Scriptures. And he said to them, "Thus it is written that the Christ would suffer and rise from the dead on the third day and that repentance, for the forgiveness of sins, would be preached in his name to all the nations, beginning from Jerusalem. You are witnesses of these things."

The Gospel of the Lord. **Praise to you, Lord Jesus Christ.**

Key Words

The God of Abraham, the God of Isaac, and the God of Jacob is a name given to the one true God who had made a covenant with each of these men (also known as the Patriarchs). Peter is telling the Jews that the God of their ancestors, whom they know from the Scriptures, is the one who raised Jesus from the dead.

The **First Letter of Saint John** was written to the Christian communities in the east. They were disagreeing among themselves, so John wrote to help them sort out their problems.

To **sin** is to knowingly turn away from God. John tells us in this letter that when we love God, we listen to God and live in a way that is pleasing to God.

The **Gospel of Luke** was written for people who, like Luke, weren't Jewish before becoming Christian. Luke also wrote the Acts of the Apostles, the book that tells us about the early days of the Christian Church.

On the day Jesus rose from the dead, he walked with two of his disciples **on the way** to Emmaus, a village near Jerusalem. They were sad because Jesus was dead. They did not recognize Jesus until he sat down at the table and broke the bread with them, as he had done at the Last Supper.

The breaking of bread here means to celebrate the Lord's Supper, as we do at every Eucharist or Mass.

April 18

4th Sunday of Easter

First Reading (Acts 4:8-12)

Peter, filled with the Holy Spirit, said: "Leaders of the people and **elders**: If we are being examined today about a good deed done to a cripple, namely, by what means he was saved, then all of you and all the people of Israel should know that it was **in the name of Jesus Christ the Nazorean** whom you crucified, whom God raised from the dead; in his name this man stands before you healed. He is *the stone rejected by you, the builders, which has become the cornerstone*. There is no salvation through anyone else, nor is there any other name under heaven given to the human race by which we are to be saved."

The word of the Lord. **Thanks be to God.**

Responsorial Psalm (Psalm 118:1, 8-9, 21-23, 26, 28, 29)

℟. **The stone rejected by the builders has become the cornerstone.** *Or* **Alleluia.**

Give thanks to the LORD, for he is good,
for his mercy endures forever.
It is better to take refuge in the LORD
than to trust in man.
It is better to take refuge in the LORD
than to trust in princes. ℟.

I will give thanks to you, for you have answered me
and have been my savior.
The stone which the builders rejected
has become the **cornerstone**.
By the LORD has this been done;
it is wonderful in our eyes. ℟.

Blessed is he who comes in the name of the LORD;
we bless you from the house of the LORD.
I will give thanks to you, for you have answered me
and have been my savior.
Give thanks to the LORD, for he is good;
for his kindness endures forever. ℟.

Second Reading (1 John 3:1-2)

Beloved: See what love the Father has bestowed on us that we may be called the children of God. Yet so we are. The reason the world does not know us is that it did not know him. Beloved, we are God's children now; what we shall be has not yet been revealed. We do know that when it is revealed we shall be like him, for we shall see him as he is.

The word of the Lord. **Thanks be to God.**

Gospel (John 10:11-18)

A reading from the holy Gospel according to John.
Glory to you, O Lord.

Jesus said: "I am the **good shepherd**. A good shepherd lays down his life for the sheep. A **hired man**, who is not a shepherd and whose sheep are not his own, sees a wolf coming and leaves the sheep and runs away, and the wolf catches and scatters them. This is because he works for pay and has no concern for the sheep. I am the good shepherd, and I know mine and mine know me, just as the Father knows me and I know the Father; and I will lay down my life for the sheep. I have other sheep that do not belong to this fold. These also I must lead, and they will hear my voice, and there will be one flock, one shepherd. This is why the Father loves me, because I lay down my life in order to take it up again. No one takes it from me, but I lay it down on my own. I have power to lay it down, and power to take it up again. This command I have received from my Father."

The Gospel of the Lord. **Praise to you, Lord Jesus Christ.**

Key Words

Peter is the apostle whose name Jesus changed from Simon, to show how important Peter would be in the life of the Church (Peter means "rock"). Although Peter let Jesus down by denying him three times when Jesus had been arrested, at other times he showed that he had great faith in Jesus. In today's reading from the Acts of the Apostles, Peter is speaking as the head of the new community.

Elders are leaders or older people who have a great deal of life experience and wisdom. They rely on their experience to help make decisions that benefit everyone.

When Peter says he healed a sick man **in the name of Jesus Christ the Nazorean**, he is saying that the power to heal does not come from him, but from Jesus, who is risen from the dead.

The **cornerstone** of a building is important: it is the stone at the base where two walls meet and therefore supports the whole building. The psalm tells us that what was a worthless stone in the eyes of the builders has become the most important stone of all! Through the resurrection, Jesus has become the cornerstone of our salvation.

A **good shepherd** is one who feeds his sheep and keeps them safe both day and night. We trust Jesus as sheep trust their shepherd, knowing that God loves us and takes care of us.

The **hired man** watches over the sheep because he is paid to do so, but doesn't love them or take risks to protect them. Unlike a hired person, Jesus will do everything he can to keep us—his sheep—safe.

April 25

5th Sunday of Easter

First Reading (Acts 9:26-31)

When **Saul** arrived in Jerusalem he tried to join the disciples, but they were all afraid of him, not believing that he was a disciple. Then **Barnabas** took charge of him and brought him to the apostles, and he reported to them how he had seen the Lord, and that he had spoken to him, and how in Damascus he had spoken out boldly in the name of Jesus. He moved about freely with them in Jerusalem, and spoke out boldly in the name of the Lord. He also spoke and debated with the Hellenists, but they tried to kill him. And when the brothers learned of this, they took him down to Caesarea and sent him on his way to Tarsus.

The church throughout all Judea, Galilee, and Samaria was at peace. It was being built up and walked in the fear of the Lord, and with the consolation of the Holy Spirit it grew in numbers.

The word of the Lord. **Thanks be to God.**

Responsorial Psalm (Psalm 22:26-27, 28, 30, 31-32)

℟. **I will praise you, Lord, in the assembly of your people.** *Or* **Alleluia.**

I will fulfill my vows before those who fear the LORD.
The lowly shall eat their fill;
they who seek the LORD shall praise him:
"May your hearts live forever!" ℟.

All the ends of the earth
shall remember and turn to the LORD;
all the families of the nations
shall bow down before him. ℟.

To him alone shall bow down
all who sleep in the earth;
before him shall bend
all who go down into the dust. ℟.

And to him my soul shall live;
my descendants shall serve him.
Let the coming generation be told of the LORD
that they may proclaim to a people yet to be born
the justice he has shown. ℟.

Second Reading (1 John 3:18-24)

Children, let us love not in word or speech but in deed and truth.

Now this is how we shall know that we belong to the truth and reassure our hearts before him in whatever our **hearts condemn**, for God is greater than our hearts and knows everything. Beloved, if our hearts do not condemn us, we have confidence in God and receive from him whatever we ask, because we keep his commandments and do what pleases him. And his commandment is this: we should believe in the name of his Son, Jesus Christ, and **love one another** just as he commanded us. Those who keep his commandments remain in him, and he in them, and the way we know that he remains in us is from the Spirit he gave us.

The word of the Lord. **Thanks be to God.**

Gospel (John 15:1-8)

A reading from the holy Gospel according to John.
Glory to you, O Lord.

Jesus said to his disciples: "I am the true vine, and my Father is the vine grower. He takes away every branch in me that does not bear fruit, and every one that does he prunes so that it bears more fruit. You are already **pruned** because of the word that I spoke to you. Remain in me, as I remain in you. Just as a branch cannot bear fruit on its own unless it remains on the vine, so neither can you unless you remain in me. I am the vine, you are the **branches**. Whoever remains in me and I in him will bear much fruit, because without me you can do nothing. Anyone who does not remain in me will be thrown out like a branch and wither; people will gather them and throw them into a fire and they will be burned. If you remain in me and my words remain in you, ask for whatever you want and it will be done for you. By this is my Father **glorified**, that you bear much fruit and become my disciples."

The Gospel of the Lord. **Praise to you, Lord Jesus Christ.**

Key Words

Saint Paul's original name was **Saul**. In the Acts of the Apostles, he is referred to by both names; usually, we think of Saul as who he was before he experienced his conversion and joined the apostles. Paul is his name as the apostle to the Gentiles and author of the New Testament letters bearing his name.

Barnabas was an important person in the early Christian community. He was Saint Paul's traveling companion and was a man of strong faith.

Saint John writes to his friends with affection; that is why he uses the word **children**. He is like a loving parent or grandparent giving advice and encouragement.

When our **hearts condemn** us, we know we have done something wrong. Perhaps we have hurt someone. Our hearts are at ease and we find peace when we repair the damage and ask for forgiveness.

Love one another. With these words, Saint John sums up all of Jesus' teaching and what every Christian must do. He explains that we show love when we help others.

Those who listen to Jesus' words and put them into practice are **pruned**. They have put aside the destructive ways of the world; their hearts are pure and full of love.

Branches are the part of the grapevine that produces grapes. If the branch does not bear fruit, it will be pruned or cut away so that the other branches can bear more fruit. By comparing us to branches on a grapevine, Jesus reminds us that our vocation is to share his message of love with others.

To **glorify** God means to praise, exalt, or give glory to him. When we follow Jesus and obey his teaching, we give glory to God.

May 2

6th Sunday of Easter

If the Ascension is celebrated on the following Sunday in your diocese, the Second Reading and Gospel from the Seventh Sunday of Easter (see page 203) may be read today.

First Reading (Acts 10:25-26, 34-35, 44-48)

When Peter entered, **Cornelius** met him and, falling at his feet, paid him homage. Peter, however, raised him up, saying, "Get up. I myself am also a human being."

Then Peter proceeded to speak and said, "In truth, I see that God shows no **partiality**. Rather, in every nation whoever fears him and acts uprightly is acceptable to him."

While Peter was still speaking these things, the Holy Spirit fell upon all who were listening to the word. The circumcised believers who had accompanied Peter were astounded that the gift of the Holy Spirit should have been poured out on the Gentiles also, for they could hear them speaking in tongues and glorifying God. Then Peter responded, "Can anyone withhold the water for baptizing these people, who have received the Holy Spirit even as we have?" He ordered them to be baptized in the name of Jesus Christ.

The word of the Lord. **Thanks be to God.**

Responsorial Psalm (Psalm 98:1, 2-3, 3-4)

℟. **The Lord has revealed to the nations his saving power.** *Or* **Alleluia.**

Sing to the LORD a new song,
for he has done wondrous deeds;
his right hand has won victory for him,
his holy arm. ℟.

The LORD has made his salvation known:
in the sight of the nations he has revealed
his justice.
He has remembered his kindness and his faithfulness
toward the house of Israel. ℟.

All the ends of the earth have seen
the salvation by our God.
Sing joyfully to the LORD, all you lands;
break into song; sing praise. ℟.

Second Reading (1 John 4:7-10)

Beloved, let us love one another, because love is of God; everyone who loves is begotten by God and knows God. Whoever is without love does not know God, for God is love. In this way the love of God was revealed to us: God sent his only Son into the world so that we might have life through him. In this is love: not that we have loved God, but that he loved us and sent his Son as **expiation** for our sins.

The word of the Lord. **Thanks be to God.**

Gospel (John 15:9-17)

A reading from the holy Gospel according to John.
Glory to you, O Lord.

Jesus said to his disciples: "As the Father loves me, so I also love you. Remain in my love. If you keep my commandments, you will remain in my love, just as I have kept my Father's commandments and remain in his love.

"I have told you this so that my **joy** may be in you and your joy might be complete. This is my commandment: love one another as I love you. No one has greater love than this, to lay down one's life for one's friends. You are my friends if you do what I command you. I no longer call you slaves, because a slave does not know what his master is doing. I have called you friends, because I have told you everything I have heard from my Father. It was not you who chose me, but I who chose you and appointed you to go and **bear fruit** that will remain, so that whatever you ask the Father in my name he may give you. This I command you: love one another."

The Gospel of the Lord. **Praise to you, Lord Jesus Christ.**

Key Words

At the time of Jesus, a Roman army or legion consisted of ten cohorts or units. Each cohort was made up of six smaller units called centuria; a centurion was the Roman military officer who was in charge of a centuria. It is because **Cornelius** was a centurion, and the Romans were the occupying force at the time, that Cornelius' actions are so remarkable.

To show **partiality** is to be nice to one person and not to another. God is impartial and treats everyone the same way: with love.

Expiation means to make up for something wrong we have done: it means the same as to atone or to be reconciled. Jesus is the expiating sacrifice for our sins: through his death our sins are forgiven and we have eternal life.

Many things can bring us **joy**, like good health, loyal friends, and peace in our family. Jesus tells us that our greatest joy is to love others as he has loved us. When we do this, his joy will be with us and we will be at one with Jesus.

We will **bear fruit** when we spread Jesus' message of love wherever we go and in all we do.

May 9

The Ascension of the Lord

If your diocese celebrates the Ascension of the Lord on Thursday, May 6, then this Sunday is the Seventh Sunday of Easter. *The readings for the Seventh Sunday of Easter can be found on page 202.*

First Reading (Acts 1:1-11)

In the first book, **Theophilus**, I dealt with all that Jesus did and taught until the day he was taken up, after giving instructions through the Holy Spirit to the apostles whom he had chosen. He presented himself alive to them by many proofs after he had suffered, appearing to them during forty days and speaking about the **kingdom of God**. While meeting with them, he enjoined them not to depart from Jerusalem, but to wait for "the promise of the Father about which you have heard me speak; for John baptized with water, but in a few days you will be **baptized with the Holy Spirit**."

When they had gathered together they asked him, "Lord, are you at this time going to restore the kingdom to Israel?" He answered them, "It is not for you to know the times or seasons that the Father has established by his own authority. But you will receive power when the Holy Spirit comes upon you, and you will be my witnesses in Jerusalem, throughout Judea and Samaria, and to the ends of the earth." When he had said this, as they were looking on, he was **lifted up**, and a cloud took him from their sight. While they were looking intently at the sky as he was going, suddenly two men dressed in white garments stood beside them. They said, "Men of Galilee, why are you standing there looking at the sky? This Jesus who has been taken up from you into heaven will return in the same way you have seen him going into heaven."

The word of the Lord. **Thanks be to God.**

Responsorial Psalm (Psalm 47:2-3, 6-7, 8-9)

℟. **God mounts his throne to shouts of joy:**
a blare of trumpets for the Lord. *Or* **Alleluia.**

All you peoples, clap your hands,
shout to God with cries of gladness.
For the LORD, the Most High, the awesome,
is the great king over all the earth. ℟.

God mounts his throne amid shouts of joy;
the LORD, amid trumpet blasts.
Sing praise to God, sing praise;
sing praise to our king, sing praise. ℟.

For king of all the earth is God;
sing hymns of praise.
God reigns over the nations,
God sits upon his holy throne. ℟.

An alternate reading follows.

Second Reading (Ephesians 1:17-23)

Brothers and sisters: May the God of our Lord Jesus Christ, the Father of glory, give you a Spirit of wisdom and revelation resulting in knowledge of him. May the eyes of your hearts be enlightened, that you may know what is the hope that belongs to his call, what are the riches of glory in his inheritance among the holy ones, and what is the surpassing greatness of his power for us who believe, in accord with the exercise of his great might: which he worked in Christ, raising him from the dead and seating him at his right hand in the heavens, far above every principality, authority, power, and dominion, and every name that is named not only in this age but also in the one to come. And he put all things beneath his feet and gave him as head over all things to the church, which is his body, the fullness of the one who fills all things in every way.

The word of the Lord. **Thanks be to God.**

Or

Second Reading (Ephesians 4:1-13 or 4:1-7, 11-13)

For the shorter version, omit the indented part in brackets.

Brothers and sisters, I, a prisoner for the Lord, urge you to live in a manner worthy of the call you have received, with all humility and gentleness, with patience, bearing with one another through love, striving to preserve the unity of the Spirit through the bond of peace: one body and one Spirit, as you were also called to the one hope of your call; one Lord, one faith, one baptism; one God and Father of all, who is over all and through all and in all.

But grace was given to each of us according to the measure of Christ's gift.

> [Therefore, it says:
> *He ascended on high and took prisoners captive;*
> *he gave gifts to men.*
>
> What does "he ascended" mean except that he also descended into the lower regions of the earth? The one who descended is also the one who ascended far above all the heavens, that he might fill all things.]

And he gave some as apostles, others as prophets, others as evangelists, others as pastors and teachers, to equip the holy ones for the work of ministry, for building up the body of Christ, until we all attain to the unity of faith and knowledge of the Son of God, to mature to manhood, to the extent of the full stature of Christ.

The word of the Lord. **Thanks be to God.**

Gospel (Mark 16:15-20)

A reading from the holy Gospel according to Mark.
Glory to you, O Lord.

Jesus said to his **disciples**: "Go into the whole world and proclaim the **gospel** to every creature. Whoever believes and is baptized will be saved; whoever does not believe will be condemned. These signs will accompany those who believe: in my name they will drive out demons, they will speak new languages. They will pick up serpents with their hands, and if they drink any deadly thing, it will not harm them. They will lay hands on the sick, and they will recover."

So then the Lord Jesus, after he spoke to them, was taken up into heaven and took his seat at the **right hand of God**. But they went forth and preached everywhere, while the Lord worked with them and confirmed the word through accompanying signs.

The Gospel of the Lord. **Praise to you, Lord Jesus Christ.**

Seventh Sunday of Easter

First Reading (Acts 1:15-17, 20a, 20c-26)

Peter stood up in the midst of the brothers—there was a group of about one hundred and twenty persons in the one place—. He said, "My brothers, the Scripture had to be fulfilled which the Holy Spirit spoke beforehand through the mouth of David, concerning Judas, who was the guide for those who arrested Jesus. He was numbered among us and was allotted a share in this ministry.

"For it is written in the Book of Psalms:
May another take his office.

"Therefore, it is necessary that one of the men who accompanied us the whole time the Lord Jesus came and went among us, beginning from the baptism of John until the day on which he was taken up from us, become with us a witness to his resurrection." So they proposed two, Judas called Barsabbas, who was also known as Justus, and Matthias. Then they prayed, "You, Lord, who know the hearts of all, show which one of these two you have chosen to take the place in this apostolic ministry from which Judas turned away to go to his own place." Then they gave lots to them, and the lot fell upon Matthias, and he was counted with the eleven apostles.

The word of the Lord. **Thanks be to God.**

Responsorial Psalm (Psalm 103:1-2, 11-12, 19-20)

℟. **The Lord has set his throne in heaven.** *Or* **Alleluia.**

Bless the LORD, O my soul;
and all my being, bless his holy name.
Bless the LORD, O my soul,
and forget not all his benefits. ℟.

For as the heavens are high above the earth,
so surpassing is his kindness toward those who fear him.
As far as the east is from the west,
so far has he put our transgressions from us. ℟.

The LORD has established his throne in heaven,
and his kingdom rules over all.
Bless the LORD, all you his angels,
you mighty in strength, who do his bidding. ℟.

Second Reading (1 John 4:11-16)

Beloved, if God so loved us, we also must love one another. No one has ever seen God. Yet, if we love one another, God remains in us, and his love is brought to perfection in us.

This is how we know that we remain in him and he in us, that he has given us of his Spirit. Moreover, we have seen and testify that the Father sent his Son as savior of the world. Whoever acknowledges that Jesus is the Son of God, God remains in him and he in God. We have come to know and to believe in the love God has for us.

God is love, and whoever remains in love remains in God and God in him.

The word of the Lord. **Thanks be to God.**

Gospel (John 17:11b-19)

A reading from the holy Gospel according to John.
Glory to you, O Lord.

Lifting up his eyes to heaven, Jesus prayed, saying: "Holy Father, keep them in your name that you have given me, so that they may be one just as we are one. When I was with them I protected them in your name that you gave me, and I guarded them, and none of them was lost except the son of destruction, in order that the Scripture might be fulfilled. But now I am coming to you. I speak this in the world so that they may share my joy completely. I gave them your word, and the world hated them, because they do not belong to the world any more than I belong to the world. I do not ask that you take them out of the world but that you keep them from the evil one. They do not belong to the world any more than I belong to the world. Consecrate them in the truth. Your word is truth. As you sent me into the world, so I sent them into the world. And I consecrate myself for them, so that they also may be consecrated in truth."

The Gospel of the Lord. **Praise to you, Lord Jesus Christ.**

Key Words

Saint Luke is the author of the Acts of the Apostles, in addition to the Gospel of Luke. He addresses the Acts of the Apostles to **Theophilus**, a name that can mean any one of us: Theophilus is Greek for "friend of God" or "beloved by God."

In the Bible, the expression **kingdom of God** describes a way of living as God asks. To enter into the kingdom means to live as children of God our Father, to do God's will, and to gain eternal life.

People who are **baptized with the Holy Spirit** have let God into their lives. The Holy Spirit is alive in them. The apostles received the Holy Spirit on the day of Pentecost. We receive the Holy Spirit in the sacraments of baptism and confirmation.

The Ascension of the Lord is the feast day when we remember how the risen Christ said goodbye to his disciples and was **lifted up** (ascended) to heaven. Jesus is still with us in spirit, but his resurrected body is with the Father. Each Sunday at Mass we celebrate Jesus, who is present among us.

Jesus appeared to his eleven **disciples**. There were twelve at first, but Judas Iscariot, who betrayed Jesus, left before Jesus died, leaving eleven followers after the resurrection.

The **gospel** refers to the message of Jesus: that God loves us and wants us to live with him forever.

The position of greatest importance next to a king is the seat at his right hand. When Saint Mark tells us Jesus sat down at the **right hand of God**, he is a saying that Jesus is very close to God the Father.

May 16

Pentecost Sunday

*For the **Mass During the Day**, turn to page 213.*

Vigil Mass

First Form: Extended Vigil
(For the Simple Form, see page 212.)

First Reading (Genesis 11:1-9)

The whole world spoke the same language, using the same words. While the people were migrating in the east, they came upon a valley in the land of Shinar and settled there. They said to one another, "Come, let us mold bricks and harden them with fire." They used bricks for stone, and bitumen for mortar. Then they said, "Come, let us build ourselves a city and a tower with its top in the sky, and so make a name for ourselves; otherwise we shall be scattered all over the earth."

The LORD came down to see the city and the tower that the people had built. Then the LORD said: "If now, while they are one people, all speaking the same language, they have started to do this, nothing will later stop them from doing whatever they presume to do. Let us then go down there and confuse their language, so that one will not understand what another says." Thus the LORD scattered them from there all over the earth, and they stopped building the city. That is why it was called Babel, because there the LORD confused the speech of all the world. It was from that place that he scattered them all over the earth.

The word of the Lord. **Thanks be to God.**

Responsorial Psalm (Psalm 33:10-11, 12-13, 14-15)

℟. **Blessed the people the Lord has chosen to be his own.**

The LORD brings to nought the plans of nations;
he foils the designs of peoples.
But the plan of the LORD stands forever;
the design of his heart, through all generations. ℟.

Blessed the nation whose God is the LORD,
    the people he has chosen for his own inheritance.
From heaven the LORD looks down;
    he sees all mankind. ℟.

From his fixed throne he beholds
    all who dwell on the earth,
He who fashioned the heart of each,
    he who knows all their works. ℟.

Second Reading (Exodus 19:3-8a, 16-20b)

Moses went up the mountain to God. Then the LORD called to him and said, "Thus shall you say to the house of Jacob; tell the Israelites: You have seen for yourselves how I treated the Egyptians and how I bore you up on eagle wings and brought you here to myself. Therefore, if you hearken to my voice and keep my covenant, you shall be my special possession, dearer to me than all other people, though all the earth is mine. You shall be to me a kingdom of priests, a holy nation. That is what you must tell the Israelites." So Moses went and summoned the elders of the people. When he set before them all that the LORD had ordered him to tell them, the people all answered together, "Everything the LORD has said, we will do."

On the morning of the third day there were peals of thunder and lightning, and a heavy cloud over the mountain, and a very loud trumpet blast, so that all the people in the camp trembled. But Moses led the people out of the camp to meet God, and they stationed themselves at the foot of the mountain. Mount Sinai was all wrapped in smoke, for the LORD came down upon it in fire. The smoke rose from it as though from a furnace, and the whole mountain trembled violently. The trumpet blast grew louder and louder, while Moses was speaking, and God answering him with thunder.

When the LORD came down to the top of Mount Sinai, he summoned Moses to the top of the mountain.

The word of the Lord. **Thanks be to God.**

An alternate Responsorial Psalm follows.

Responsorial Psalm (Daniel 3:52, 53, 54, 55, 56)

℟. **Glory and praise forever!**

"Blessed are you, O Lord, the God of our fathers,
praiseworthy and exalted above all forever;
And blessed is your holy and glorious name,
praiseworthy and exalted above all for all ages." ℟.

"Blessed are you in the temple of your holy glory,
praiseworthy and glorious above all forever." ℟.

"Blessed are you on the throne of your Kingdom,
praiseworthy and exalted above all forever." ℟.

"Blessed are you who look into the depths
from your throne upon the cherubim,
praiseworthy and exalted above all forever." ℟.

"Blessed are you in the firmament of heaven,
praiseworthy and glorious forever." ℟.

Or

Responsorial Psalm (Psalm 19:8, 9, 10, 11)

℟. **Lord, you have the words of everlasting life.**

The law of the LORD is perfect,
refreshing the soul;
The decree of the LORD is trustworthy,
giving wisdom to the simple. ℟.

The precepts of the LORD are right,
rejoicing the heart;
The command of the LORD is clear,
enlightening the eye. ℟.

The fear of the LORD is pure,
enduring forever;
The ordinances of the LORD are true,
all of them just. ℟.

They are more precious than gold,
than a heap of purest gold;
Sweeter also than syrup
or honey from the comb. ℟.

Third Reading (Ezekiel 37:1-14)

The hand of the LORD came upon me, and he led me out in the spirit of the LORD and set me in the center of the plain, which was now filled with bones. He made me walk among the bones in every direction so that I saw how many they were on the surface of the plain. How dry they were! He asked me: Son of man, can these bones come to life? I answered, "Lord GOD, you alone know that." Then he said to me: Prophesy over these bones, and say to them: Dry bones, hear the word of the LORD! Thus says the Lord GOD to these bones: See! I will bring spirit into you, that you may come to life. I will put sinews upon you, make flesh grow over you, cover you with skin, and put spirit in you so that you may come to life and know that I am the LORD. I, Ezekiel, prophesied as I had been told, and even as I was prophesying I heard a noise; it was a rattling as the bones came together, bone joining bone. I saw the sinews and the flesh come upon them, and the skin cover them, but there was no spirit in them. Then the LORD said to me: Prophesy to the spirit, prophesy, son of man, and say to the spirit: Thus says the Lord GOD: From the four winds come, O spirit, and breathe into these slain that they may come to life. I prophesied as he told me, and the spirit came into them; they came alive and stood upright, a vast army. Then he said to me: Son of man, these bones are the whole house of Israel. They have been saying, "Our bones are dried up, our hope is lost, and we are cut off." Therefore, prophesy and say to them: Thus says the Lord GOD: O my people, I will open your graves and have you rise from them, and bring you back to the land of Israel. Then you shall know that I am the LORD, when I open your graves and have you rise from them, O my people! I will put my spirit in you that you may live, and I will settle you upon your land; thus you shall know that I am the LORD. I have promised, and I will do it, says the LORD.

The word of the Lord. **Thanks be to God.**

Responsorial Psalm (Psalm 107:2-3, 4-5, 6-7, 8-9)

℟. **Give thanks to the Lord; his love is everlasting.**
Or **Alleluia.**

Let the redeemed of the LORD say,
those whom he has redeemed from the hand
of the foe
And gathered from the lands,
from the east and the west, from the north
and the south. ℟.

They went astray in the desert wilderness;
the way to an inhabited city they did not find.
Hungry and thirsty,
their life was wasting away within them. ℟.

They cried to the LORD in their distress;
from their straits he rescued them.
And he led them by a direct way
to reach an inhabited city. ℟.

Let them give thanks to the LORD for his mercy
and his wondrous deeds to the children of men,
Because he satisfied the longing soul
and filled the hungry soul with good things. ℟.

Fourth Reading (Joel 3:1-5)

Thus says the LORD:
I will pour out my spirit upon all flesh.
Your sons and daughters shall prophesy,
your old men shall dream dreams,
your young men shall see visions;
even upon the servants and the handmaids,
in those days, I will pour out my spirit.
And I will work wonders in the heavens and on the earth,
blood, fire, and columns of smoke;
the sun will be turned to darkness,
and the moon to blood,
at the coming of the day of the LORD,
the great and terrible day.
Then everyone shall be rescued

who calls on the name of the LORD;
for on Mount Zion there shall be a remnant,
as the LORD has said,
and in Jerusalem survivors
whom the LORD shall call.

The word of the Lord. **Thanks be to God.**

Responsorial Psalm (Psalm 104:1-2, 24, 35, 27-28, 29, 30)

℟. **Lord, send out your Spirit, and renew the face of the earth.** *Or* **Alleluia.**

Bless the LORD, O my soul!
O LORD, my God, you are great indeed!
You are clothed with majesty and glory,
robed in light as with a cloak. ℟.

How manifold are your works, O LORD!
In wisdom you have wrought them all —
the earth is full of your creatures;
bless the LORD, O my soul! Alleluia. ℟.

Creatures all look to you
to give them food in due time.
When you give it to them, they gather it;
when you open your hand, they are filled
with good things. ℟.

If you take away their breath, they perish
and return to their dust.
When you send forth your spirit, they are created,
and you renew the face of the earth. ℟.

Epistle (Romans 8:22-27)

Brothers and sisters: We know that all creation is groaning in labor pains even until now; and not only that, but we ourselves, who have the firstfruits of the Spirit, we also groan within ourselves as we wait for adoption, the redemption of our bodies. For in hope we were saved. Now hope that sees is not hope. For who hopes for what one sees? But if we hope for what we do not see, we wait with endurance.

In the same way, the Spirit too comes to the aid of our weakness; for we do not know how to pray as we ought, but the Spirit himself intercedes with inexpressible groanings. And the one who searches hearts knows what is the intention of the Spirit, because he intercedes for the holy ones according to God's will.

The word of the Lord. **Thanks be to God.**

Gospel (John 7:37-39)

A reading from the holy Gospel according to John.
Glory to you, O Lord.

On the last and greatest day of the feast, Jesus stood up and exclaimed, "Let anyone who thirsts come to me and drink. As Scripture says:
Rivers of living water will flow from within him
who believes in me."
He said this in reference to the Spirit that those who came to believe in him were to receive. There was, of course, no Spirit yet, because Jesus had not yet been glorified.

The Gospel of the Lord. **Praise to you, Lord Jesus Christ.**

Simple Form

First Reading

A First Reading is chosen from among the Old Testament readings prescribed for the Extended Vigil on pages 206-210 (Genesis 11:1-9; Exodus 19:3-8a, 16-20b; Ezekiel 37:1-14; or Joel 3:1-5).

Responsorial Psalm

Use Psalm 104, page 211.

Second Reading

Use Romans 8:22-27, page 211.

Gospel

Use John 7:37-39, above.

Mass During the Day

First Reading (Acts 2:1-11)

When the time for **Pentecost** was fulfilled, they were all in one place together. And suddenly there came from the sky a noise like a strong driving wind, and it filled the entire house in which they were. Then there appeared to them tongues as of **fire**, which parted and came to rest on each one of them. And they were all filled with the Holy Spirit and began to speak in different tongues, as the Spirit enabled them to proclaim.

Now there were devout Jews from every nation under heaven staying in Jerusalem. At this sound, they gathered in a large crowd, but they were confused because each one heard them speaking in his own language. They were astounded, and in amazement they asked, "Are not all these people who are speaking Galileans? Then how does each of us hear them in his native language? We are Parthians, Medes, and Elamites, inhabitants of Mesopotamia, Judea and Cappadocia, Pontus and Asia, Phrygia and Pamphylia, Egypt and the districts of Libya near Cyrene, as well as travelers from Rome, both Jews and **converts** to Judaism, Cretans and Arabs, yet we hear them speaking in our own tongues of the **mighty acts** of God."

The word of the Lord. **Thanks be to God.**

Responsorial Psalm (Psalm 104:1, 24, 29-30, 31, 34)

℟. **Lord, send out your Spirit, and renew the face of the earth.** *Or* **Alleluia.**

Bless the LORD, O my soul!
O LORD, my God, you are great indeed!
How manifold are your works, O LORD!
The earth is full of your creatures. ℟.

If you take away their breath, they perish
and return to their dust.
When you send forth your spirit, they are created,
and you renew the face of the earth. ℟.

May the glory of the LORD endure forever;
may the LORD be glad in his works!
Pleasing to him be my theme;
I will be glad in the LORD. R.

An alternate reading follows.

Second Reading (1 Corinthians 12:3b-7, 12-13)

Brothers and sisters: No one can say, "Jesus is Lord," except by the Holy Spirit.

There are different kinds of spiritual gifts but the same Spirit; there are different forms of service but the same Lord; there are different workings but the same God who produces all of them in everyone. To each individual the manifestation of the Spirit is given for some benefit.

As a body is one though it has many parts, and all the parts of the body, though many, are one body, so also Christ. For in one Spirit we were all baptized into one body, whether Jews or Greeks, slaves or free persons, and we were all given to drink of one Spirit.

The word of the Lord. **Thanks be to God.**

Or

Second Reading (Galatians 5:16-25)

Brothers and sisters, live by the Spirit and you will certainly not gratify the desire of the flesh. For the flesh has desires against the Spirit, and the Spirit against the flesh; these are opposed to each other, so that you may not do what you want. But if you are guided by the Spirit, you are not under the law. Now the works of the flesh are obvious: immorality, impurity, lust, idolatry, sorcery, hatreds, rivalry, jealousy, outbursts of fury, acts of selfishness, dissensions, factions, occasions of envy, drinking bouts, orgies, and the like. I warn you, as I warned you before, that those who do such things will not inherit the kingdom of God. In contrast, the fruit of the Spirit is love, joy, peace, patience, kindness, generosity, faithfulness, gentleness, self-control. Against such there is no law. Now those who belong to Christ Jesus have crucified their flesh with its passions and desires. If we live in the Spirit, let us also follow the Spirit.

The word of the Lord. **Thanks be to God.**

Sequence (Veni, Sancte Spiritus)

Come, Holy Spirit, come!
And from your celestial home
    Shed a ray of light divine!
Come, Father of the poor!
Come, source of all our store!
    Come, within our bosoms shine.
You, of comforters the best;
You, the soul's most welcome guest;
    Sweet refreshment here below.
In our labor, rest most sweet;
Grateful coolness in the heat;
    Solace in the midst of woe.
O most blessed Light divine,
Shine within these hearts of yours,
    And our inmost being fill!
Where you are not, we have naught,
Nothing good in deed or thought,
    Nothing free from taint of ill.
Heal our wounds, our strength renew;
On our dryness pour your dew;
    Wash the stains of guilt away.
Bend the stubborn heart and will;
Melt the frozen, warm the chill;
    Guide the steps that go astray.
On the faithful, who adore
And confess you, evermore
    In your sevenfold gift descend.
Give them virtue's sure reward;
Give them your salvation, Lord;
    Give them joys that never end. Amen.
    Alleluia.

An alternate reading follows.

Gospel (John 20:19-23)

A reading from the holy Gospel according to John.
Glory to you, O Lord.

On the evening of that first day of the week, when the doors were locked, where the disciples were, for fear of the Jews, Jesus came and stood in their midst and said to them, "Peace be with you." When he had said this, he showed them his hands and his side. The disciples rejoiced when they saw the Lord. Jesus said to them again, "Peace be with you. As the Father has sent me, so I send you." And when he had said this, he breathed on them and said to them, "Receive the Holy Spirit. Whose sins you forgive are forgiven them, and whose sins you retain are retained."

The Gospel of the Lord. **Praise to you, Lord Jesus Christ.**

Or

Gospel (John 15:26-27; 16:12-15)

A reading from the holy Gospel according to John.
Glory to you, O Lord.

Jesus said to his disciples: "When the **Advocate** comes whom I will send you from the Father, the Spirit of truth that proceeds from the Father, he will testify to me. And you also testify, because you have been with me from the beginning.

"I have much more to tell you, but you cannot bear it now. But when he comes, the Spirit of truth, he will guide you to all truth. He will not speak on his own, but he will speak what he hears, and will declare to you the things that are coming. He will glorify me, because he will take from what is mine and declare it to you. Everything that the Father has is mine; for this reason I told you that he will take from what is mine and declare it to you."

The Gospel of the Lord. **Praise to you, Lord Jesus Christ.**

Key Words

Pentecost is the Greek word for the Jewish festival that takes place fifty days after Passover. Fifty days after Jesus' resurrection, the Holy Spirit descended upon Mary and the apostles. For Christians, Pentecost is the feast celebrating the coming of the Holy Spirit.

Saint Luke describes the coming of the Holy Spirit like **fire**—full of energy and power, dazzling everyone.

People from all over the world are amazed at the apostles' message. Saint Luke reminds us that Jesus came for all humankind—for Jews, **converts** (Jews who were not born Jewish), and people from every country on earth.

God's **mighty acts** are so great that they cannot be counted, but the greatest of these is that God sent Jesus to save us. The disciples proclaimed God's marvelous deed—the death and resurrection of Jesus.

The **Advocate** is another name for the Holy Spirit, sent by Jesus to be our helper and guide until the end of time. An advocate is someone who speaks on another's behalf, often to make their case for them. Jesus promises that the Holy Spirit will be our advocate.

May 23

The Most Holy Trinity

First Reading (Deuteronomy 4:32-34, 39-40)

Moses said to the people: "Ask now of the days of old, before your time, ever since God created man upon the earth; ask from one end of the sky to the other: Did anything so great ever happen before? Was it ever heard of? Did a people ever hear the voice of God speaking from the midst of fire, as you did, and live? Or did any god venture to go and take a nation for himself from the midst of another nation, by testings, by signs and wonders, by war, with strong hand and outstretched arm, and by great terrors, all of which the LORD, your God, did for you in **Egypt** before your very eyes? This is why you must now know, and fix in your heart, that the LORD is God in the heavens above and on earth below, and that there is no other. You must keep his statutes and commandments that I enjoin on you today, that you and your children after you may prosper, and that you may have long life on the land which the LORD, your God, is giving you forever."

The word of the Lord. **Thanks be to God.**

Responsorial Psalm (Psalm 33:4-5, 6, 9, 18-19, 20, 22)

℟. **Blessed the people the Lord has chosen to be his own.**

Upright is the word of the LORD,
  and all his works are trustworthy.
He loves justice and right;
  of the kindness of the LORD the earth is full. ℟.

By the word of the LORD the heavens were made;
  by the breath of his mouth all their host.
For he spoke, and it was made;
  he commanded, and it stood forth. ℟.

See, the eyes of the LORD are upon those who fear him,
  upon those who hope for his kindness,
to deliver them from death
  and preserve them in spite of famine. ℟.

Our soul waits for the LORD,
  who is our help and our shield.
May your kindness, O LORD, be upon us
  who have put our hope in you. ℟.

Second Reading (Romans 8:14-17)

Brothers and sisters: Those who are led by the Spirit of God are sons of God. For you did not receive a spirit of slavery to fall back into fear, but you received a Spirit of adoption, through whom we cry, "Abba, Father!" The Spirit himself bears witness with our spirit that we are **children of God**, and if children, then heirs, **heirs of God** and joint heirs with Christ, if only we suffer with him so that we may also be glorified with him.

The word of the Lord. **Thanks be to God.**

Gospel (Matthew 28:16-20)

A reading from the holy Gospel according to Matthew.
Glory to you, O Lord.

The eleven disciples went to **Galilee**, to the mountain to which Jesus had ordered them. When they all saw him, they worshiped, but they doubted. Then Jesus approached and said to them, "All power in heaven and on earth has been given to me. Go, therefore, and make disciples of all nations, baptizing them in the name of the Father, and of the Son, and of the Holy Spirit, teaching them to observe all that I have commanded you. And behold, **I am with you always**, until the end of the age."

The Gospel of the Lord. **Praise to you, Lord Jesus Christ.**

Key Words

The **Trinity** is three persons in one God: the Father, the Son, and the Holy Spirit. Today, on Trinity Sunday, we celebrate this mystery.

Deuteronomy is the fifth book in the Old Testament. It is a Greek word meaning "the second law," or the second time God gave Moses his law. It tells us that God is one and so the people of God must be united.

God freed the people of Israel, who were slaves in **Egypt**. This important event shows how God fulfills the promises made to us, God's people.

Children of God describes all of us: God our Father loves us and takes care of us.

We are **heirs of God** because we are God's children and children inherit from their parents. All God's riches are ours—not only the things God has created, but also God's promise of eternal life.

Galilee is a province in the north of Palestine. Nazareth, the town where Jesus lived with his parents, is in Galilee. So is the Sea of Galilee, where some of Jesus' disciples worked as fishermen. Jesus spent a lot of time preaching in this area. In Jerusalem, to the south, Jesus was known as a Galilean, because of his northern accent.

"I am with you always" is the promise Jesus made to us when he appeared after his resurrection. Jesus is with us when we gather in his name as a community, when we listen to God's word, when we celebrate the Eucharist, and when we share his love with others.

May 30

The Most Holy Body and Blood of Christ

First Reading (Exodus 24:3-8)

When Moses came to the people and related all the words and ordinances of the LORD, they all answered with one voice, "We will do everything that the LORD has told us." Moses then wrote down all the words of the LORD and, rising early the next day, he erected at the foot of the mountain an altar and twelve pillars for the **twelve tribes of Israel**. Then, having sent certain young men of the Israelites to offer holocausts and sacrifice **young bulls** as peace offerings to the LORD, Moses took half of the blood and put it in large bowls; the other half he splashed on the altar. Taking the book of the covenant, he read it aloud to the people, who answered, "All that the LORD has said, we will **heed and do**." Then he took the blood and sprinkled it on the people, saying, "This is the blood of the covenant that the LORD has made with you in accordance with all these words of his."

The word of the Lord. **Thanks be to God.**

Responsorial Psalm (Psalm 116:12-13, 15-16, 17-18)

℟. **I will take the cup of salvation, and call on the name of the Lord.** *Or* **Alleluia.**

How shall I make a return to the LORD
for all the good he has done for me?
The cup of salvation I will take up,
and I will call upon the name of the LORD. ℟.

Precious in the eyes of the LORD
is the death of his faithful ones.
I am your servant, the son of your handmaid;
you have loosed my bonds. ℟.

To you will I offer sacrifice of thanksgiving,
and I will call upon the name of the LORD.
My **vows** to the LORD I will pay
in the presence of all his people. ℟.

Second Reading (Hebrews 9:11-15)

Brothers and sisters: When Christ came as high priest of the good things that have come to be, passing through the greater and more perfect tabernacle not made by hands, that is, not belonging to this creation, he entered once for all into the sanctuary, not with the blood of goats and calves but with his own blood, thus obtaining eternal redemption. For if the blood of goats and bulls and the sprinkling of a heifer's ashes can sanctify those who are defiled so that their flesh is cleansed, how much more will the blood of Christ, who through the eternal Spirit offered himself unblemished to God, cleanse our consciences from dead works to worship the living God.

For this reason he is **mediator** of a new covenant: since a death has taken place for deliverance from transgressions under the first covenant, those who are called may receive the promised eternal inheritance.

The word of the Lord. **Thanks be to God.**

Sequence (Optional)

The shorter version begins at the asterisks.

Laud, O Zion, your salvation,
Laud with hymns of exultation,
    Christ, your king and shepherd true:

Bring him all the praise you know,
He is more than you bestow.
    Never can you reach his due.

Special theme for glad thanksgiving
Is the quick'ning and the living
    Bread today before you set:

From his hands of old partaken,
As we know, by faith unshaken,
    Where the Twelve at supper met.

Full and clear ring out your chanting,
Joy nor sweetest grace be wanting,
    From your heart let praises burst:

For today the feast is holden,
When the institution olden
    Of that supper was rehearsed.

Here the new law's new oblation,
By the new king's revelation,
    Ends the form of ancient rite:

Now the new the old effaces,
Truth away the shadow chases,
    Light dispels the gloom of night.

What he did at supper seated,
Christ ordained to be repeated,
    His memorial ne'er to cease:

And his rule for guidance taking,
Bread and wine we hallow, making
    Thus our sacrifice of peace.

This the truth each Christian learns,
Bread into his flesh he turns,
    To his precious blood the wine:

Sight has fail'd, nor thought conceives,
But a dauntless faith believes,
    Resting on a pow'r divine.

Here beneath these signs are hidden
Priceless things to sense forbidden;
    Sign, not things are all we see:

Blood is poured and flesh is broken,
Yet in either wondrous token
    Christ entire we know to be.

Whoso of this food partakes,
Does not rend the Lord nor breaks;
    Christ is whole to all that taste:

Thousands are, as one, receivers,
One, as thousands of believers,
    Eats of him who cannot waste.

Bad and good the feast are sharing,
Of what divers dooms preparing,
    Endless death, or endless life.

Life to these, to those damnation,
See how like participation
    Is with unlike issues rife.

When the sacrament is broken,
Doubt not, but believe 'tis spoken
    That each sever'd outward token
        doth the very whole contain.

Nought the precious gift divides,
Breaking but the sign betides
    Jesus still the same abides,
        still unbroken does remain.

* * *

Lo! the angel's food is given
To the pilgrim who has striven;
    See the children's bread from heaven,
        which on dogs may not be spent.

Truth the ancient types fulfilling,
Isaac bound, a victim willing,
    Paschal lamb, its lifeblood spilling,
    manna to the fathers sent.

Very bread, good shepherd, tend us,
Jesu, of your love befriend us,
    You refresh us, you defend us,
    Your eternal goodness send us
In the land of life to see.

You who all things can and know,
Who on earth such food bestow,
    Grant us with your saints, though lowest,
    Where the heav'nly feast you show,
Fellow heirs and guests to be. Amen. Alleluia.

Gospel (Mark 14:12-16, 22-26)

A reading from the holy Gospel according to Mark.
Glory to you, O Lord.

On the first day of the Feast of Unleavened Bread, when they sacrificed the **Passover lamb**, Jesus' disciples said to him, "Where do you want us to go and prepare for you to eat the Passover?" He sent two of his disciples and said to them, "Go into the city and a man will meet you, carrying a jar of water. Follow him. Wherever he enters, say to the master of the house, 'The Teacher says, "Where is my guest room where I may eat the Passover with my disciples?" ' Then he will show you a large upper room furnished and ready. Make the preparations for us there." The disciples then went off, entered the city, and found it just as he had told them; and they prepared the Passover.

While they were eating, he took bread, said the blessing, broke it, gave it to them, and said, "Take it; this is my body." Then he took a cup, gave thanks, and gave it to them, and they all drank from it. He said to them, "This is my blood of the covenant, which will be shed for many. Amen, I say to you, I shall not drink again the fruit of the vine until the day when I drink it new in the kingdom of God." Then, after singing a hymn, they went out to the **Mount of Olives**.

The Gospel of the Lord. **Praise to you, Lord Jesus Christ.**

Key Words

The **twelve tribes of Israel** were the descendants of the twelve sons of Jacob, who was also called Israel. The Bible often uses this term to refer to the whole Jewish people.

Young bulls were strong, valuable animals: they pulled the plough to prepare the land for seeding and then pulled the wagons to bring in the crops at harvest time. Sacrificing (killing) a bull meant giving up something important.

When the people of Israel say, "We will **heed and do**," they are promising to do God's will for the rest of their lives.

A **vow** is a solemn promise to be faithful. When a man and a woman marry, they vow to love God and each other. Priests and religious brothers and sisters vow to be faithful to God. Vows are "paid" when people keep their promises.

A **mediator** brings together two people who don't know each other or who cannot agree. Christ is our mediator; he acts as a link between human beings and God.

For Passover, or the Feast of Unleavened Bread, each Jewish family prepares a **Passover lamb**. At the festival dinner, they gather to recall how God freed their ancestors from slavery in Egypt. This follows the instructions that the angel of God gave to the Israelites to sacrifice a spring lamb as they prepared to flee Egypt.

The **Mount of Olives** is a hillside near Jerusalem on which olive trees grow. Jesus often went there to pray and rest after he had been teaching. The Garden of Gethsemane is at the base of the Mount of Olives, and Jesus was praying there when the soldiers came to arrest him.

June 6

10th Sunday in Ordinary Time

First Reading (Genesis 3:9-15)

After **the man**, Adam, had eaten of the tree, the LORD God called to the man and asked him, "Where are you?" He answered, "I heard you in the garden; but I was afraid, because I was naked, so I hid myself." Then he asked, "Who told you that you were naked? You have you eaten, then, from the tree of which I had forbidden you to eat!" The man replied, "The woman whom you put here with me—she gave me fruit from the tree, and so I ate it." The LORD God then asked to **the woman**, "Why did you do such a thing?" The woman answered, "The serpent tricked me into it, so I ate it."

Then the LORD God said to the serpent:
"Because you have done this, you shall be banned
from all the animals
and from all the wild creatures;
on your belly shall you crawl,
and dirt you shall eat
all the days of your life.
I will put enmity between you and the woman,
and between your offspring and hers;
he will strike your head,
while you strike at his heel."

The word of the Lord. **Thanks be to God.**

Responsorial Psalm (Psalm 130:1-2, 3-4, 4-6, 7-8)

℟. **With the Lord there is mercy, and fullness of redemption.**

Out of the depths I cry to you, O LORD;
LORD, hear my voice!
Let your ears be attentive
to my voice in supplication. ℟.

If you, O LORD, mark **iniquities,**
LORD, who could stand?
But with you is forgiveness,
that you may be revered. ℟.

I trust in the LORD;
    my soul trusts in his word.
More than **sentinels** wait for the dawn,
    let Israel wait for the LORD. ℟.

For with the LORD is kindness
    and with him is plenteous redemption;
an he will redeem Israel
    from all their iniquities. ℟.

Second Reading (2 Corinthians 4:13-5:1)

Brothers and sisters: Since we have the same spirit of faith, according to what is written, *I believed, therefore I spoke,* we too believe and therefore we speak, knowing that the one who raised the Lord Jesus will raise us also with Jesus and place us with you in his presence. Everything indeed is for you, so that the grace bestowed in abundance on more and more people may cause the thanksgiving to overflow for the glory of God. Therefore, we are not discouraged; rather, although our outer self is wasting away, our inner self is being renewed day by day. For this momentary light affliction is producing us for an eternal weight of glory beyond all comparison, as we look not to what is seen but to what is unseen; for what can is seen is transitory, but what is unseen is eternal. For we know that if our earthly dwelling, a tent, should be destroyed, we have a building from God, a dwelling not made with hands, eternal in heaven.

The word of the Lord. **Thanks be to God.**

Gospel (Mark 3:20-25)

A reading from the holy Gospel according to Mark.
Glory to you, O Lord.

Jesus came with his disciples into the house. Again the crowd gathered, making it impossible for them even to eat. When his relatives heard of this they set out to seize him, for they said, "He is out of his mind." The scribes who had come from Jerusalem said, "He is possessed by **Beelzebul**," and "By the prince of **demons** he drives out demons."

Summoning them, he began to speak to them in parables, "How can Satan drive out Satan? If a kingdom is divided against itself, that kingdom cannot stand. And if a house is divided against itself, that house will not be able to stand. And if Satan has risen up against himself and is divided, he cannot stand; that is the end of him. But no one can enter a strong man's house and plunder his property unless he first ties up the strong man. Then he can plunder the house. Amen, I say to you, all sins and all **blasphemies** that people utter will be forgiven them. But whoever blasphemes against the Holy Spirit will never have forgiveness, but is guilty of an everlasting sin." For they had said, "He has an unclean spirit."

His mother and his brothers arrived. Standing outside they sent word to him and called him. A crowd seated around him told him, "Your mother and your brothers and your sisters are outside asking for you." But he said to them in reply, "Who are my mother and my brothers?" And looking at those seated in the circle he said, "Here are my mother and my brothers. For whoever does the will of God is my brother and sister and mother."

The Gospel of the Lord. **Praise to you, Lord Jesus Christ.**

Key Words

In the first reading, taken from Genesis (the first book of the Bible), we hear of **the man** and **the woman**—these are Adam and Eve, and they are in the Garden of Eden. They have just disobeyed God and eaten the forbidden fruit. Already sin has taken root: notice how the man blames the woman, and the woman blames the serpent. Neither of them takes responsibility for their actions.

Iniquities are our sins, our wrongdoings—when we act unfairly, or when we try to hurt someone. The psalmist knows that all people make bad choices from time to time, and if God kept track of all of these sins, we all would be lost. Fortunately, God is full of mercy and forgiveness.

When **sentinels** are given the job of standing guard overnight, in order to keep a community safe from its enemies, the night can seem very long. No doubt they are eager for morning light, which will signal the end of their duty. The psalmist says that his soul is more eager to see God than the sentinel is to see the dawn.

In the gospel, the scribes accuse Jesus of being in league with the devil or **Beelzebul**. They say only someone ruled by Satan can cast out evil spirits or **demons**. But Jesus shows how illogical this is—why would Satan want to destroy himself? In fact, God is more powerful than Satan, and it is through God's power that Jesus is able to cast out evil spirits.

Blasphemies are evil acts and words against God. Jesus says that God will forgive all sins and even blasphemies—except the greatest sin, which is saying the Holy Spirit comes from Satan and not from God. This one sin, against the Holy Spirit, cannot be forgiven.

June 13

11th Sunday in Ordinary Time

First Reading (Ezekiel 17:22-24)

Thus says the Lord God:
I, too, will take from the crest of the cedar,
from its topmost branches tear off a tender shoot,
and plant it on a high and lofty mountain;
on the mountain heights of Israel I will plant it.
It shall put forth branches and bear fruit,
and become a majestic cedar.
Birds of every kind shall dwell beneath it,
every winged thing in the shade of its boughs.
And all the trees of the field shall know
that I, the Lord,
bring low the high tree,
lift high the lowly tree,
wither up the green tree,
and make the withered tree bloom.
As I, the Lord, have **spoken**, so will I do.

The word of the Lord. **Thanks be to God.**

Responsorial Psalm (Psalm 92:2-3, 13-14, 15-16)

℟. **Lord, it is good to give thanks to you.**

It is good to give thanks to the Lord,
to sing praise to your name, Most High,
to proclaim your kindness at dawn
and your faithfulness throughout the night. ℟.

The just one shall flourish like the palm tree,
like a **cedar of Lebanon** shall he grow.
They that are planted in the house of the Lord
shall flourish in the courts of our God. ℟.

They shall bear fruit even in old age;
vigorous and sturdy shall they be,
declaring how just is the Lord,
my rock, in whom there is no wrong. ℟.

Second Reading (2 Corinthians 5:6-10)

Brothers and sisters: We are always courageous, although we know that while we are **at home in the body** we are away from the Lord, for we walk by faith, not by sight. Yet we are courageous, and we would rather leave the body and go home to the Lord. Therefore, we aspire to please him, whether we are at home or away. For we must all appear before the judgment seat of Christ, so that each may receive recompense, according to what he did in the body, whether good or evil.

The word of the Lord. **Thanks be to God.**

Gospel (Mark 4:26-34)

A reading from the holy Gospel according to Mark.
Glory to you, O Lord.

Jesus said to the **crowds**: "This is how it is with the kingdom of God; it is as if a man were to scatter seed on the land and would sleep and rise night and day and through it all the seed would sprout and grow, he knows not how. Of its own accord the land yields fruit, first the blade, then the ear, then the full grain in the ear. And when the grain is ripe, he wields the **sickle** at once, for the harvest has come."

He said, "To what shall we compare the kingdom of God, or what parable can we use for it? It is like a mustard seed that, when it is sown in the ground, is the smallest of all the seeds on the earth. But once it is sown, it springs up and becomes the largest of plants and puts forth large branches, so that the birds of the sky can dwell in its shade." With many such parables he spoke the word to them as they were able to understand it. Without parables he did not speak to them, but to his own disciples he explained everything in private.

The Gospel of the Lord. **Praise to you, Lord Jesus Christ.**

Key Words

When the Bible wants to show God's power, it often says that God has **spoken**. In the Creation story, for example, God says "Let there be light," and there is light. God speaks the word, and it is so. Ezekiel likens the people of God to a forest that is growing and spreading; God says the word, and the trees either flourish or die.

A **cedar of Lebanon** is an ancient tree that can be seen on the flag of Lebanon today. It is famous for its size and hardiness. There are some trees today that stand 130 feet tall and whose trunks are over 8 feet wide. At the time today's psalm was written, it was a great compliment to be compared to a cedar of Lebanon.

Saint Paul reminds us that while we are **at home in the body**—while we enjoy the gift of life that God gives us— our true home is with God. We must never forget to avoid sin and follow God's laws while we live in the body.

When Jesus was teaching the **crowds**, sometimes there were so many people that he couldn't be seen or heard. In today's gospel, Jesus gets into a boat instead. This way, everyone could stand on the shore in order to see and hear Jesus as he spoke to them from the boat.

A **sickle** is a crescent-shaped hand tool that is used to cut the stalks of grains and grasses. It is a good sign in today's parable that the man is using his sickle, because this means his crop is ready to be harvested.

June 20

12th Sunday in Ordinary Time

First Reading (Job 38:1, 8-11)

The Lord addressed Job out of the storm and said:
Who shut within doors the sea,
when it burst forth **from the womb**;
when I made the clouds its garment
and thick darkness its swaddling bands?
When I set limits for it
and fastened the bar of its door,
and said: Thus far shall you come but no farther,
and here shall your proud waves be stilled!

The word of the Lord. **Thanks be to God.**

Responsorial Psalm (Psalm 107:23-24, 25-26, 28-29, 30-31)

℟. **Give thanks to the Lord, his love is everlasting.**
Or **Alleluia.**

They who sailed the sea in ships,
trading on the deep waters,
these saw the works of the LORD
and his wonders in the abyss. ℟.

His command raised up a storm wind
which tossed its waves on high.
They mounted up to heaven; they sank to the depths;
their hearts melted away in their plight. ℟.

They cried to the LORD in their distress;
from their straits he rescued them,
he hushed the storm to a gentle breeze,
and the billows of the sea were stilled. ℟.

They rejoiced that they were calmed,
and he brought them to their desired **haven**.
Let them give thanks to the LORD for his kindness
and his wondrous deeds to the children of men. ℟.

Second Reading (2 Corinthians 5:14-17)

Brothers and sisters: The love of Christ impels us, once we have come to the conviction that one died for all; therefore, all have died. He indeed died for all, so that those who live might no longer live for themselves but for him who for their sake died and was raised.

Consequently, from now on we regard no one **according to the flesh**; even if we once knew Christ according to the flesh, yet now we know him so no longer. So whoever is in Christ is a new creation: the old things have passed away; behold, new things have come.

The word of the Lord. **Thanks be to God.**

Gospel (Mark 4:35-41)

A reading from the holy Gospel according to Mark.
Glory to you, O Lord.

On that day, as evening drew on, Jesus said to his disciples: "Let us cross to the other side." Leaving the crowd, they took Jesus with them in the boat just as he was. And other boats were with him. A violent **squall** came up and waves were breaking over the boat, so that it was already filling up. Jesus was in the stern, asleep on a cushion. They woke him and said to him, "Teacher, do you not care that we are perishing?" He woke up, rebuked the wind, and said to the sea, "Quiet! Be still!" The wind ceased and there was great calm. Then he asked them, "Why are you terrified? Do you not yet have faith?" They were filled with great awe and said to one another, "Who then is this whom even wind and sea obey?"

The Gospel of the Lord. **Praise to you, Lord Jesus Christ.**

Key Words

The **Book of Job** is well known because it talks about why people suffer and where God is when people suffer. In today's reading, we hear God question Job about whether he, a mortal, can fully understand God's power and wisdom. Job has been questioning God about the apparent unfairness of life. God replies that Job does not have sufficient knowledge to understand God's ways.

God compares the creation of the sea to a birth, with the sea bursting out **from the womb** and then clothed in clouds as a baby is wrapped. God also keeps the sea safe by setting boundaries for it, just as parents look to keep their children safe. God cares deeply for all of creation.

A **haven** is a safe harbor, where boats and fishermen are protected from storms and destructive waves. The psalmist knows that God can command the seas either to rise up or be still; in the end, God will bring us through the seas to safety.

Saint Paul tells the people of Corinth not to live **according to the flesh**. Before his conversion, when Paul first looked at Jesus' teaching in this way, he felt threatened and tried to stamp out the early Church. But once he understood the meaning of Jesus' resurrection, he saw everyone and everything in a new way—as a new creation.

A **squall** is a violent windy storm that moves in suddenly without warning. Caught off-guard, sailors must act quickly to keep the boat and passengers safe.

June 27

13th Sunday in Ordinary Time

First Reading (Wisdom 1:13-15; 2:23-24)

God did not make death,
nor does he rejoice in the destruction of the living.
For he fashioned all things that they might have being;
and the creatures of the world are wholesome,
and there is not a destructive drug among them
nor any domain of the **netherworld** on earth,
for justice is undying.
For God formed man to be imperishable;
the image of his own nature he made him.
But by the envy of the devil, death entered the world,
and they who belong to his company experience it.

The word of the Lord. **Thanks be to God.**

Responsorial Psalm (Psalm 30:2, 4, 5-6, 11, 12, 13)

℟. **I will praise you, Lord, for you have rescued me.**

I will extol you, O LORD, for you drew me clear
and did not let my enemies rejoice over me.
O LORD, you brought me up from the **netherworld**;
you preserved me from among those going down
into the **pit**. ℟.

Sing praise to the LORD, you his faithful ones,
and give thanks to his holy name.
For his anger lasts but a moment;
a lifetime, his good will.
At nightfall, weeping enters in,
but with the dawn, rejoicing. ℟.

Hear, O LORD, and have pity on me;
O LORD, be my helper.
You changed my mourning into dancing;
O LORD, my God, forever will I give you thanks. ℟.

Second Reading (2 Corinthians 8:7, 9, 13-15)

Brothers and sisters: As you excel in every respect, in faith, discourse, knowledge, all earnestness, and in the love we have for you, may you excel in this gracious act also.

For you know the gracious act of our Lord Jesus Christ, that though he was rich, for your sake he became poor, so that by his poverty you might become rich. Not that others should have relief while you are burdened, but that as a matter of equality your **abundance** at the present time should supply their needs, so that their abundance may also supply your needs, that there may be equality. As it is written:

Whoever had much did not have more,
and whoever had little did not have less.

The word of the Lord. **Thanks be to God.**

Gospel (Mark 5:21-43 or 5:21-24, 35b-43)

For the shorter version, omit the indented part in brackets.

A reading from the holy Gospel according to Mark.
Glory to you, O Lord.

When Jesus had crossed again in the boat to the other side, a large crowd gathered around him, and he stayed close to the sea. One of the synagogue officials, named Jairus, came forward. Seeing him he fell at his feet and pleaded earnestly with him, saying, "My daughter is at the point of death. Please, come lay your hands on her that she may get well and live." He went off with him, and a large crowd followed him and pressed upon him.

> [There was a woman afflicted with hemorrhages for twelve years. She had suffered greatly at the hands of many doctors and had spent all that she had. Yet she was not helped but only grew worse. She had heard about Jesus and came up behind him in the crowd and touched his cloak. She said, "If I but touch his clothes, I shall be cured." Immediately her flow of blood dried up. She felt in her body that she was healed of her affliction. Jesus, aware at once that power had gone out from him, turned around in the crowd and asked, "Who has touched my clothes?" But his disciples said to Jesus, "You see how the crowd is

pressing upon you, and yet you ask, 'Who touched me?' " And he looked around to see who had done it. The woman, realizing what had happened to her, approached in fear and trembling. She fell down before Jesus and told him the whole truth. He said to her, "Daughter, your faith has saved you. Go in peace and be cured of your affliction."]

While he was still speaking, people from the synagogue official's house arrived and said, "Your daughter has died; why trouble the teacher any longer?" Disregarding the message that was reported, Jesus said to the synagogue official, "Do not be afraid; just have faith." He did not allow anyone to accompany him inside except Peter, James, and John, the brother of James. When they arrived at the house of the synagogue official, he caught sight of a commotion, people weeping and wailing loudly. So he went in and said to them, "Why this commotion and weeping? The child is not dead but asleep." And they ridiculed him. Then he put them all out. He took along the child's father and mother and those who were with him and entered the room where the child was. He took the child by the hand and said to her, "***Talitha koum***," which means, "Little girl, I say to you, arise!" The girl, a child of twelve, arose immediately and walked around. At that they were utterly astounded. He gave strict orders that no one should know this and said that she should be given something to eat.

The Gospel of the Lord. **Praise to you, Lord Jesus Christ.**

Key Words

The **netherworld**, which we sometimes call Hell, is a place of death. The book of Wisdom tells us that death and destruction do not control our world. God created the world and knows that it is good.

The phrase **the image of his own nature** here refers to the eternal nature of God. Eternity means time without beginning or end: a past, present, and future that always exist. God is eternal because there is no limit to God's existence. God created us to share this infinite time, rejoicing in eternity.

The Israelites believed that when people died, their soul went down into the **netherworld**, which was described as a **pit**. It was a silent place, where people could no longer worship God. The psalmist is happy because God's saving power has drawn him up out of this pit.

Many people are fortunate to live with **abundance** or more than they need; others are not so lucky and have very little upon which to live. Saint Paul teaches us to share with others from our abundance, so that everyone can have enough to live on.

Talitha koum is Aramaic for "Little girl, get up!" While the gospels of Matthew and Luke also include this miracle, only Mark gives us the Aramaic words that Jesus spoke. This can help us feel closer in time to Jesus.

July 4

14th Sunday in Ordinary Time

First Reading (Ezekiel 2:2-5)

As the LORD spoke to me, the spirit entered into me and set me on my feet, and I heard the one who was speaking say to me: Son of man, I am sending you to the Israelites, rebels who have rebelled against me; they and their ancestors have revolted against me to this very day. **Hard of face and obstinate of heart** are they to whom I am sending you. But you shall say to them: Thus says the Lord GOD! And whether they heed or resist—for they are a rebellious house—they shall know that a prophet has been among them.

The word of the Lord. **Thanks be to God.**

Responsorial Psalm (Psalm 123:1-2, 2, 3-4)

℟. **Our eyes are fixed on the Lord, pleading for his mercy.**

To you I lift up my eyes
who are enthroned in heaven—
as the eyes of servants
are on the hands of their masters. ℟.

As the eyes of a maid
are on the hands of her mistress,
so are our eyes on the LORD, our God,
till he have pity on us. ℟.

Have pity on us, O LORD, have pity on us,
for we are more than sated with contempt;
our souls are more than sated
with the mockery of the arrogant,
with the contempt of the proud. ℟.

Second Reading (2 Corinthians 12:7-10)

Brothers and sisters: That I, Paul, might not become too elated, because of the abundance of the revelations, a thorn in the flesh was given to me, an angel of Satan, to beat me, to keep me from being too elated. Three times I begged the Lord about this, that it might leave me, but he said to me, "My grace is sufficient for you, for power is made perfect in weakness." I will rather boast most gladly of my weaknesses, in order that the power of Christ may dwell with me. Therefore, I am content with **weaknesses**, insults, hardships, persecutions, and constraints, for the sake of Christ; for when I am weak, then I am strong.

The word of the Lord. **Thanks be to God.**

Gospel (Mark 6:1-6)

A reading from the holy Gospel according to Mark.
Glory to you, O Lord.

Jesus departed from there and came to his native place, accompanied by his disciples. When the sabbath came he began to teach in the **synagogue**, and many who heard him were astonished. They said, "Where did this man get all this? What kind of wisdom has been given him? What **mighty deeds** are wrought by his hands! Is he not the carpenter, the son of Mary, and the brother of James and Joses and Judas and Simon? And are not his sisters here with us?" And they took offense at him. Jesus said to them, "A prophet is not without honor except in his native place and among his own kin and in his own house." So he was not able to perform any mighty deed there, apart from curing a few sick people by laying his hands on them. He was amazed at their lack of faith.

The Gospel of the Lord. **Praise to you, Lord Jesus Christ.**

Key Words

Ezekiel was one of the most important prophets in Israel. He lived during a time when many of the people in Jerusalem were taken prisoner and forced to live in another place, Babylon. The king and Ezekiel were taken away, too. Ezekiel helped the people follow God's ways far from home.

The people of Israel had turned away from God and were **hard of face and obstinate of heart** (not showing God proper respect and refusing to change). Ezekiel was sent as a prophet to bring them back to God. We all need to be willing to change our hearts if we love God.

Saint Paul endured hardship and imprisonment for the sake of the gospel, but he didn't complain of his sufferings. Instead, he says he can boast of his **weaknesses** because they make him rely on God who gives him everything. Saint Paul is thankful for all God's gifts and finds strength in the grace of God.

The **synagogue** is a place where Jews gather to read the Scriptures and pray. Sometimes it is called a temple.

Mighty deeds are extraordinary events that cannot be explained except by the grace and power of God. Jesus performed many miracles to show that he was sent by God and to let people know that God cares about those who suffer. When Jesus performed a miracle, it was always so that people could have faith.

July 11

15th Sunday in Ordinary Time

First Reading (Amos 7:12-15)

Amaziah, priest of Bethel, said to **Amos**, "Off with you, visionary, flee to the land of Judah! There earn your bread by prophesying, but never again prophesy in Bethel; for it is the king's sanctuary and a royal temple." Amos answered Amaziah, "I was no **prophet**, nor have I belonged to a company of prophets; I was a shepherd and a dresser of sycamores. The LORD took me from following the flock, and said to me, Go, prophesy to my people Israel."

The word of the Lord. **Thanks be to God.**

Responsorial Psalm (Psalm 85:9-10, 11-12, 13-14)

℟. **Lord, let us see your kindness, and grant us your salvation.**

I will hear what God proclaims;
the LORD—for he proclaims peace.
Near indeed is his salvation to those who fear him,
glory dwelling in our land. ℟.

Kindness and truth shall meet;
justice and peace shall kiss.
Truth shall spring out of the earth,
and justice shall look down from heaven. ℟.

The LORD himself will give his benefits;
our land shall yield its increase.
Justice shall walk before him,
and prepare the way of his steps. ℟.

Second Reading (Ephesians 1:3-14 or 1:3-10)

The shorter version ends at the asterisks.

Blessed be the God and Father of our Lord Jesus Christ, who has blessed us in Christ with every spiritual blessing in the heavens, as he chose us in him, before the foundation of the world, to be holy and without blemish before him. In love he destined us for adoption to himself through Jesus Christ, in accord with the favor of his will, for the praise of the glory of his grace that he granted us in the beloved.

In him we have **redemption** by his blood, the forgiveness of transgressions, in accord with the riches of his grace that he lavished upon us. In all wisdom and insight, he has made known to us the mystery of his will in accord with his favor that he set forth in him as a plan for the fullness of times, to sum up all things in Christ, in heaven and on earth.

* * *

In him we were also chosen, destined in accord with the purpose of the One who accomplishes all things according to the intention of his will, so that we might exist for the praise of his glory, we who first hoped in Christ. In him you also, who have heard the word of truth, the gospel of your salvation, and have believed in him, were sealed with the promised holy Spirit, which is the first installment of our inheritance toward redemption as God's possession, to the praise of his glory.

The word of the Lord. **Thanks be to God.**

Gospel (Mark 6:7-13)

A reading from the holy Gospel according to Mark.
Glory to you, O Lord.

Jesus summoned the Twelve and began to send them out two by two and gave them authority over **unclean spirits**. He instructed them to take nothing for the journey but a walking stick—no food, no sack, no money in their belts. They were, however, to wear sandals but not a second tunic. He said to them, "Wherever you enter a house, stay there until you leave. Whatever place does not welcome you or listen to you, leave there and shake the dust off your feet in testimony against them." So they went off and preached repentance. The Twelve drove out many demons, and they anointed with oil many who were sick and cured them.

The Gospel of the Lord. **Praise to you, Lord Jesus Christ.**

Key Words

Amos was a prophet, a friend of God. He lived about 800 years before Jesus. Some people he met were rich because they made the poor work hard for them and paid them very little. Amos taught these rich people that they must treat others fairly and help the poor.

Amos is a good example of how a **prophet** speaks for God. His message reminds people that they need to focus on God and love everyone they meet. Prophets do not choose to be God's messengers: God chooses them for this important job.

Saying "**Blessed be** God" is a way of praising God. We are saying, "Let the whole world know how great and wonderful God is!"

Redemption is another word for setting someone free. Long ago, slaves could be set free if someone bought, or redeemed, them. God redeems us so that we are no longer slaves to anyone or anything.

Long ago, it was thought that people who acted strangely were evil or had **unclean spirits**. Jesus showed that he had the power to heal both body and spirit, and he shared this power with the apostles.

July 18

16th Sunday in Ordinary Time

First Reading (Jeremiah 23:1-6)

Woe to the **shepherds** who mislead and scatter the flock of my pasture, says the LORD. Therefore, thus says the LORD, the God of Israel, against the shepherds who shepherd my people: You have scattered my sheep and driven them away. You have not cared for them, but I will take care to punish your evil deeds. I myself will gather the remnant of my flock from all the lands to which I have driven them and bring them back to their meadow; there they shall increase and multiply. I will appoint shepherds for them who will shepherd them so that they need no longer fear and tremble; and none shall be missing, says the LORD.

Behold, the days are coming, says the LORD,
when I will raise up a righteous **shoot** to David;
as king he shall reign and govern wisely,
he shall **do what is just** and right in the land.
In his days Judah shall be saved,
Israel shall dwell in security.
This is the name they give him:
"The LORD our justice."

The word of the Lord. **Thanks be to God.**

Responsorial Psalm (Psalm 23:1-3, 3-4, 5, 6)

℟. **The Lord is my shepherd; there is nothing I shall want.**

The LORD is my shepherd; I shall not want.
In verdant pastures he gives me repose;
beside restful waters he leads me;
he refreshes my soul. ℟.

He guides me in right paths
for his name's sake.
Even though I walk in the dark valley
I fear no evil; for you are at my side
with your rod and your staff
that give me courage. ℟.

You spread the table before me
in the sight of my foes;
you anoint my head with oil;
my cup overflows. ℟.

Only goodness and kindness follow me
all the days of my life;
and I shall dwell in the house of the LORD
for years to come. ℟.

Second Reading (Ephesians 2:13-18)

Brothers and sisters: In Christ Jesus you who once were far off have become near by the blood of Christ.

For he is our peace, he who made **both** one and broke down the dividing wall of enmity, through his flesh, abolishing the law with its commandments and legal claims, that he might create in himself one new person in place of the two, thus establishing peace, and might reconcile both with God, in one body, through the cross, putting that enmity to death by it. He came and preached peace to you who were far off and peace to those who were near, for through him we both have access in one Spirit to the Father.

The word of the Lord. **Thanks be to God.**

Gospel (Mark 6:30-34)

A reading from the holy Gospel according to Mark.
Glory to you, O Lord.

The apostles gathered together with Jesus and reported all they had done and taught. He said to them, "Come away by yourselves to a deserted place and rest a while." People were coming and going in great numbers, and they had no opportunity even to eat. So they went off in the boat by themselves to a deserted place. People saw them leaving and many came to know about it. They hastened there on foot from all the towns and arrived at the place before them.

When he disembarked and saw the vast crowd, his heart was moved with pity for them, for they were like sheep without a shepherd; and he began to teach them many things.

The Gospel of the Lord. **Praise to you, Lord Jesus Christ.**

Key Words

Good **shepherds** take care of their sheep and keep them safe day and night. Jeremiah is angry at the bad shepherds (the leaders of Israel who have led the people away from God). Today we call a church leader a pastor, a word that literally means "shepherd."

A **shoot** to David is the family that comes from David: his children and all who are born from them. When Jeremiah announces that God will raise up a new shoot, or branch, he is foretelling the birth of Jesus, who will be born of the House of David.

To **do what is just** is to make sure that God's law of love is observed all the time. This is the only way people can live in peace and joy. By calling us to love one another as God has loved us, Jesus shows us how to do this.

Saint Paul is known as the Apostle to the Gentiles (non-Jewish people). Before the time of Jesus, the Jewish people understood God to be the God of Israel only. But in Saint Paul's letters and in the Acts of the Apostles, we see how the disciples in the early Church came to understand that everyone—**both** Jews and Gentiles alike—are made one in the blood of Christ. This was a difficult and radical new teaching.

July 25

17th Sunday in Ordinary Time

First Reading (2 Kings 4:42-44)

A man came from Baal-shalishah bringing to **Elisha**, the man of God, twenty barley loaves made from the firstfruits, and fresh grain in the ear. Elisha said, "Give it to the people to eat." But his servant objected, "How can I set this before a hundred people?" Elisha insisted, "Give it to the people to eat." "For thus says the LORD, 'They shall eat and there shall be some left over.' " And when they had eaten, there was some left over, as the LORD had said.

The word of the Lord. **Thanks be to God.**

Responsorial Psalm (Psalm 145:10-11, 15-16, 17-18)

℟. **The hand of the Lord feeds us; he answers all our needs.**

Let all your works give you thanks, O LORD,
and let your faithful ones bless you.
Let them discourse of the glory of your kingdom
and speak of your might. ℟.

The eyes of all look hopefully to you,
and you give them their food in due season;
you open your hand
and satisfy the desire of every living thing. ℟.

The LORD is just in all his ways
and holy in all his works.
The LORD is near to all who call upon him,
to all who call upon him in truth. ℟.

Second Reading (Ephesians 4:1-6)

Brothers and sisters: I, a prisoner for the Lord, urge you to live in a manner worthy of the call you have received, with all **humility** and gentleness, with patience, bearing with one another through love, striving to preserve the unity of the spirit through the **bond** of peace: one body and one Spirit, as you were also called to the one hope of your call; **one Lord**, one faith, one baptism; one God and Father of all, who is over all and through all and in all.

The word of the Lord. **Thanks be to God.**

Gospel (John 6:1-15)

A reading from the holy Gospel according to John.
Glory to you, O Lord.

Jesus went across the Sea of Galilee. A large crowd followed him, because they saw the signs he was performing on the sick. Jesus went up on the **mountain**, and there he sat down with his disciples. The Jewish feast of Passover was near. When Jesus raised his eyes and saw that a large crowd was coming to him, he said to Philip, "Where can we buy enough food for them to eat?" He said this to test him, because he himself knew what he was going to do. Philip answered him, "Two hundred days' wages worth of food would not be enough for each of them to have a little." One of his disciples, Andrew, the brother of Simon Peter, said to him, "There is a boy here who has five barley loaves and two fish; but what good are these for so many?" Jesus said, "Have the people recline." Now there was a great deal of grass in that place. So the men reclined, about five thousand in number. Then Jesus took the loaves, gave thanks, and distributed them to those who were reclining, and also as much of the fish as they wanted. When they had had their fill, he said to his disciples, "Gather the fragments left over, so that nothing will be wasted." So they collected them, and filled twelve wicker baskets with fragments from the five barley loaves that had been more than they could eat. When the people saw the sign he had done, they said, "This is truly the Prophet, the one who is to come into the world." Since Jesus knew that they were going to come and carry him off to make him king, he withdrew again to the mountain alone.

The Gospel of the Lord. **Praise to you, Lord Jesus Christ.**

Key Words

In the Bible, the two **Books of Kings** tell the story of a time when Israel was ruled by kings. The books begin with the death of King David, nearly 1,000 years before Jesus was born, and end when the Babylonians capture Jerusalem, nearly 600 years before Jesus. The writer wants us to see how God helps his people throughout history.

Toward the end of Elijah's life, God told Elijah to anoint **Elisha** to be prophet after him, to guide the people so they would not stray from God. Elisha lived about 850 years before Jesus and was a prophet in Israel for 60 years.

Humility means helping or serving others without expecting any reward or recognition. Jesus is our model of humility—helping others, feeding the crowd, and healing the sick.

A **bond** is a link to someone we care about. In his letter to the Ephesians, Saint Paul helps us to see that building a bond of peace between each other is one of the best ways to maintain unity.

There are many different Christian churches today. Because we have **one Lord**, who is Jesus, Christians are always working to become one community of faith. We do this by getting to know each other and praying together, nurturing the faith that Jesus taught us.

Although the word **mountain** is used, in Israel there are no high mountains. Rather, when the gospel speaks of a "mountain," we can imagine a hill. Jesus often went up into the hills to pray and to speak to the people who followed him.

August 1

18th Sunday in Ordinary Time

First Reading (Exodus 16:2-4, 12-15)

The whole **Israelite community** grumbled against Moses and Aaron. The Israelites said to them, "Would that we had died at the LORD's hand in the land of Egypt, as we sat by our **fleshpots** and ate our fill of bread! But you had to lead us into this desert to make the whole community die of famine!"

Then the LORD said to Moses, "I will now rain down bread from heaven for you. Each day the people are to go out and gather their daily portion; thus will I test them, to see whether they follow my instructions or not.

"I have heard the grumbling of the Israelites. Tell them: In the evening twilight you shall eat flesh, and in the morning you shall have your fill of bread, so that you may know that I, the LORD, am your God."

In the evening quail came up and covered the camp. In the morning a dew lay all about the camp, and when the dew evaporated, there on the surface of the desert were fine flakes like hoarfrost on the ground. On seeing it, the Israelites asked one another, "What is this?" for they did not know what it was. But Moses told them, "This is the bread that the LORD has given you to eat."

The word of the Lord. **Thanks be to God.**

Responsorial Psalm (Psalm 78:3-4, 23-24, 25, 54)

℟. **The Lord gave them bread from heaven.**

What we have heard and know,
  and what our fathers have declared to us,
We will declare to the generation to come,
  the glorious deeds of the LORD and his strength
  and the wonders that he wrought. ℟.

He commanded the skies above
  and opened the doors of heaven;
he rained manna upon them for food
  and gave them heavenly bread. ℟.

Man ate the bread of angels,
food he sent them in abundance.
And he brought them to his holy land,
to the mountains his right hand had won. R.

Second Reading (Ephesians 4:17, 20-24)

Brothers and sisters: I declare and testify in the Lord that you must no longer live as the Gentiles do, in the futility of their minds; that is not how you learned Christ, assuming that you have heard of him and were taught in him, as truth is in Jesus, that you should put away the old self of your former way of life, corrupted through deceitful desires, and be renewed in the spirit of your minds, and put on the new self, created in God's way in righteousness and holiness of truth.

The word of the Lord. **Thanks be to God.**

Gospel (John 6:24-35)

A reading from the holy Gospel according to John.
Glory to you, O Lord.

When the crowd saw that neither Jesus nor his disciples were there, they themselves got into boats and came to Capernaum looking for Jesus. And when they found him across the sea they said to him, "Rabbi, when did you get here?" Jesus answered them and said, "Amen, amen, I say to you, you are looking for me not because you saw **signs** but because you ate the loaves and were filled. Do not work for food that perishes but for the food that endures for eternal life, which the Son of Man will give you. For on him the Father, God, has **set his seal**." So they said to him, "What can we do to accomplish the works of God?" Jesus answered and said to them, "This is the work of God, that you believe in the one he sent." So they said to him, "What sign can you do, that we may see and believe in you? What can you do? Our ancestors ate manna in the desert, as it is written:

He gave them bread from heaven to eat."

So Jesus said to them, "Amen, amen, I say to you, it was not Moses who gave the bread from heaven; my Father gives you the **true bread** from heaven. For the bread of God is that which comes down from heaven and gives life to the world."

So they said to him, "Sir, give us this bread always." Jesus said to them, "I am the bread of life; whoever comes to me will never hunger, and whoever believes in me will never thirst."

The Gospel of the Lord. **Praise to you, Lord Jesus Christ.**

Key Words

The **Israelite community** was chosen by God to help everyone in the world know God's love. God made a covenant or promise with the Israelites, and God is always faithful to his promises.

Fleshpots were sinful or evil places. The Israelites are saying that they would rather return to Egypt with its slavery and sin, because in the desert they are starving while in Egypt they had enough to eat. God came to their aid and gave them meat (quail) and bread from heaven (manna). God listens to our prayers!

In the Gospel according to Saint John, the miracles that Jesus performs are called **signs**. When Jesus changes water into wine, or heals someone, or feeds the multitude, this is a sign that he is the Son of God.

To **set your seal** upon someone is to say that this person is authorized to speak and act on your behalf. It is like a seal of approval or a guarantee.

While God gave his people manna in the desert, Jesus gives us his very self—**true bread** from heaven. Jesus is the Bread of Life and he gives us eternal life.

August 8

19th Sunday in Ordinary Time

First Reading (1 Kings 19:4-8)

Elijah went a day's journey into the desert, until he came to a **broom tree** and sat beneath it. He **prayed for death** saying: "This is enough, O LORD! Take my life, for I am no better than my fathers." He lay down and fell asleep under the broom tree, but then an angel touched him and ordered him to get up and eat. Elijah looked and there at his head was a hearth cake and a jug of water. After he ate and drank, he lay down again, but the angel of the LORD came back a second time, touched him, and ordered, "Get up and eat, else the journey will be too long for you!" He got up, ate, and drank; then strengthened by that food, he walked forty days and forty nights to the **mountain** of God, Horeb.

The word of the Lord. **Thanks be to God.**

Responsorial Psalm (Psalm 34:2-3, 4-5, 6-7, 8-9)

℟. **Taste and see the goodness of the Lord.**

I will bless the LORD at all times;
his praise shall be ever in my mouth.
Let my soul glory in the LORD;
the lowly will hear me and be glad. ℟.

Glorify the LORD with me,
let us together extol his name.
I sought the LORD, and he answered me
and delivered me from all my fears. ℟.

Look to him that you may be radiant with joy,
and your faces may not blush with shame.
When the afflicted man called out, the LORD heard,
and from all his distress he saved him. ℟.

The angel of the LORD encamps
around those who fear him and delivers them.
Taste and see how good the LORD is;
blessed the man who takes refuge in him. ℟.

Second Reading (Ephesians 4:30–5:2)

Brothers and sisters: Do not **grieve the Holy Spirit of God**, with which you were sealed for the day of redemption. All bitterness, fury, anger, shouting, and reviling must be removed from you, along with all malice. And be kind to one another, compassionate, forgiving one another as God has forgiven you in Christ.

So be imitators of God, as beloved children, and live in love, as Christ loved us and handed himself over for us as a sacrificial offering to God for a fragrant aroma.

The word of the Lord. **Thanks be to God.**

Gospel (John 6:41-51)

A reading from the holy Gospel according to John.
Glory to you, O Lord.

The Jews murmured about Jesus because he said, "I am the bread that came down from heaven," and they said, "Is this not Jesus, the **son of Joseph?** Do we not know his father and mother? Then how can he say, 'I have come down from heaven'?" Jesus answered and said to them, "Stop murmuring among yourselves. No one can come to me unless the Father who sent me draw him, and I will raise him on the last day. It is written in the prophets:

They shall all be taught by God.

Everyone who listens to my Father and learns from him comes to me. Not that anyone has seen the Father except the one who is from God; he has seen the Father. Amen, amen, I say to you, whoever believes has eternal life. I am the bread of life. Your ancestors ate the manna in the desert, but they died; this is the bread that comes down from heaven so that one may eat it and not die. I am the living bread that came down from heaven; whoever eats this bread will live forever; and the bread that I will give is my flesh for the life of the world."

The Gospel of the Lord. **Praise to you, Lord Jesus Christ.**

Key Words

A **broom tree** is a kind of tree that grows near the River Jordan and on the Sinai Peninsula. It has a few thin branches and very small leaves, and so it doesn't give much shade.

Elijah **prayed for death** because he was weary and discouraged, and he did not want to continue being a prophet. People were not listening to his message and wanted to kill him. God sent his angel to take care of Elijah by giving him food, drink, and, most importantly, hope.

Important events in the history of the people of Israel took place on hilltops or **mountains** such as Mount Horeb. For example, Moses received the revelation of God's name as well as the Ten Commandments on Mount Sinai, and Jesus was transfigured on a high mountain.

We **grieve the Holy Spirit of God**, or make God sad, when we do things that set us apart from God and from other people. Although God is much greater than we can ever imagine, Saint Paul tells us to be imitators of God in our daily lives by loving others and walking in God's ways.

We know that Jesus was the son of the Virgin Mary, who became pregnant by the Holy Spirit. People in Jesus' time thought he was the **son of Joseph**, because Joseph was married to Mary and raised Jesus as his son. Joseph was a descendant of King David, thus fulfilling the prophecy that the Messiah would come from the House of David.

August 15

The Assumption of the Blessed Virgin Mary

For the **Mass During the Day**, turn to page 273

Vigil Mass

First Reading (1 Chronicles 15:3-4, 15-16; 16:1-2)

David assembled all Israel in Jerusalem to bring the ark of the LORD to the place which he had prepared for it. David also called together the sons of Aaron and the Levites.

The Levites bore the ark of God on their shoulders with poles, as Moses had ordained according to the word of the LORD.

David commanded the chiefs of the Levites to appoint their kinsmen as chanters, to play on musical instruments, harps, lyres, and cymbals, to make a loud sound of rejoicing.

They brought in the ark of God and set it within the tent which David had pitched for it. Then they offered up burnt offerings and peace offerings to God. When David had finished offering up the burnt offerings and peace offerings, he blessed the people in the name of the LORD.

The word of the Lord. **Thanks be to God.**

Responsorial Psalm (Psalm 132:6-7, 9-10, 13-14)

℟. **Lord, go up to the place of your rest,**
you and the ark of your holiness.

Behold, we heard of it in Ephrathah;
we found it in the fields of Jaar.
Let us enter his dwelling,
let us worship at his footstool. ℟.

May your priests be clothed with justice;
let your faithful ones shout merrily for joy.
For the sake of David your servant,
reject not the plea of your anointed. ℟.

For the LORD has chosen Zion;
he prefers her for his dwelling.
“Zion is my resting place forever;
in her will I dwell, for I prefer her.” ℟.

Second Reading (1 Corinthians 15:54b-57)

Brothers and sisters: When that which is mortal clothes itself with immortality, then the word that is written shall come about:

Death is swallowed up in victory.
Where, O death, is your victory?
Where, O death, is your sting?

The sting of death is sin, and the power of sin is the law. But thanks be to God who gives us the victory through our Lord Jesus Christ.

The word of the Lord. **Thanks be to God.**

Gospel (Luke 11:27-28)

A reading from the holy Gospel according to Luke.
Glory to you, O Lord.

While Jesus was speaking, a woman from the crowd called out and said to him, "Blessed is the womb that carried you and the breasts at which you nursed." He replied, "Rather, blessed are those who hear the word of God and observe it."

The Gospel of the Lord. **Praise to you, Lord Jesus Christ.**

Mass During the Day

First Reading (Revelation 11:19a; 12:1-6a, 10ab)

God's temple in heaven was opened, and the ark of his covenant could be seen in the temple.

A great sign appeared in the sky, a **woman clothed with the sun**, with the moon under her feet, and on her head a crown of twelve stars. She was with child and wailed aloud in pain as she labored to give birth. Then another sign appeared in the sky; it was a huge red dragon, with seven heads and ten horns, and on its heads were seven diadems. Its tail swept away a third of the stars in the sky and hurled them down to the earth. Then the dragon stood before the woman about to give birth, to devour her child when she gave birth. She gave birth to a son, a male child, destined to rule all the nations with an iron rod. Her child was caught up to God and his throne. The woman herself fled into the desert where she had a place prepared by God.

Then I heard a loud voice in heaven say:
"Now have salvation and power come,
and the Kingdom of our God
and the authority of his Anointed One."

The word of the Lord. **Thanks be to God.**

Responsorial Psalm (Psalm 45:10, 11, 12, 16)

℟. **The queen stands at your right hand, arrayed in gold.**

The queen takes her place at your right hand
in gold of Ophir. ℟.

Hear, O daughter, and see; turn your ear,
forget your people and your father's house. ℟.

So shall the king desire your beauty;
for he is your lord. ℟.

They are borne in with gladness and joy;
they enter the palace of the king. ℟.

Second Reading (1 Corinthians 15:20-27)

Brothers and sisters: Christ has been raised from the dead, the **firstfruits** of those who have fallen asleep. For since death came through man, the resurrection of the dead came also through man. For just as in Adam all die, so too in Christ shall all be brought to life, but each one in proper order: Christ the firstfruits; then, at his coming, those who belong to Christ; then comes the end, when he hands over the Kingdom to his God and Father, when he has destroyed every sovereignty and every authority and power. For he must reign until he has put all his enemies under his feet. The last enemy to be destroyed is death, for "he subjected everything under his feet."

The word of the Lord. **Thanks be to God.**

Gospel (Luke 1:39-56)

A reading from the holy Gospel according to Luke.
Glory to you, O Lord.

Mary set out and traveled to the hill country in haste to a town of Judah, where she entered the house of Zechariah and greeted Elizabeth. When Elizabeth heard Mary's greeting, the infant leaped in her womb, and Elizabeth, filled with the Holy Spirit, cried out in a loud voice and said, "Blessed are you among women, and blessed is the fruit of your womb. And how does this happen to me, that the mother of my Lord should come to me? For at the moment the sound of your greeting reached my ears, the infant in my womb leaped for joy. Blessed are you who believed that what was spoken to you by the Lord would be fulfilled."

And Mary said:

"**My soul proclaims the greatness of the Lord**;
my spirit rejoices in God my Savior
for he has looked with favor on his lowly servant.
From this day all generations will call me blessed:
the Almighty has done great things for me,
and holy is his Name.
He has mercy on those who fear him
in every generation.
He has shown the strength of his arm,
and has scattered the proud in their conceit.
He has cast down the mighty from their thrones,
and has lifted up the lowly.
He has filled the hungry with good things,
and the rich he has sent away empty.
He has come to the help of his servant Israel
for he has remembered his promise of mercy,
the promise he made to our fathers,
to Abraham and his children forever."

Mary remained with her about three months and then returned to her home.

The Gospel of the Lord. **Praise to you, Lord Jesus Christ.**

Key Words

Today's first reading portrays the conflict between Jesus Christ and the power of evil (Satan) through the story of a huge red dragon and a **woman clothed with the sun**. The woman could represent God's people—either as Israel giving birth to the Messiah or as the Church being persecuted by Satan—or Mary, enduring the pain of birth for a son "destined to rule all the nations."

The **firstfruits** were the first crops collected at harvest time. These were offered to God. Saint Paul tells us that Jesus is the firstfruits of salvation, the first to die and rise again. Jesus Christ is our guarantee that death is not the end but rather a transition to new life.

Mary's prayer that begins, "**My soul proclaims the greatness of the Lord...**" is known as the Magnificat (the first word in the Latin version of this prayer). It is an ancient prayer of triumph through humility that leads us to Christ. When we make it our prayer, too, it calls us to recognize God's saving work in our lives. It teaches us the true meaning of humility and invites us to submit our will to God. Mary recognized that God's design for the world will reverse the way humans have set things up.

August 22

21st Sunday in Ordinary Time

First Reading (Joshua 24:1-2a, 15-17, 18b)

Joshua gathered together all the tribes of Israel at Shechem, summoning their elders, their leaders, their judges, and their officers. When they stood in ranks before God, Joshua addressed all the people: "If it does not please you to serve the LORD, decide today whom you will serve, the gods your fathers served beyond the River or the gods of the **Amorites** in whose country you are now dwelling. As for me and my household, we will serve the LORD."

But the people answered, "Far be it from us to forsake the LORD for the service of other gods. For it was the LORD, our God, who brought us and our fathers up out of the land of Egypt, out of a state of slavery. He performed those great miracles before our very eyes and protected us along our entire journey and among the peoples through whom we passed. Therefore we also will serve the LORD, for he is our God."

The word of the Lord. **Thanks be to God.**

Responsorial Psalm (Psalm 34:2-3, 16-17, 18-19, 20-21)

℟. **Taste and see the goodness of the Lord.**

I will bless the LORD at all times;
his praise shall be ever in my mouth.
Let my soul glory in the LORD;
the lowly will hear me and be glad. ℟.

The LORD has eyes for the just,
and ears for their cry.
The LORD confronts the evildoers,
to destroy remembrance of them from the earth. ℟.

When the just cry out, the LORD hears them,
and from all their distress he rescues them.
The LORD is close to the brokenhearted;
and those who are crushed in spirit he saves. ℟.

Many are the troubles of the just one,
but out of them all the LORD delivers him;
he watches over all his bones;
not one of them shall be broken. ℟.

Second Reading (Ephesians 5:21-32 or 5:2a, 25-32)

The shorter version begins at the asterisks.

Brothers and sisters: Be subordinate to one another out of reverence for Christ. Wives should **be subordinate to their husbands** as to the Lord. For the husband is head of his wife just as Christ is head of the church, he himself the savior of the body. As the church is subordinate to Christ, so wives should be subordinate to their husbands in everything.

* * *

[Brothers and sisters: Live in love, as Christ loved us.]

Husbands, **love your wives**, even as Christ loved the church and handed himself over for her to sanctify her, cleansing her by the bath of water with the word, that he might present to himself the church in splendor, without spot or wrinkle or any such thing, that she might be holy and without blemish. So also husbands should love their wives as their own bodies. He who loves his wife loves himself. For no one hates his own flesh but rather nourishes and cherishes it, even as Christ does the church, because we are members of his body.

For this reason a man shall leave his father and his mother
and be joined to his wife,
and the two shall become one flesh.

This is a great **mystery**, but I speak in reference to Christ and the church.

The word of the Lord. **Thanks be to God.**

Gospel (John 6:60-69)

A reading from the holy Gospel according to John.
Glory to you, O Lord.

Many of Jesus' disciples who were listening said, "This saying is hard; who can accept it?" Since Jesus knew that his disciples were murmuring about this, he said to them, "Does this shock you? What if you were to see the Son of Man ascending to where he was before? It is the spirit that gives life, while the flesh is of no avail. The words I have spoken to you are Spirit and life. But there are some of you who do not believe." Jesus knew from the beginning the ones who would not believe and the one who would betray him. And he said, "For this reason I have told you that no one can come to me unless it is granted him by my Father."

As a result of this, many of his disciples returned to their former way of life and no longer accompanied him. Jesus then said to the Twelve, "Do you also want to leave?" Simon Peter answered him, "Master, to whom shall we go? You have the words of eternal life. We have come to believe and are convinced that you are the Holy One of God."

The Gospel of the Lord. **Praise to you, Lord Jesus Christ.**

Key Words

After Moses died, God told Joshua to take the people of Israel and conquer the Promised Land. In the Bible, the **Book of Joshua** tells the story of this battle of conquest and describes how the twelve tribes of Israel divided up the land among them.

The **Amorites** lived in the Promised Land before the Israelites. Many Israelites were attracted by the Amorites' religion and were tempted to leave their own. But Joshua is firm: he and his household will not follow the gods of the Amorites or anyone else but will worship the one God of Israel.

Saint Paul tells the women of his time to **be subordinate to their husbands**. He tells the men: **love your wives**. While we might say it differently, Saint Paul is encouraging husbands and wives to grow in respect and love for each other.

Saint Paul calls marriage a **mystery**—something wonderful that is hard to understand. Marriage is also a sacrament—an outward sign of God's grace and a vocation to holiness—and a symbol of God's relationship to his people.

August 29

22nd Sunday in Ordinary Time

First Reading (Deuteronomy 4:1-2, 6-8)

Moses said to the people: "Now, Israel, hear the statutes and decrees which I am teaching you to observe, that you may live, and may enter in and take possession of the land which the LORD, the God of your fathers, is giving you. In your observance of the commandments of the LORD, your God, which I enjoin upon you, you shall not add to what I command you nor subtract from it. Observe them carefully, for thus will you give evidence of your **wisdom** and intelligence to the nations, who will hear of all these statutes and say, 'This great nation is truly a wise and intelligent people.' For what great nation is there that has gods so close to it as the LORD, our God, is to us whenever we call upon him? Or what great nation has statutes and decrees that are as just as this whole law which I am setting before you today?"

The word of the Lord. **Thanks be to God.**

Responsorial Psalm (Psalm 15:2-3, 3-4, 4-5)

℟. **The one who does justice will live in the presence of the Lord.**

Whoever walks blamelessly and does justice;
who thinks the truth in his heart
and slanders not with his tongue. ℟.

Who harms not his fellow man,
nor takes up a reproach against his neighbor;
by whom the reprobate is despised,
while he honors those who fear the LORD. ℟.

Who lends not his money at usury
and accepts no bribe against the innocent.
Whoever does these things
shall never be disturbed. ℟.

Second Reading (James 1:17-18, 21b-22, 27)

Dearest brothers and sisters: All good giving and every perfect gift is from above, coming down from the Father of lights, with whom there is no alteration or shadow caused by change. He willed to give us birth by the word of truth that we may be a kind of firstfruits of his creatures.

Humbly welcome the word that has been planted in you and is able to save your souls

Be doers of the word and not hearers only, deluding yourselves.

Religion that is pure and undefiled before God and the Father is this: to care for **orphans and widows** in their affliction and to keep oneself unstained by the world.

The word of the Lord. **Thanks be to God.**

Gospel (Mark 7:1-8, 14-15, 21-23)

A reading from the holy Gospel according to Mark.
Glory to you, O Lord.

When the Pharisees with some scribes who had come from Jerusalem gathered around Jesus, they observed that some of his disciples ate their meals with unclean, that is, unwashed, hands.—For the Pharisees and, in fact, all Jews, do not eat without carefully washing their hands, keeping the tradition of the elders. And on coming from the marketplace they do not eat without purifying themselves. And there are many other things that they have traditionally observed, the purification of cups and jugs and kettles and beds.—So the Pharisees and scribes questioned him, "Why do your disciples not follow the tradition of the elders but instead eat a meal with unclean hands?" He responded, "Well did Isaiah prophesy about you **hypocrites**, as it is written:

This people honors me with their lips,
but their hearts are far from me;
in vain do they worship me,
teaching as doctrines human precepts.

You disregard God's commandment but cling to human tradition." He summoned the crowd again and said to them, "Hear me, all of you, and understand. Nothing that enters one from outside can defile that person; but the things that come out from within are what defile.

"From within people, from their hearts, come evil thoughts, unchastity, theft, murder, adultery, greed, malice, deceit, licentiousness, envy, blasphemy, arrogance, folly. All these evils come from within and they defile."

The Gospel of the Lord. **Praise to you, Lord Jesus Christ.**

Key Words

Deuteronomy is the fifth book in the Old Testament. The word means "the second law," or the second time God gave Moses his law. It tells us that God is one and that the people of God must be united.

Wisdom is a deep understanding of things. It does not come from studying many books: it comes from experience and understanding life as God understands it.

The **Letter of Saint James** teaches us that we show our faith both by our words and in the things we do, particularly in the way we treat others. We are called as people of faith especially to care for the poor and oppressed.

When Saint James reminds us to care for **orphans and widows**, he is speaking about people whom society leaves behind. In the time of Jesus, it was the male head of the household who provided food, security, and social standing for the whole family. A widow had no husband, and an orphan no father; neither of them had anyone to protect them or provide for them. It is the Christian duty to care for such members of our society.

Hypocrites are people whose actions don't match their words. They may say they love God, but they don't act in a loving way. Such behavior hurts that person, others around them, and God.

September 5

23rd Sunday in Ordinary Time

First Reading (Isaiah 35:4-7a)

Thus says the LORD:
Say to those whose **hearts are frightened**:
Be strong, fear not!
Here is your God,
he comes with **vindication**;
with divine recompense
he comes to save you.
Then will the eyes of the blind be opened,
the ears of the deaf be cleared;
then will the lame leap like a stag,
then the tongue of the mute will sing.
Streams will burst forth in the desert,
and rivers in the steppe.
The burning sands will become pools,
and the thirsty ground, springs of water.

The word of the Lord. **Thanks be to God.**

Responsorial Psalm (Psalm 146:6-7, 8-9, 9-10)

℟. **Praise the Lord, my soul!** *Or* **Alleluia.**

The God of Jacob **keeps faith** forever,
secures justice for the oppressed,
gives food to the hungry.
The LORD sets captives free. ℟.

The LORD gives sight to the blind;
the LORD raises up those who were bowed down.
The LORD loves the just;
the LORD protects strangers. ℟.

The fatherless and the widow the LORD sustains,
but the way of the wicked he thwarts.
The LORD shall reign forever;
your God, O Zion, through all generations.
Alleluia. ℟.

Second Reading (James 2:1-5)

My brothers and sisters, show no **partiality** as you adhere to the faith in our glorious Lord Jesus Christ. For if a man with gold rings and fine clothes comes into your assembly, and a **poor person** in shabby clothes also comes in, and you pay attention to the one wearing the fine clothes and say, "Sit here, please," while you say to the poor one, "Stand there," or "Sit at my feet," have you not made distinctions among yourselves and become judges with evil designs?

Listen, my beloved brothers and sisters. Did not God choose those who are poor in the world to be rich in faith and heirs of the kingdom that he promised to those who love him?

The word of the Lord. **Thanks be to God.**

Gospel (Mark 7:31-37)

A reading from the holy Gospel according to Mark.
Glory to you, O Lord.

Again Jesus left the district of Tyre and went by way of Sidon to the Sea of Galilee, into the district of the **Decapolis**. And people brought to him a deaf man who had a speech impediment and begged him to **lay his hand** on him. He took him off by himself away from the crowd. He put his finger into the man's ears and, spitting, touched his tongue; then he looked up to heaven and groaned, and said to him, *"Ephphatha!"*—that is, "Be opened!"—And immediately the man's ears were opened, his speech impediment was removed, and he spoke plainly. He ordered them not to tell anyone. But the more he ordered them not to, the more they proclaimed it. They were exceedingly astonished and they said, "He has done all things well. He makes the deaf hear and the mute speak."

The Gospel of the Lord. **Praise to you, Lord Jesus Christ.**

Key Words

People whose **hearts are frightened** feel they are alone and are afraid of everything. Isaiah tells the people not to be afraid, because God is with them. They will find their strength and courage in God.

When Isaiah describes God coming with **vindication** (or punishment), he is trying to comfort the people who are afraid. God is on their side; God will bring justice and healing; and God will help set them free.

To **keep faith** is to honor a promise. God made a promise, or covenant, with the people of Israel; God also made a New Covenant in Jesus. God always keeps his promises!

Partiality means treating some people better than others, so that one group gets more than another. We may find ourselves doing this, but God does not have favorites. God loves all his children equally.

The Bible teaches that every person has dignity, including a **poor person**. When we ignore the poor and care only for the wealthy, we are turning our back on God. When we treat the poor with kindness and justice, we show our love for Jesus.

Decapolis is a Greek word meaning "ten cities." This group of cities was near where Jesus lived.

Often when Jesus healed people, he would **lay his hand** on their heads. This gesture is now part of certain sacraments, such as confirmation and holy orders (priesthood). It is a sign that the power of God, the Holy Spirit, is being given to the person.

September 12

24th Sunday in Ordinary Time

First Reading (Isaiah 50:5-9a)

The Lord GOD opens my ear that I may hear;
and I have not rebelled,
have not turned back.
I gave my back to those who beat me,
my cheeks to those who plucked my beard;
my face I did not shield
from buffets and spitting.

The Lord GOD is my help,
therefore I am not disgraced;
I have set my face like flint,
knowing that I shall not be put to shame.
He is near who **upholds my right**;
if anyone wishes to oppose me,
let us appear together.
Who disputes my right?
Let that man confront me.
See, the Lord GOD is my help;
who will prove me wrong?

The word of the Lord. **Thanks be to God.**

Responsorial Psalm (Psalm 116:1-2, 3-4, 5-6, 8-9)

℟. **I will walk before the Lord, in the land of the living.**
Or **Alleluia.**

I love the LORD because he has heard
my voice in supplication,
Because he has inclined his ear to me
the day I called. ℟.

The cords of death encompassed me;
the snares of the netherworld seized upon me;
I fell into distress and sorrow,
and I called upon the name of the LORD,
"O LORD, save my life!" ℟.

Gracious is the LORD and just;
yes, our God is merciful.
The LORD keeps the little ones;
I was brought low, and he saved me. ℟.

For he has freed my soul from death,
my eyes from tears, my feet from stumbling.
I shall walk before the LORD
in the land of the living. ℟.

Second Reading (James 2:14-18)

What good is it, my brothers and sisters, if someone says he has faith but does not have **works**? Can that faith save him? If a brother or sister has nothing to wear and has no food for the day, and one of you says to them, "Go in peace, keep warm, and eat well," but you do not give them the necessities of the body, what good is it? So also faith of itself, if it does not have works, is dead.

Indeed someone might say, "You have faith and I have works." Demonstrate your faith to me without works, and I will demonstrate my faith to you from my works.

The word of the Lord. **Thanks be to God.**

Gospel (Mark 8:27-35)

A reading from the holy Gospel according to Mark.
Glory to you, O Lord.

Jesus and his disciples set out for the villages of Caesarea Philippi. Along the way he asked his disciples, "Who do people say that I am?" They said in reply, "**John the Baptist**, others Elijah, still others one of the prophets." And he asked them, "But who do you say that I am?" Peter said to him in reply, "You are the Christ." Then he warned them not to tell anyone about him.

He began to teach them that the Son of Man must suffer greatly and be rejected by the elders, the chief priests, and the scribes, and be killed, and rise after three days. He spoke this openly. Then Peter took him aside and began to rebuke him. At this he turned around and, looking at his disciples, rebuked Peter and said, "Get behind me, **Satan**. You are thinking not as God does, but as human beings do."

He summoned the crowd with his disciples and said to them, "Whoever wishes to come after me must deny himself, **take up his cross**, and follow me. For whoever wishes to save his life will lose it, but whoever loses his life for my sake and that of the gospel will save it."

The Gospel of the Lord. **Praise to you, Lord Jesus Christ.**

Key Words

To **uphold one's right** means to defend someone when they are being treated unfairly. Isaiah knows he can stand with courage and hope because God is at his side.

Saint James's teaching in his letter is important for everyone. He shows us that it is not what we say that proves our belief; faith shows itself in **works** or deeds that prove we are living the way Jesus taught us to live.

John the Baptist was the son of Zechariah and Elizabeth, and the cousin of Jesus. He prepared the way for Jesus, telling the people that the Messiah, Jesus, was coming. He is called the Baptist because he baptized people as a sign of their willingness to change their lives. He was a great prophet.

Satan is one of the names given to the enemy of God and our strongest enemy. Satan works against God and tries to lead people away from God's love. In today's gospel, when Peter argues with Jesus over whether it is necessary for Jesus to die, Jesus calls Peter "Satan" because it is God's will that Jesus should suffer, die, and rise again, and Peter wants to reject it.

When Jesus says whoever wants to be his follower must **take up his cross**, he is challenging us to accept everything that comes with being Christian. We proudly mark ourselves with the sign of the cross and we accept whatever comes our way as a result. We must be prepared to let go of our life if we want to save our life.

September 19

25th Sunday in Ordinary Time

First Reading (Wisdom 2:12, 17-20)

The wicked say:
Let us beset the just one, because he is obnoxious to us;
he sets himself against our doings,
reproaches us for transgressions of the law
and charges us with violations of our training.
Let us see whether his words be true;
let us find out what will happen to him.
For if the just one be the son of God, God will defend him
and deliver him from the hand of his foes.
With revilement and torture let us put the just one to the test
that we may have proof of his gentleness
and try his patience.
Let us condemn him to a shameful death;
for according to his own words, God will take care of him.

The word of the Lord. **Thanks be to God.**

Responsorial Psalm (Psalm 54:3-4, 5, 6-8)

℟. **The Lord upholds my life.**

O God, by your name save me,
and by your might defend my cause.
O God, hear my prayer;
hearken to the words of my mouth. ℟.

For the haughty men have risen up against me,
the ruthless seek my life;
they set not God before their eyes. ℟.

Behold, God is my helper;
the Lord sustains my life.
Freely will I offer you sacrifice;
I will praise your name, O Lord, for its goodness. ℟.

Second Reading (James 3:16-4:3)

Beloved: Where jealousy and selfish ambition exist, there is disorder and every foul practice. But the wisdom from above is first of all pure, then peaceable, gentle, compliant, full of **mercy** and good fruits, without inconstancy or insincerity. And the fruit of righteousness is sown in peace for those who cultivate peace.

Where do the wars and where do the conflicts among you come from? Is it not from your passions that make war within your members? You covet but do not possess. You kill and envy but you cannot obtain; you **fight and wage war**. You do not possess because you do not ask. You ask but do not receive, because you ask wrongly, to spend it on your passions.

The word of the Lord. **Thanks be to God.**

Gospel (Mark 9:30-37)

A reading from the holy Gospel according to Mark.
Glory to you, O Lord.

Jesus and his disciples left from there and began a journey through Galilee, but he did not wish anyone to know about it. He was teaching his disciples and telling them, "The Son of Man is to be handed over to men and they will kill him, and three days after his death the Son of Man will rise." But they did not understand the saying, and they were afraid to question him.

They came to **Capernaum** and, once inside the house, he began to ask them, "What were you arguing about on the way?" But they remained silent. They had been discussing among themselves on the way who was the greatest. Then he sat down, called the Twelve, and said to them, "If anyone wishes to be first, he shall be the last of all and the servant of all." Taking a **child**, he placed it in their midst, and putting his arms around it, he said to them, "Whoever receives one child such as this in my name, receives me; and whoever receives me, receives not me but the One who sent me."

The Gospel of the Lord. **Praise to you, Lord Jesus Christ.**

Key Words

The **Book of Wisdom** was written not long before Jesus was born. It is one of seven biblical books called wisdom literature (the others are Job, the Psalms, Proverbs, Ecclesiastes, the Song of Solomon, and Sirach). It urges God's people to stand firm in faith, even when life is difficult or hostile.

Mercy is God's loving concern for everyone, but most especially for the poor and the weak. Saint James lists mercy as one of the characteristics of heavenly wisdom: if we truly are God's children, then we will be merciful as God is merciful.

People **fight and wage war** when they think only of themselves and not of the needs of others. Fighting prevents the community from growing together in love. If we are to make peace, as Saint James says, we must first live in a peaceable manner.

Capernaum was a fishing village on the shore of the Sea of Galilee. Jesus frequently taught in Capernaum and performed miracles there.

Young children are defenseless and depend on adults to care for them. This gospel shows how important each **child** is to God. Jesus says that when we welcome children, we welcome Jesus and God his Father.

September 26

26th Sunday in Ordinary Time

First Reading (Numbers 11:25-29)

The LORD came down in the cloud and spoke to Moses. Taking some of the spirit that was on Moses, the LORD bestowed it on the seventy elders; and as the spirit came to rest on them, they **prophesied**.

Now two men, one named Eldad and the other Medad, were not in the gathering but had been left in the camp. They too had been on the list, but had not gone out to the tent; yet the spirit came to rest on them also, and they prophesied in the camp. So, when a young man quickly told Moses, "Eldad and Medad are prophesying in the camp," **Joshua**, son of Nun, who from his youth had been Moses' aide, said, "Moses, my lord, stop them." But Moses answered him, "Are you jealous for my sake? Would that all the people of the LORD were prophets! Would that the LORD might bestow his spirit on them all!"

The word of the Lord. **Thanks be to God.**

Responsorial Psalm (Psalm 19:8, 10, 12-13, 14)

℟. **The precepts of the Lord give joy to the heart.**

The law of the LORD is perfect,
refreshing the soul;
the decree of the LORD is trustworthy,
giving wisdom to the simple. ℟.

The fear of the LORD is pure,
enduring forever;
the ordinances of the LORD are true,
all of them just. ℟.

Though your servant is careful of them,
very diligent in keeping them,
Yet who can detect failings?
Cleanse me from my unknown faults! ℟.

From wanton sin especially, restrain your servant;
let it not rule over me.
Then shall I be blameless and innocent
of serious sin. ℟.

Second Reading (James 5:1-6)

Come now, you rich, weep and wail over your impending miseries. Your wealth has rotted away, your clothes have become moth-eaten, your gold and silver have corroded, and that corrosion will be a testimony against you; it will devour your flesh like a fire. You have stored up treasure for the last days. Behold, the wages you withheld from the workers who harvested your fields are crying aloud; and the cries of the harvesters have reached the ears of the Lord of hosts. You have lived on earth in luxury and pleasure; you have fattened your hearts for the day of slaughter. You have condemned; you have murdered the righteous one; he offers you no resistance.

The word of the Lord. **Thanks be to God.**

Gospel (Mark 9:38-43, 45, 47-48)

A reading from the holy Gospel according to Mark.
Glory to you, O Lord.

At that time, John said to Jesus, "Teacher, we saw someone driving out demons in your name, and we tried to prevent him because he does not follow us." Jesus replied, "Do not prevent him. There is no one who performs a mighty deed in my name who can at the same time speak ill of me. For whoever is not against us is for us. Anyone who gives you a cup of water to drink because you belong to Christ, amen, I say to you, will surely not lose his reward.

"Whoever causes one of these little ones who believe in me to sin, it would be better for him if a great millstone were put around his neck and he were thrown into the sea. If your hand causes you to sin, **cut it off**. It is better for you to enter into life maimed than with two hands to go into Gehenna, into the unquenchable fire. And if your foot causes you to sin, cut if off. It is better for you to enter into life crippled than with two feet to be thrown into Gehenna. And if your eye causes you to sin, pluck it out. Better for you to enter into the kingdom of God with one eye than with two eyes to be thrown into Gehenna, where 'their worm does not die, and the fire is not quenched.' "

The Gospel of the Lord. **Praise to you, Lord Jesus Christ.**

Key Words

The **Book of Numbers** is found in the Old Testament. It is called "Numbers" because it talks about many numbers and times when the people of Israel were counted. In Hebrew, it is called "In the Desert" because it tells of the travels of the Israelites after they left slavery in Egypt.

To **prophesy** can sometimes mean to announce what is going to happen in the future. In the Bible, however, prophets speak for God, reminding the people of God's promises and their own need to remain faithful to the covenant.

Joshua helped Moses lead the people of Israel to the Promised Land. Moses died before they got there, and so Joshua became the leader of the Israelites as they conquered the land. He is the central person in the book of Joshua.

When Jesus tells people to **cut off** their hand or their foot if it is causing them to sin, he means we must sometimes let go of valuable things in order to obey God. No one should cut off a part of their body, unless it is to save their lives.

October 3

27th Sunday in Ordinary Time

First Reading (Genesis 2:18-24)

The LORD God said: "It is not good for **the man** to be alone. I will make a suitable partner for him." So the LORD God formed out of the ground various wild animals and various birds of the air, and he brought them to the man to see what he would call them; whatever the man called each of them would be its **name**. The man gave names to all the cattle, all the birds of the air, and all wild animals; but none proved to be the suitable partner for the man.

So the LORD God cast a deep sleep on the man, and while he was asleep, he took out **one of his ribs** and closed up its place with flesh. The LORD God then built up into a woman the rib that he had taken from the man. When he brought her to the man, the man said:

"This one, at last, is bone of my bones
and flesh of my flesh;
this one shall be called 'woman,'
for out of 'her man' this one has been taken."

That is why a man leaves his father and mother and clings to his wife, and the two of them become one flesh.

The word of the Lord. **Thanks be to God.**

Responsorial Psalm (Psalm 128:1-2, 3, 4-5, 6)

℟. **May the Lord bless us all the days of our lives.**

Blessed are you who fear the LORD,
who walk in his ways!
For you shall eat the fruit of your handiwork;
blessed shall you be, and favored. ℟.

Your wife shall be like a fruitful vine
in the recesses of your home,
your children like olive plants
around your table. ℟.

Behold, thus is the man blessed
who fears the LORD.
The LORD bless you from Zion:
may you see the prosperity of Jerusalem
all the days of your life. ℟.

May you see your children's children.
Peace be upon Israel! ℟.

Second Reading (Hebrews 2:9-11)

Brothers and sisters: He "for a little while" was made "**lower than the angels**," that by the grace of God he might taste death for everyone.

For it was fitting that he, for whom and through whom all things exist, in bringing many children to glory, should make the leader to their salvation perfect through suffering. He who consecrates and those who are being consecrated all have one origin. Therefore, he is not ashamed to call them "brothers."

The word of the Lord. **Thanks be to God.**

Gospel (Mark 10:2-16 or 10:2-12)

The shorter version ends at the asterisks.

A reading from the holy Gospel according to Mark.
Glory to you, O Lord.

The Pharisees approached Jesus and asked, "Is it lawful for a husband to **divorce** his wife?" They were testing him. He said to them in reply, "What did Moses command you?" They replied, "Moses permitted a husband to write a bill of divorce and dismiss her." But Jesus told them, "Because of the hardness of your hearts he wrote you this commandment. But from the beginning of creation, *God made them male and female. For this reason a man shall leave his father and mother and be joined to his wife, and the two shall become one flesh.* So they are no longer two but one flesh. Therefore what God has joined together, no human being must separate." In the house the disciples again questioned Jesus about this. He said to them, "Whoever divorces his wife and marries another commits adultery against her; and if she divorces her husband and marries another, she commits adultery."

* * *

And people were bringing children to him that he might touch them, but the disciples rebuked them. When Jesus saw this he became indignant and said to them, "Let the children come to me; do not prevent them, for the kingdom of God belongs to such as these. Amen, I say to you, whoever does not accept the kingdom of God like a child will not enter it." Then he embraced them and blessed them, placing his hands on them.

The Gospel of the Lord. **Praise to you, Lord Jesus Christ.**

Key Words

The man (in Hebrew, *adam*) is the name that the book of Genesis gives to the first human being God created from the earth (in Hebrew, *adama*). We call him Adam. The first woman was called Eve ("living one"). They are the first parents of all people.

In the Bible, to **name** something is to be responsible for it. God let Adam name the animals he created. It was then Adam's job to take care of them. We are all asked to care for God's creation.

When God takes **one of the man's ribs** to form a woman, God shows that women and men share the same human nature. God wants us to work side by side to care for the world and one another.

The writer of the Letter to the Hebrews is speaking, in today's reading, about the hierarchy of beings in heaven. The angels are close to God, but Jesus is the closest. In becoming human, Jesus was made "**lower than the angels**"; but after his resurrection, he was crowned with glory and honor and returned to his rightful place with God.

The law that was given to Moses allowed **divorce**, but Jesus teaches that when a man and a woman are joined in marriage, in God's eyes their love never ends and they cannot be separated until death. In the Catholic Church, marriage is a sacrament—an outward sign of God's grace and a vocation to holiness.

October 10

28th Sunday in Ordinary Time

First Reading (Wisdom 7:7-11)

I prayed, and prudence was given me;
I pleaded, and the spirit of **wisdom** came to me.
I preferred her to **scepter and throne**,
and deemed riches nothing in comparison with her,
nor did I liken any priceless gem to her;
because all gold, in view of her, is a little sand,
and before her, silver is to be accounted mire.
Beyond health and comeliness I loved her,
and I chose to have her rather than the light,
because the splendor of her never yields to sleep.
Yet all good things together came to me in her company,
and countless riches at her hands.

The word of the Lord. **Thanks be to God.**

Responsorial Psalm (Psalm 90:12-13, 14-15, 16-17)

℟. Fill us with your love, O Lord, and we will sing for joy!

Teach us to number our days aright,
that we may gain wisdom of heart.
Return, O LORD! How long?
Have pity on your servants! ℟.

Fill us at daybreak with your kindness,
that we may shout for joy and gladness all our days.
Make us glad, for the days when you afflicted us,
for the years when we saw evil. ℟.

Let your work be seen by your servants
and your glory by their children;
and may the gracious care of the LORD our God be ours;
prosper the work of our hands for us!
Prosper the work of our hands! ℟.

Second Reading (Hebrews 4:12-13)

Brothers and sisters: Indeed the word of God is living and effective, sharper than any two-edged sword, penetrating even between soul and spirit, joints and marrow, and able to discern reflections and thoughts of the heart. No creature is concealed from him, but everything is naked and exposed to the eyes of him to whom we must render an account.

The word of the Lord. **Thanks be to God.**

Gospel (Mark 10:17-30 or 10:17-27)

The shorter version ends at the asterisks.

A reading from the holy Gospel according to Mark.
Glory to you, O Lord.

As Jesus was setting out on a journey, a man ran up, **knelt** down before him, and asked him, "Good teacher, what must I do to inherit eternal life?" Jesus answered him, "Why do you call me good? No one is good but God alone. You know the commandments: *You shall not kill; you shall not commit adultery; you shall not steal; you shall not bear false witness; you shall not defraud; honor your father and your mother.*" He replied and said to him, "Teacher, all of these I have observed from my youth." Jesus, looking at him, loved him and said to him, "You are lacking in one thing. Go, sell what you have, and give to the poor and you will have treasure in heaven; then **come, follow me.**" At that statement his face fell, and he went away **sad**, for he had many possessions.

Jesus looked around and said to his disciples, "How hard it is for those who have wealth to enter the kingdom of God!" The disciples were amazed at his words. So Jesus again said to them in reply, "Children, how hard it is to enter the kingdom of God! It is easier for a camel to pass through the **eye of a needle** than for one who is rich to enter the kingdom of God." They were exceedingly astonished and said among themselves, "Then who can be saved?" Jesus looked at them and said, "For human beings it is impossible, but not for God. All things are possible for God."

* * *

Peter began to say to him, "We have given up everything and followed you." Jesus said, "Amen, I say to you, there is no one who has given up house or brothers or sisters or mother or father or children or lands for my sake and for the sake of the gospel who will not receive a hundred times more now in this present age: houses and brothers and sisters and mothers and children and lands, with persecutions, and eternal life in the age to come."

The Gospel of the Lord. **Praise to you, Lord Jesus Christ.**

Key Words

Wisdom is a deep understanding of things. It does not come from studying books: it comes from experience. Wisdom is one of the seven gifts of the Holy Spirit—it allows us to see God in everyone and everything around us.

Scepters and thrones are two signs of a king or queen's power. A scepter is a decorative wand held in the hand. It represents authority. The Bible says it is better to have wisdom than to have worldly power.

When we kneel before someone, we are showing reverence and obedience to that person. In today's gospel, the man **knelt** before Jesus because he believed Jesus to be a great teacher deserving of his respect.

When Jesus says to the rich man, "**Come, follow me**," he is also inviting us to follow him: sharing the good news of God's love with everyone and sharing our wealth with the poor.

We sometimes feel **sad** because we have lost something or someone important to us. The man in the gospel story was saddened by the thought of giving up his belongings—but he might also have been sad because he wasn't strong enough to leave his possessions and follow Jesus.

The **eye of a needle** is the opening at the top of a needle through which thread is looped. Surely it is impossible for a camel to pass through the eye! By using this saying, Jesus is showing us that we have no other option: we must not merely think about giving to the poor, we must do it, if we are to have eternal life.

October 17

29th Sunday in Ordinary Time

First Reading (Isaiah 53:10-11)

The LORD was pleased
to crush him in infirmity.

If he gives his life as an offering for sin,
he shall see his **descendants** in a long life,
and the will of the LORD shall be accomplished
through him.

Because of his **affliction**
he shall see the light in fullness of days;
through his suffering, my servant shall justify many,
and their guilt he shall bear.

The word of the Lord. **Thanks be to God.**

Responsorial Psalm (Psalm 33:4-5, 18-19, 20, 22)

℟. **Lord, let your mercy be on us,**
as we place our trust in you.

Upright is the word of the LORD,
and all his works are trustworthy.
He loves justice and right;
of the kindness of the LORD the earth is full. ℟.

See, the eyes of the LORD are upon those who fear him,
upon those who hope for his kindness,
To deliver them from death
and preserve them in spite of **famine**. ℟.

Our soul waits for the LORD,
who is our help and our shield.
May your kindness, O LORD, be upon us
who have put our hope in you. ℟.

Second Reading (Hebrews 4:14-16)

Brothers and sisters: Since we have a great high priest who has passed through the heavens, Jesus, the Son of God, let us hold fast to our confession. For we do not have a high priest who is unable to sympathize with our weaknesses, but one who has similarly been tested in every way, yet without sin. So let us confidently approach the throne of grace to receive **mercy** and to find grace for timely help.

The word of the Lord. **Thanks be to God.**

Gospel (Mark 10:35-45 or 10:42-45)

The shorter version begins at the asterisks.

A reading from the holy Gospel according to Mark.
Glory to you, O Lord.

James and John, the sons of Zebedee, came to Jesus and said to him, "Teacher, we want you to do for us whatever we ask of you." He replied, "What do you wish me to do for you?" They answered him, "Grant that in your glory we may sit one at your right and the other at your left." Jesus said to them, "You do not know what you are asking. Can you drink the cup that I drink or be baptized with the baptism with which I am baptized?" They said to him, "We can." Jesus said to them, "The cup that I drink, you will drink, and with the baptism with which I am baptized, you will be baptized; but to sit at my right or at my left is not mine to give but is for those for whom it has been prepared." When the ten heard this, they became indignant at James and John.

* * *

Jesus summoned them [the Twelve] and said to them, "You know that those who are recognized as rulers over the **Gentiles** lord it over them, and their great ones make their authority over them felt. But it shall not be so among you. Rather, whoever wishes to be great among you will be your servant; whoever wishes to be first among you will be the slave of all. For the Son of Man did not come to be served but to serve and to give his life as a **ransom** for many."

The Gospel of the Lord. **Praise to you, Lord Jesus Christ.**

Key Words

Descendants are a person's children and grandchildren. They were important to the Jewish people because they carried the faith of the people into the future. To have many children was a sign of God's blessing. In the book of Isaiah, the person who is suffering will be blessed by God: he will live to see his children for many days.

An **affliction** is a great mental or physical pain. Isaiah tells us that people who suffer will gain wisdom from their experience and will one day find peace. We can trust in God to help us endure our pain.

Famine is a long period of time when there is not enough food in a country. The people go hungry day after day. Flooding, drought, insects, or war are some reasons crops cannot grow. The psalmist trusts that God will keep his people alive in time of famine.

Mercy is God's loving forgiveness of our sins. God is always merciful. At the beginning of Mass we say, "Lord, have mercy; Christ, have mercy; Lord, have mercy," both to ask for God's mercy and to remind us of how merciful God is.

The **Gentiles** were non-Jewish people. Their faith, government, and customs were different from those of the Jewish people. Jesus tells his disciples not to act like the leaders of the Gentiles, who do not always treat their people fairly.

Ransom is a sum of money or other valuable thing that is paid to save someone's life or free a prisoner. Jesus gave the most valuable thing he had—his life—in order to ransom, or save, everyone from sin and death. He chose to do this because he loves us.

October 24

30th Sunday in Ordinary Time

First Reading (Jeremiah 31:7-9)

Thus says the LORD:
Shout with joy for **Jacob**,
exult at the head of the nations;
proclaim your praise and say:
The LORD has delivered his people,
the remnant of Israel.
Behold, I will bring them back
from the land of the north;
I will gather them from the ends of the world,
with the blind and the lame in their midst,
the mothers and those with child;
they shall return as an immense throng.
They departed in tears,
but I will console them and guide them;
I will lead them to brooks of water,
on a level road, so that none shall stumble.
For I am a father to Israel,
Ephraim is my first-born.

The word of the Lord. **Thanks be to God.**

Responsorial Psalm (Psalm 126:1-2, 2-3, 4-5, 6)

℟. **The Lord has done great things for us;
we are filled with joy.**

When the LORD brought back the captives of Zion,
we were like men dreaming.
Then our mouth was filled with laughter,
and our tongue with rejoicing. ℟.

Then they said among the nations,
"The LORD has done great things for them."
The LORD has done great things for us;
we are glad indeed. ℟.

Restore our fortunes, O LORD,
like the torrents in the southern desert.
Those that sow in tears
shall reap rejoicing. ℟.

Although they go forth weeping,
carrying the seed to be sown,
They shall come back rejoicing,
carrying their sheaves. R.

Second Reading (Hebrews 5:1-6)

Brothers and sisters: Every high priest is taken from among men and made their representative before God, to offer gifts and sacrifices for sins. He is able to deal patiently with the ignorant and erring, for he himself is beset by weakness and so, for this reason, must make sin offerings for himself as well as for the people. No one takes this honor upon himself but only when called by God, just as **Aaron** was. In the same way, it was not Christ who glorified himself in becoming high priest, but rather the one who said to him:

You are my son:
this day I have begotten you;

just as he says in another place:

You are a priest forever
according to the order of Melchizedek.

The word of the Lord. **Thanks be to God.**

Gospel (Mark 10:46-52)

A reading from the holy Gospel according to Mark.
Glory to you, O Lord.

As Jesus was leaving Jericho with his disciples and a sizable crowd, Bartimaeus, a blind man, the son of Timaeus, sat by the roadside begging. On hearing that it was Jesus of Nazareth, he began to cry out and say, "Jesus, **son of David**, have pity on me." And many rebuked him, telling him to be silent. But he kept calling out all the more, "Son of David, have pity on me." Jesus stopped and said, "Call him." So they called the blind man, saying to him, "Take courage; get up, Jesus is calling you." He threw aside his cloak, sprang up, and came to Jesus. Jesus said to him in reply, "What do you want me to do for you?" The blind man replied to him, "Master, I want to see." Jesus told him, "Go your way; your faith has saved you." Immediately he received his sight and followed him on the way.

The Gospel of the Lord. **Praise to you, Lord Jesus Christ.**

Key Words

Jacob was the grandson of Abraham and the father of many children. His twelve sons were the first people in the twelve tribes of the Jewish people. In this reading, Jacob represents all of the people of Israel.

Ephraim was a son of Joseph (one of Jacob's sons) who was later adopted by Jacob and became the head of one of the twelve tribes of Israel. The Bible sometimes uses the name Ephraim to mean the whole people of Israel.

Aaron, Moses' older brother, helped him free the Israelites from slavery in Egypt. Aaron and Moses were Levites, the priestly tribe of the Hebrew people. The chief priest and all other priests were chosen from the tribe of Levi. Aaron is considered to be the first high priest of the Israelites.

Son of David (or descendant of King David) is a name the Hebrew people used to describe the Messiah. They were expecting the Messiah to be born of the House of David. In today's gospel, Bartimaeus knows in his heart that the person who is passing by is the Messiah, so he calls Jesus "son of David."

October 31

31st Sunday in Ordinary Time

First Reading (Deuteronomy 6:2-6)

Moses spoke to the people, saying: "Fear the LORD, your God, and keep, throughout the days of your lives, all his statutes and commandments which I enjoin on you, and thus have long life. Hear then, Israel, and be careful to observe them, that you may grow and prosper the more, in keeping with the promise of the LORD, the God of your fathers, to give you a land flowing with **milk and honey**.

"Hear, O Israel! The LORD is our God, the LORD alone! Therefore, you shall love the LORD, your God, with all your heart, and with all your soul, and with all your strength. Take to heart these words which I enjoin on you today."

The word of the Lord. **Thanks be to God.**

Responsorial Psalm (Psalm 18:2-3, 3-4, 47, 51)

℟. **I love you, Lord, my strength.**

I love you, O LORD, my strength,
O LORD, my rock, my fortress, my deliverer. ℟.

My God, my rock of refuge,
my shield, the horn of my salvation, my stronghold!
Praised be the LORD, I exclaim,
and I am safe from my enemies. ℟.

The LORD lives! And blessed be my rock!
Extolled be God my savior,
you who gave great victories to your king
and showed kindness to your anointed. ℟.

Second Reading (Hebrews 7:23-28)

Brothers and sisters: The levitical priests were many because they were prevented by death from remaining in office, but Jesus, because he remains forever, has a priesthood that does not pass away. Therefore, he is always able to save those who approach God through him, since he lives forever to make intercession for them.

It was fitting that we should have such a **high priest**: holy, innocent, undefiled, separated from sinners, higher than the heavens. He has no need, as did the high priests, to offer sacrifice day after day, first for his own sins and then for those of the people; he did that once for all when he offered himself. For the law appoints men subject to weakness to be high priests, but the word of the oath, which was taken after the law, appoints a son, who has been made perfect forever.

The word of the Lord. **Thanks be to God.**

Gospel (Mark 12:28b-34)

A reading from the holy Gospel according to Mark.
Glory to you, O Lord.

One of the **scribes** came to Jesus and asked him, "Which is the first of all the commandments?" Jesus replied, "The first is this: *Hear, O Israel! The Lord our God is Lord alone! You shall love the Lord your God with all your heart, with all your soul, with all your mind, and with all your strength.* The second is this: *You shall love your neighbor as yourself.* There is no other commandment greater than these." The scribe said to him, "Well said, teacher. You are right in saying, 'He is One and there is no other than he.' And 'to love him with all your heart, with all your understanding, with all your strength, and to love your neighbor as yourself' is worth more than all **burnt offerings** and sacrifices." And when Jesus saw that he answered with understanding, he said to him, "You are not far from the kingdom of God." And no one dared to ask him any more questions.

The Gospel of the Lord. **Praise to you, Lord Jesus Christ.**

Key Words

A land flowing with **milk and honey** is rich and fertile. There is abundant plant life allowing for grazing sheep and goats as well as flowering plants. The animals provide milk, and the plants and trees are key for the production of honey and syrups. For a people without a fixed home, this is indeed paradise!

The **high priest** was the chief of all the priests who were the links between God and his people. When the high priest died, his son became high priest after him. In the Letter to the Hebrews, the writer shows us how Jesus, as both God and a human being, is the perfect high priest, interceding for us with God. There is no need for another, for Jesus is our high priest forever.

In Jesus' time, **scribes** wrote letters and kept records for the community. They also studied the Law of Moses. In the Gospels, scribes often asked Jesus hard questions. This was how they learned and tested their knowledge of the Law.

A **burnt offering** is a sacrifice to God made in the temple, where a whole animal was offered on the fire. It was the highest form of sacrifice, since the animal was wholly consumed by fire and nothing was left over. The scribe in today's gospel acknowledges that Jesus has indeed spoken the greatest commandment —it is more important to love God and our neighbor than it is to give the highest sacrifice.

November 1

All Saints

First Reading (Revelation 7:2-4, 9-14)

I, John, saw another angel come up from the East, holding the seal of the living God. He cried out in a loud voice to the four angels who were given power to damage the land and the sea, "Do not damage the land or the sea or the trees until we put the seal on the foreheads of the servants of our God." I heard the number of those who had been marked with the seal, one hundred and forty-four thousand marked from every tribe of the children of Israel.

After this I had a vision of a great multitude, which no one could count, from every nation, race, people, and tongue. They stood before the throne and before the Lamb, wearing white robes and holding palm branches in their hands. They cried out in a loud voice:

"Salvation comes from our God, who is seated on the throne,
and from the Lamb."

All the angels stood around the throne and around the elders and the four living creatures. They prostrated themselves before the throne, worshiped God, and exclaimed:

"Amen. Blessing and glory, wisdom and thanksgiving,
honor, power, and might
be to our God forever and ever. Amen."

Then one of the elders spoke up and said to me, "Who are these **wearing white robes**, and where did they come from?" I said to him, "My lord, you are the one who knows." He said to me, "These are the ones who have survived the time of great distress; they have washed their robes and made them white in the Blood of the Lamb."

The word of the Lord. **Thanks be to God.**

Responsorial Psalm (Psalm 24:1bc-2, 3-4ab, 5-6)

℟. **Lord, this is the people that longs to see your face.**

The LORD's are the earth and its fullness;
the world and those who dwell in it.
For he founded it upon the seas
and established it upon the rivers. ℟.

Who can ascend the mountain of the LORD?
   or who may stand in his holy place?
One whose hands are sinless, whose heart is clean,
   who desires not what is vain. ℟.

He shall receive a blessing from the LORD,
   a reward from God his savior.
Such is the race that seeks him,
   that seeks the face of the God of Jacob. ℟.

Second Reading (1 John 3:1-3)

Beloved: See what love the Father has bestowed on us that we may be called the children of God. Yet so we are. The reason the world does not know us is that it did not know him. Beloved, we are God's children now; what we shall be has not yet been revealed. We do know that when it is revealed we shall be like him, for we shall see him as he is. Everyone who has this hope based on him makes himself pure, as he is pure.

The word of the Lord. **Thanks be to God.**

Gospel (Matthew 5:1-12a)

A reading from the holy Gospel according to Matthew.
Glory to you, O Lord.

When Jesus saw the crowds, he went **up the mountain**, and after he had sat down, his disciples came to him. He began to teach them, saying:

"Blessed are the poor in spirit,
   for theirs is the Kingdom of heaven.
Blessed are they who mourn,
   for they will be comforted.
Blessed are the meek,
   for they will inherit the land.
Blessed are they who hunger and thirst for righteousness,
   for they will be satisfied.
Blessed are the merciful,
   for they will be shown mercy.
Blessed are the clean of heart,
   for they will see God.

Blessed are the peacemakers,
for they will be called children of God.
Blessed are they who are persecuted for the sake
of righteousness,
for theirs is the Kingdom of heaven.

Blessed are you when they insult you and persecute you and utter every kind of evil against you falsely because of me. Rejoice and be glad, for your reward will be great in heaven."

The Gospel of the Lord. **Praise to you, Lord Jesus Christ.**

Key Words

All Saints is the day when we remember all the saints who live with God in heaven. This includes all the men and women we officially call saints but also all the holy people whose sainthood is known only by God.

The **Book of Revelation** is the last book of the Bible. Its messages are hidden in symbols that often seem very strange to us. Everything has a hidden meaning—the colors, numbers, even the dragons and monsters. The early Christians understood what the writer was trying to tell them. They were facing difficult times, but Revelation told them not to be discouraged, for in the end, Jesus would win over all their enemies.

Those **wearing white robes** are the ones who belong to Jesus. When you were baptized, you were dressed in a white garment to show that you too are part of his people.

Just as Moses went **up a mountain** to get the Ten Commandments from God, Jesus goes up the mountain to proclaim his beatitudes ("Blessed are..."). These beatitudes show us how to live today and help us move even more deeply into God's love.

November 7

32nd Sunday in Ordinary Time

First Reading (1 Kings 17:10-16)

In those days, Elijah the prophet went to Zarephath. As he arrived at the entrance of the city, a widow was gathering sticks there; he called out to her, "Please bring me a small cupful of water to drink." She left to get it, and he called out after her, "Please bring along a bit of bread." She answered, "As the LORD, your God, lives, I have nothing baked; there is only a handful of flour in my jar and a little oil in my jug. Just now I was collecting a couple of sticks, to go in and prepare something for myself and my son; when we have eaten it, we shall die." Elijah said to her, "Do not be afraid. Go and do as you propose. But first make me a little cake and bring it to me. Then you can prepare something for yourself and your son. For the LORD, the God of Israel, says, 'The jar of flour shall not go empty, nor the jug of oil run dry, until the day when the LORD sends rain upon the earth.' " She left and did as Elijah had said. She was able to eat for a year, and he and her son as well; the jar of flour did not go empty, nor the jug of oil run dry, as the LORD had foretold through Elijah.

The word of the Lord. **Thanks be to God.**

Responsorial Psalm (Psalm 146:7, 8-9, 9-10)

℟. **Praise the Lord, my soul!** Or **Alleluia.**

The LORD keeps faith forever,
secures justice for the **oppressed**,
gives food to the hungry.
The LORD sets captives free. ℟.

The LORD gives sight to the blind;
the LORD raises up those who were bowed down.
The LORD loves the just;
the LORD protects strangers. ℟.

The fatherless and the widow he sustains,
but the way of the wicked he thwarts.
The LORD shall reign forever;
your God, O **Zion**, through all generations.
Alleluia. ℟.

Second Reading (Hebrews 9:24-28)

Christ did not enter into a **sanctuary** made by hands, a copy of the true one, but heaven itself, that he might now appear before God on our behalf. Not that he might offer himself repeatedly, as the high priest enters each year into the sanctuary with blood that is not his own; if that were so, he would have had to suffer repeatedly from the foundation of the world. But now once for all he has appeared at the end of the ages to take away sin by his sacrifice. Just as it is appointed that human beings die once, and after this the judgment, so also Christ, offered once to take away the sins of many, will appear a second time, not to take away sin but to bring salvation to those who eagerly await him.

The word of the Lord. **Thanks be to God.**

Gospel (Mark 12:38-44 or 12:41-44)

The shorter version begins at the asterisks.

A reading from the holy Gospel according to Mark.
Glory to you, O Lord.

In the course of his teaching Jesus said to the crowds, "Beware of the scribes, who like to go around in long robes and accept greetings in the marketplaces, seats of honor in synagogues, and places of honor at banquets. They devour the houses of widows and, as a pretext, recite lengthy prayers. They will receive a very severe condemnation."

* * *

He [Jesus] sat down opposite the **treasury** and observed how the crowd put money into the treasury. Many rich people put in large sums. A poor **widow** also came and put in two small coins worth a few cents. Calling his disciples to himself, he said to them, "Amen, I say to you, this poor widow put in more than all the other contributors to the treasury. For they have all contributed from their **surplus** wealth, but she, from her poverty, has contributed all she had, her whole livelihood."

The Gospel of the Lord. **Praise to you, Lord Jesus Christ.**

Key Words

The **oppressed** are people who are treated unfairly by others. God never forgets the oppressed and desires their freedom from oppression. There are many oppressed people in our world today. When we work to help them, we are working with God to set them free.

Zion is the name of a hill in Jerusalem where the temple was built, but the entire city was often called Zion. The name Zion can also mean the whole people of Israel.

A **sanctuary** is a holy place in a temple or church. In a temple, it is where the Ark of the Covenant is kept. In Catholic churches, it is where the altar and tabernacle are found. In heaven, Jesus appears before God in the heavenly sanctuary to intercede for us as our high priest.

The **treasury** was the place where people gave money for the upkeep of the temple. It is similar to the collection that is taken up at Mass in our day.

A **widow** is a woman whose husband has died. A widow in Israel had no one to care for her. God made a law saying that the people of Israel had to care for widows and orphans (children without parents). In today's gospel, a widow gives as much as she can to the temple in Jerusalem. Even though she is poor, she is generous towards God because she loves God and recognizes how good God is to her.

To have a **surplus** means to have more than enough. Jesus noticed that many people gave to the temple treasury from their extra money, not from the money they used for their basic needs. To be generous means to give from our abundance, but also from our need.

November 14

33rd Sunday in Ordinary Time

First Reading (Daniel 12:1-3,)

In those days, I Daniel, heard this word of the Lord:
"At that time there shall arise
Michael, the great prince,
guardian of your people;
it shall be a time unsurpassed in distress
since nations began until that time.
At that time your people shall escape,
everyone who is found written in the book.

"Many of those who sleep in the dust of the earth shall awake;
some shall live forever,
others shall be an everlasting horror and disgrace.

"But the wise shall shine brightly
like the splendor of the firmament,
and those who lead the many to justice
shall be like the stars forever."

The word of the Lord. **Thanks be to God.**

Responsorial Psalm (Psalm 16:5, 8, 9-10, 11)

℟. **You are my inheritance, O Lord!**

O Lord, my allotted portion and my cup,
you it is who hold fast my lot.
I set the Lord ever before me;
with him at my right hand I shall not be
disturbed. ℟.

Therefore my heart is glad and my soul rejoices,
my body, too, abides in confidence;
because you will not abandon my soul to the
netherworld,
nor will you suffer your faithful one to undergo
corruption. ℟.

You will show me the path to life,
fullness of joys in your presence,
the delights at your right hand forever. ℟.

Second Reading (Hebrews 10:11-14, 18)

Brothers and sisters: Every priest stands daily at his ministry, offering frequently those same sacrifices that can never take away sins. But this one offered one sacrifice for sins, and took his seat forever at the right hand of God; now he waits until his enemies are made his footstool. For by one offering he has made perfect forever those who are being **consecrated**.

Where there is forgiveness of these, there is no longer offering for sin.

The word of the Lord. **Thanks be to God.**

Gospel (Mark 13:24-32)

A reading from the holy Gospel according to Mark.
Glory to you, O Lord.

Jesus said to his disciples: "In those days after that tribulation
the sun will be darkened,
and the moon will not give its light,
and the stars will be falling from the sky,
and the powers in the heavens will be shaken.

"And then they will see 'the Son of Man coming in the clouds' with great power and glory, and then he will send out the angels and gather his elect from the four winds, from the end of the earth to the end of the sky.

"Learn a lesson from the fig tree. When its branch becomes tender and sprouts leaves, you know that summer is near. In the same way, when you see these things happening, know that he is near, at the gates. Amen, I say to you, this generation will not pass away until all these things have taken place. Heaven and earth will pass away, but my words will not pass away.

"But of that **day or hour**, no one knows, neither the angels in heaven, nor the Son, but only the Father."

The Gospel of the Lord. **Praise to you, Lord Jesus Christ.**

Key Words

The **Book of Daniel** gave the Hebrew people comfort and hope in hard times. It was written about 160 years before Jesus was born, and is the first book of the Bible to talk about the resurrection of the dead.

Michael is the name of the angel who is the head of the heavenly angels and the protector of the people of Israel. His name means "who is like God." At the end of time, Michael will lead an army and help the people overcome all suffering.

To be **consecrated** is to be made holy, as God is holy. We say people who are close to God are consecrated, or sanctified, because they love everyone the way God does. The Letter to the Hebrews tells us that because Jesus has offered his life as a sacrifice for us, we are made holy for all time.

Although no one knows the **day or hour** when history will end, we trust in God. If we live as God's people and follow the life and teachings of Jesus, we will be ready whenever it happens.

November 21

Our Lord Jesus Christ, King of the Universe (Christ the King)

First Reading (Daniel 7:13-14)

As the visions during the night continued, I saw
one like a Son of man coming,
on the clouds of heaven;
when he reached the **Ancient One**
and was presented before him,
the one like a Son of man received dominion, glory, and kingship;
all peoples, nations, and languages serve him.
His dominion is an everlasting **dominion**
that shall not be taken away,
his kingship shall not be destroyed.

The word of the Lord. **Thanks be to God.**

Responsorial Psalm (Psalm 93:1, 1-2, 5)

℟. **The Lord is king; he is robed in majesty.**

The LORD is king, in splendor robed;
robed is the LORD and girt about with strength. ℟.

And he has made the world firm,
not to be moved.
Your throne stands firm from of old;
from everlasting you are, O LORD. ℟.

Your decrees are worthy of trust indeed;
holiness befits your house,
O LORD, for length of days. ℟.

Second Reading (Revelation 1:5-8)

Jesus Christ is the faithful witness, the firstborn of the dead and ruler of the kings of the earth. To him who loves us and has freed us from our sins by his blood, who has made us into a kingdom, priests for his God and Father, to him be glory and power forever and ever. Amen.

Behold, he is coming amid the clouds,
and every eye will see him,
even those who pierced him.
All the peoples of the earth will lament him.
Yes. Amen.

"I am the **Alpha** and the **Omega**," says the Lord God, "the one who is and who was and who is to come, the almighty."

The word of the Lord. **Thanks be to God.**

Gospel (John 18:33b-37)

A reading from the holy Gospel according to John.
Glory to you, O Lord.

Pilate said to Jesus, "Are you the King of the Jews?" Jesus answered, "Do you say this on your own or have others told you about me?" Pilate answered, "I am not a Jew, am I? Your own nation and the chief priests handed you over to me. What have you done?" Jesus answered, "My kingdom does not belong to this world. If my kingdom did belong to this world, my attendants would be fighting to keep me from being handed over to the Jews. But as it is, my kingdom is not here." So Pilate said to him, "Then you are a king?" Jesus answered, "You say I am a king. For this I was born and for this I came into the world, to testify to the truth. Everyone who belongs to the truth listens to my voice."

The Gospel of the Lord. **Praise to you, Lord Jesus Christ.**

Key Words

The liturgical year, or Church year, has five seasons: Advent, Christmas, Lent, Easter, and Ordinary Time. See page 349 of this book to learn more. With the Solemnity of **Our Lord Jesus Christ, King of the Universe**, we come to the end of Ordinary Time and the liturgical year. Next Sunday we begin a new liturgical year with Advent.

Daniel calls God the **Ancient One** as a way to show how God is eternal—God's kingdom will have no end.

Dominion is a word meaning the authority to govern. To the Hebrew people, God's dominion extended to all peoples, all creation, heaven, and hell. God is ruler over all.

The **Book of Revelation**, also called the Apocalypse, is the last book in the Bible. It uses symbols and colorful images to tell its story. It was written at a time when the Church was being persecuted and gives a vision of the end of time.

Alpha and **Omega** (A and Ω) are the first and last letters of the Greek alphabet. This expression describing Jesus means he is "the beginning and the end"—the most important person in all of history.

Children's Prayers for Various Occasions

A Child's Prayer for Morning

Now, before I run to play,
let me not forget to pray
to God who kept me through the night
and waked me with the morning light.
Help me, Lord, to love you more
than I have ever loved before.
In my work and in my play
please be with me through the day. Amen.

Morning Prayer

Dear God, we thank you for this day. We thank you for our families and friends. We thank you for our classmates. Be with us as we work and play today. Help us always to be kind to each other. We pray in the name of the Father, and of the Son and of the Holy Spirit. Amen.

Heather Reid, *Let's Pray! Prayers for the Elementary Classroom* (Toronto: Novalis, 2006).

Guardian Angel Prayer

Angel of God, my guardian dear, to whom God's love entrusts me here, ever this day be at my side, to light and guard, to rule and guide. Amen.

Children's Bedtime Prayer

Now I lay me down to sleep,
I pray you, Lord, your child to keep.
Your love will guard me through the night
and wake me with the morning light. Amen.

Child's Evening Prayer

I hear no voice, I feel no touch, I see no glory bright;
but yet I know that God is near, in darkness as in light.
He watches ever by my side, and hears my whispered prayer:
the Father for his little child both night and day does care. Amen.

God, Hear My Prayer

God in heaven hear my prayer, keep me in your loving care.
Be my guide in all I do, bless all those who love me too. Amen.

PRAYERS FOR FAMILY

A Family Prayer

Father, what love you have given us. May we love as you would have us love. Teach us to be kind to each other, patient and gentle with one another. Help us to bear all things together, to see in our love, your love, through Christ our Lord. Amen.

Prayer for Families

God and Father of us all,
in Jesus, your Son and our Savior,
you have made us your sons and daughters
in the family of the Church.

May your grace and love
help our families in every part of the world
be united to one another in fidelity to the Gospel.

May the example of the Holy Family,
with the aid of your Holy Spirit,
guide all families, especially those most troubled,
to be homes of communion and prayer
and to always seek your truth and live in your love.

Through Christ our Lord. Amen.

Jesus, Mary and Joseph, Pray for us!

World Meeting of Families, 2015

Prayer of Gratitude for Family

Loving God,

Thank you for the gift of my family.
(Pause to name each person in the family.)

Thank you for the times we have to be together.
(Pause to name a particular way of being together.)

Thank you for the ways in which we care for each other.
(Pause to name a specific act of kindness.)

May the joy and affection we share increase each and every day.
With gratitude for your bountiful love, I pray. Amen.

Kathy Hendricks, *Pocket Prayers for Parents* (Toronto: Novalis, 2014).

Grace Before Meals

Bless us, O Lord,
and these your gifts
which we are about to receive
from your bounty.
Through Christ our Lord. Amen.

* * *

For food in a world where many walk in hunger,
for friends in a world where many walk alone,
for faith in a world where many walk in fear,
we give you thanks, O God. Amen.

* * *

God is great, God is good!
Let us thank God for our food.
Amen.

* * *

Be present at our table, Lord.
Be here and everywhere adored.
Your creatures bless
and grant that we may feast
in paradise with you. Amen.

Grace After Meals

We give you thanks, Almighty God,
for these and all the benefits we receive
from your bounty. Through Christ our Lord. Amen.

* * *

Blessed be the name of the Lord.
Now and forever. Amen.

Peace Prayer of Saint Francis

Lord, make me an instrument of your peace.
Where there is hatred, let me sow love;
where there is injury, pardon;
where there is doubt, faith;
where there is despair, hope;
where there is darkness, light;
where there is sadness, joy.

Divine Master,
grant that I may not so much seek
to be consoled, as to console;
to be understood as to understand;
to be loved as to love.
For it is in giving that we receive;
it is in pardoning that we are pardoned;
and it is in dying that we are born
to eternal life. Amen.

Prayer of Saint Dominic

May God the Father, who made us, bless us.
May God the Son send his healing among us.
May God the Holy Spirit move within us
and give us eyes to see with, ears to hear with,
and hands that your work might be done.
May we walk and preach the word of God to all.
May the angel of peace watch over us
and lead us at last by God's grace to the Kingdom. Amen.

Night Prayer of Saint Augustine of Hippo

Watch, dear Lord,
with those who wake or watch or weep this night,
and give your angels charge over those who sleep.
Tend your sick ones,
O Lord Jesus Christ,
rest your weary ones,
bless your dying ones,
soothe your suffering ones,
shield your joyous ones,
and all for your love's sake. Amen.

Prayer of Saint Elizabeth Ann Seton

O Father, the first rule of our dear Savior's life was to do your will. Let his will of the present moment be the first rule of our daily life and work, with no other desire but for its most full and complete accomplishment. Help us to follow it faithfully, so that doing what you wish, we will be pleasing to you. Amen.

Prayer of Saint Columba of Ireland

O Lord,
grant us that love which can never die,
which will enkindle our lamps but not extinguish them,
so that they may shine in us and bring light to others.

Most dear Savior,
enkindle our lamps that they may shine forever in your temple.
May we receive unquenchable light from you
so that our darkness will be illuminated
and the darkness of the world will be made less. Amen.

Prayer of Saint Philippine Duchesne

O eternal Father, we come to you
through the heart of our Lord Jesus,
who is the way, the truth and the life.
Through his divine heart,
we adore you for those who do not adore you,
we love you for those who do not love you.
we gratefully acknowledge you to be our God. Amen.

Prayer of Saint Thérèse of Lisieux

Breathe into me, Holy Spirit,
that my thoughts may all be holy.
Move in me, Holy Spirit,
that my work, too, may be holy.
Attract my heart, Holy Spirit,
that I may love only what is holy.
Strengthen me, Holy Spirit,
that I may defend all that is holy.
Protect me, Holy Spirit,
that I may always be holy. Amen.

THE ROSARY

In the Rosary we focus on 20 events or mysteries in the life and death of Jesus and meditate on how we share with Mary in the saving work of Christ. Reading a relevant passage from the Bible can help us to understand better a particular mystery of the Rosary. The Bible references below are suggestions; other biblical texts can also be used for meditation.

- Begin the Rosary at the crucifix by praying the Apostles' Creed.
- At each large bead, pray the Lord's Prayer. *(page 352)*
- At each small bead, pray the Hail Mary. *(page 352)*
- At the first three beads it is customary to pray a Hail Mary for each of the gifts of faith, hope, and love.
- For each mystery, begin with the Lord's Prayer, then recite the Hail Mary ten times, and end with Glory Be to the Father. *(page 352)*

The Five Joyful Mysteries:

The Annunciation (Luke 1.26-38)
The Visitation (Luke 1.39-56)
The Nativity (Luke 2.1-20)
The Presentation (Luke 2.22-38)
The Finding in the Temple (Luke 2.41-52)

The Five Mysteries of Light:

The Baptism in the Jordan (Matthew 3.13-17)
The Wedding at Cana (John 2.1-12)
The Proclamation of the Kingdom (Mark 1.15)
The Transfiguration (Luke 9.28-36)
The First Eucharist (Matthew 26.26-29)

The Five Sorrowful Mysteries:

The Agony in the Garden (Matthew 26.36-56)
The Scourging at the Pillar (Matthew 27.20-26)
The Crowning with Thorns (Matthew 27.27-30)
The Carrying of the Cross (Matthew 27.31-33)
The Crucifixion (Matthew 27.34-60)

The Five Glorious Mysteries:

The Resurrection (John 20.1-18)
The Ascension (Acts 1.9-11)
The Descent of the Holy Spirit (John 20.19-23)
The Assumption of Mary (John 11.26)
The Crowning of Mary (Philippians 2.1-11)

Prayer for Friends

Loving God, you are the best friend we can have.
We ask today that you help us to be good friends to each other.
Help us to be fair, kind and unselfish.
Keep our friends safe and happy.
Bless us and bless all friends in this community.
We pray in the name of Jesus,
who was always the friend of children. Amen.

Heather Reid, *Let's Pray! Prayers for the Elementary Classroom* (Toronto: Novalis, 2006).

Prayer for the Birthday Child

May God bless you with every good gift
and surround you with love and happiness.
May Jesus be your friend and guide
all the days of your life.
May the Spirit of God
guide your footsteps
in the path of truth. Amen.

Prayer for Pets

Dear Father, hear and bless
your beasts and singing birds,
and guard with care and tenderness
small things that have no words. Amen.

Prayer for a Student / Teacher Who Is Sick

Gracious God, ______________ is sick right now. We pray for (him/her/them) and ask that they get better quickly and be able to return to us. Bless all nurses, doctors, and everyone who cares for people who are ill. May all sick people find comfort through their families and friends. We ask this in the name of Jesus, who healed many people. Amen.

Heather Reid, *Let's Pray: Prayers for the Elementary Classroom* (Ottawa: Novalis, 2007).

Prayer for When I Feel Bullied by Others

Heavenly Father, there are people in my life who reject me and break my heart. I feel down and ashamed. Give me the courage to withstand the hurtful words (and actions) of others. No matter what persecutions I endure, help me to remember your great love for me. Remind me that I am a beloved child of God. You made me in your image. With you, I am confident.

Help me to journey through each day peacefully, with purpose and joy. Place your protective angels around me at all times. Bless the person who is hurting me with your light, and help them realize their wrong actions and amend their ways. Help each one of us to spread love and kindness in this world, to make it a better place for everyone. In Jesus' name I pray. Amen.

Help Me Find the Way

Dear Lord, we often find it difficult to know what to choose and how to respond to many situations in our lives. Give us the discipline to acquire the knowledge we need to make good decisions. Grant us the ability and willingness to open our minds and hearts to the Holy Spirit as well as to follow the path upon which we are led. We also pray that we use the gift of prudence to discern between that which is constructive and that which is destructive. Amen.

When Someone Has Died

Lord God, hear our cries.
Grant us comfort in our sadness,
gently wipe away our tears,
and give us courage in the days ahead.
We ask this through Christ our Lord. Amen.

Thank You, Creator

I am thankful that the Creator gave us a sun for warmth, a moon to light the darkness, food to fill our hunger, families for comfort, trees for air and the stars in the sky that will never stop shining. Amen.

My Catholic Prayer Book (Novalis, 2017).

Let Go and Let God

God of peace and acceptance, things do not often go the way we want them to go. We can be disappointed, particularly when we want something really badly and it doesn't work out. We pray today to be granted the ability to accept things that we are not able to change. We pray for peace of mind and heart. Please grant us the faith to trust in you. Help us to follow the words in the Serenity Prayer: "God, grant me the serenity to accept the things I cannot change, courage to change the things I can, and wisdom to know the difference." Amen.

Let's Feel the Love

Loving Jesus, we are often in awe when we look at the compassion and mercy that you demonstrated during your life on earth. You reached out to the downtrodden, the sinner, the loner, the leper, and the rejected. You did not judge these people; instead you showed your love and the love of your Father. Guide us to reach out to all who are in need. May we refrain from judging, gossip, and criticizing others. Amen.

Commitment Is Key

Dear God, help us to be committed to all those aspects of our lives that are in need of our attention and gifts. When we agree to be a part of some group, project, team, or club, grant us the discipline and the wisdom we need to make our commitment real and meaningful. Keep us focused and on track so that we can reach our goals and feel good about the contributions we have made. Amen.

EXAMINATION OF CONSCIENCE

For use in preparing for the Sacrament of Reconciliation, based on The Ten Commandments.

1. **God Comes First**
   - *Did I pray each day?*
   - *Did I act with respect in church?*
   - *Did I participate at Mass?*
2. **God's Name Is Holy**
   - *Did I always use God's name in the right way?*
   - *Did I treat and talk about holy things with respect?*
3. **God's Day Is Holy**
   - *Did I go to Mass on Sundays and Holy Days?*
   - *Did I miss Mass through my own fault?*
4. **Honor Mom & Dad**
   - *Did I obey my parents?*
   - *Did I treat them with respect?*
   - *Was I obedient and respectful to my teachers?*
5. **Do Not Kill**
   - *Have I been kind to my siblings and friends?*
   - *Did I hit or hurt anyone?*
   - *Did I harm anyone with mean or cruel words, whether in person or online?*
6. **Be Pure**
   - *Were my thoughts and actions good and pure?*
   - *Have I been careful to watch good movies and TV shows?*
7. **Do Not Steal**
   - *Have I always been honest?*
   - *Did I take anything that doesn't belong to me?*
8. **Do Not Lie**
   - *Have I always told the truth?*
   - *Have I spread rumors?*
   - *Have I been quiet about something when I should have spoken up?*

9. **Do Not Want Other People** and
10. **Do Not Want Their Things**
   - *Have I been satisfied with what I have?*
   - *Have I been jealous of another's toys or belongings?*
   - *Am I thankful for what I have?*

THE LITURGICAL YEAR

The readings for Sunday Mass and feast days change according to the liturgical calendar.

What is the liturgical year?

Throughout the year, Christians celebrate together important moments in Jesus' life. This is the liturgical year. There are five seasons: Advent, Christmas, Lent, Easter, and Ordinary Time.

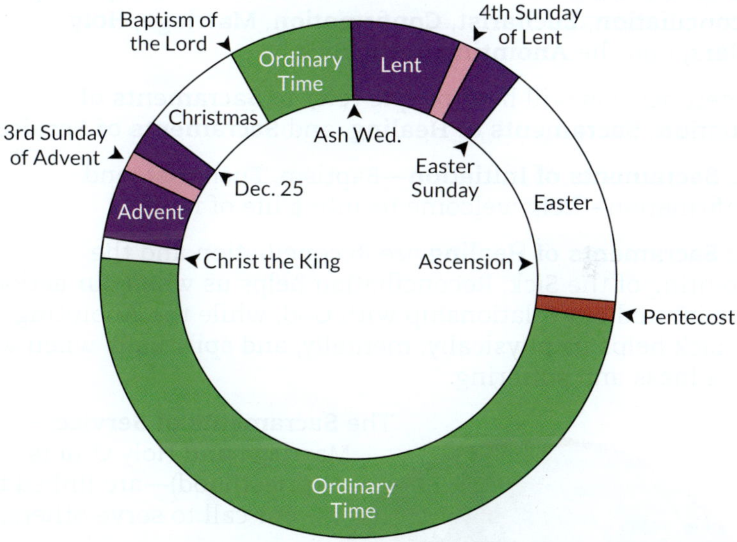

Advent is a time of waiting. It begins 4 weeks before Christmas. We prepare to welcome Jesus.

Christmas time celebrates the life of Jesus from his birth to his baptism. It includes Epiphany: Jesus welcomes the whole world.

During the 40 days of **Lent** we prepare for the great feast of Easter, the most important moment of the year.

Easter time is a season to celebrate Jesus' victory over death. It lasts from Easter Sunday to Pentecost, when the Holy Spirit comes upon the disciples.

The season in green above is called **Ordinary Time** because the Sundays are arranged using "ordinal numbers." It recounts many of the things Jesus did and said during his lifetime.

SACRAMENTS: A GIFT FROM GOD

Sacraments are rituals through which we receive God's grace. Grace is the gift of God's love and strength, given freely to us to help us lead good and just lives. Sacraments always involve signs appealing to our senses that point to God's saving presence in our lives. Baptism requires water, for example, and when we are confirmed, we are anointed with a special oil called chrism.

The seven sacraments of the Catholic Church are **Baptism, Reconciliation**, **Eucharist**, **Confirmation**, **Marriage**, **Holy Orders,** and the **Anointing of the Sick**.

Sometimes you will hear people refer to **Sacraments of Initiation**, **Sacraments of Healing,** and **Sacraments of Service**.

The **Sacraments of Initiation**—Baptism, Eucharist, and Confirmation—help welcome us into a life of faith.

The **Sacraments of Healing** are Reconciliation and the Anointing of the Sick. Reconciliation helps us when our actions have injured our relationship with God, while the Anointing of the Sick helps us physically, mentally, and spiritually when we face illness and suffering.

The **Sacraments of Service**—Marriage and Holy Orders (priesthood)—are linked to our call to serve others.

The sacraments of Baptism, Confirmation, and Holy Orders can only be received once. As Catholics, we believe that when these sacraments are received, they leave a lasting mark—or seal—on the soul.